Social Mobility and Education in Britain

Building upon extensive research into modern British society, this book traces out trends in social mobility and their relation to educational inequalities, with surprising results. Contrary to what is widely supposed, Bukodi and Goldthorpe's findings show there has been no overall decline in social mobility – though downward mobility is tending to rise and upward mobility to fall – and Britain is not a distinctively low mobility society. However, the inequalities of mobility chances among individuals, in relation to their social origins, have not been reduced and remain in some respects extreme. Exposing the widespread misconceptions that prevail in political and policy circles, this book shows that educational policy alone cannot break the link between inequality of condition and inequality of opportunity. It will appeal to students, researchers, policy makers, and anyone interested in the issues surrounding social inequality, social mobility and education.

ERZSÉBET BUKODI is an Associate Professor in Quantitative Social Policy and Professorial Fellow of Nuffield College, Oxford. She is also a Senior Research Fellow at the Institute for New Economic Thinking, The Oxford Martin School.

JOHN H. GOLDTHORPE is an Emeritus Fellow of Nuffield College Oxford, a Fellow of the British Academy, a Member of the Royal Swedish Academy of Sciences, and an Honorary Fellow of the Royal Statistical Society. He has written extensively on social class and social mobility since the 1960s.

GW00775895

Social Mobility and Education in Britain

Research, Politics and Policy

ERZSÉBET BUKODI
University of Oxford

JOHN H. GOLDTHORPE
University of Oxford

CAMBRIDGE
UNIVERSITY PRESS

CAMBRIDGE
UNIVERSITY PRESS

University Printing House, Cambridge CB2 8BS, United Kingdom

One Liberty Plaza, 20th Floor, New York, NY 10006, USA

477 Williamstown Road, Port Melbourne, VIC 3207, Australia

314–321, 3rd Floor, Plot 3, Splendor Forum, Jasola District Centre, New Delhi – 110025, India

79 Anson Road, #06–04/06, Singapore 079906

Cambridge University Press is part of the University of Cambridge.

It furthers the University's mission by disseminating knowledge in the pursuit of education, learning, and research at the highest international levels of excellence.

www.cambridge.org
Information on this title: www.cambridge.org/9781108474962
DOI: 10.1017/9781108567404

© Erzsébet Bukodi and John H. Goldthorpe 2019

First published 2019

Printed and bound in Great Britain by Clays Ltd, Elcograf S.p.A.

A catalogue record for this publication is available from the British Library.

ISBN 978-1-108-47496-2 Hardback
ISBN 978-1-108-46821-3 Paperback

Contents

Figures

Tables

Acknowledgements

The research on which our book is primarily based derives from the following projects, for each of which Erzsébet Bukodi was principal investigator: 'The Role of Education in Intergenerational Social Mobility', supported by the Economic and Social Research Council, grant ES/1038187/1; 'Social Origins, Cognitive Ability and Educational Attainment: A Life-Course Perspective', supported by the Nuffield Foundation, grant EDU/42195; and 'Social Inequalities in Education in Historical and Comparative Perspective: The Changing Effects of Different Components of Social Origins', supported by the Oxford University Press John Fell Research Fund, grant 122/673. We are duly grateful to the funding bodies that made our research possible. The projects were based in the Department of Social Policy and Intervention, University of Oxford, and we wish to acknowledge the support of the Department and, especially, the help of the Finance and Research Administration in ensuring that the projects ran smoothly.

In addition, the research reported on in Chapter 10 resulted from Erzsébet Bukodi's participation in the Employment, Equity and Growth Programme at the Oxford Martin School Institute for New Economic Thinking, supported by the Resolution Foundation and directed by Professor Brian Nolan, whom we wish to thank for his valuable co-operation.

We are both fortunate to be Fellows of Nuffield College, Oxford, and we have benefited greatly from the research allowances made to us by the College, from the excellent services of its library and IT staff, and from the enriching intellectual and social environment that the College provides.

Finally, we would wish to acknowledge, with our warmest thanks, the contributions of the following colleagues who at various times were members of the research teams working on the several projects: Bastian Betthäuser, Mollie Bourne, Ferdinand Eibl, Heather Joshi, Magda Karyda, Jouni Kuha, Marii Paskov, Nhat An Trinh and Lorraine

Waller. Other colleagues who significantly contributed to the research and in co-authoring papers were Robert Erikson, Alexi Gugushvili and Brendan Halpin. And we also received helpful information, advice and commentary from – among others whom we may have regretfully forgotten – Richard Breen, Tak-Wing Chan, David Cox, Geoff Evans, Duncan Gallie, Colin Mills, Madeline Nightingale and Brian Nolan.

Introduction

In 1927 Pitirim Sorokin, a former Russian revolutionary exiled by Lenin, who had become Professor of Sociology at the University of Minnesota, published the first major academic work on social mobility.[1] Drawing on research findings from a wide range of historical and contemporary societies, he attempted to find regularities in mobility patterns and processes over time and place. Perhaps the two most striking conclusions that he reached – and that still have resonance today – were the following. First, there was no evidence of any tendency for mobility either to increase or to decrease in a sustained fashion, only evidence of 'trendless fluctuation'. Second, although in modern societies education had become the main agency of social selection, there was no reason to suppose that in this way a new age of greater social mobility was being brought into being. Selection by education could in itself serve to block as much as to promote mobility.

Sorokin was, however, well aware that the data at his disposal were of a limited and indeed quite fragmentary nature. They related for the most part to mobility in particular localities or industries or to mobility in the sense of recruitment into various elite groupings, such as those of political and business leaders or eminent scientists and literary figures. He lacked what he called 'the statistical material' necessary to put his arguments to a serious test at a population level.

In the years following the Second World War major progress in social mobility research was achieved. For the first time, studies of mobility were carried out based on representative samples of national populations – and in this regard Britain took the lead through research directed by David Glass from the London School of Economics in 1949. Further improvements have then steadily been made in the design of mobility surveys, in methods of data collection, and in the

---

[1] See Sorokin (1927). Sorokin (1959) is in effect a substantially enlarged second edition.

1

conceptualisation and measurement of mobility rates and patterns. And at the same time a greater understanding has been gained of the actual social processes through which mobility occurs or is impeded.[2]

While these developments brought growing numbers of sociologists into the research field – the twice-yearly meetings of an international Research Committee on Social Stratification and Mobility now attract several hundred participants – any wider interest in issues of social mobility for long remained only occasional and ephemeral. But, in the recent past this situation has rather dramatically changed. In Britain, then in the US, and by now in a number of other economically advanced societies, social mobility has ceased to be merely the subject of some rather esoteric academic research and has become a central political concern, while at the same time attracting a rapidly increasing amount of media attention. Anyone in doubt of these claims is invited to enter 'social mobility' into a web search engine.

Why has this change come about? Although there are some cross-national differences, a general underlying explanation can be given on the following lines. From the mid 1970s economic and social inequality, as measured in terms of income or living standards or by various indicators of quality of life, began to widen – initially and most sharply, it would appear, in Britain and the US but then more generally across most of the western world. In response, parties and governments across the political spectrum, whether unwilling to oppose this rising inequality or simply doubtful about the political possibility of doing so, have been drawn towards an essentially similar default position. It has been found attractive to suppose that *a greater inequality of condition* will become more acceptable if *a greater equality of opportunity*, leading to higher rates of social mobility, can be created. Families will then be less likely to appear as fixed in positions of advantage or disadvantage across generations, and inequality will be more readily legitimated insofar as it can in some way be seen as reflecting differences in achievement rather than the mere accidents of birth.[3]

---

[2] For reviews, see Goldthorpe (2005), Hout and DiPrete (2006) and Torche (2015).
[3] On increasing inequality, see Piketty (2015), Atkinson (2015), Milanovic (2016). Perhaps the most striking expression of the political stance in question can be found in a speech by Tony Blair in which he claimed that mobility was in itself 'the great force for social equality in dynamic market economies' (*The Guardian*, 10 June 2002).

It has at the same time become a further matter of political consensus that in widening opportunity and increasing mobility, it is *education* that must play the crucial role. Governments can best take action, it is supposed, through policies of educational expansion and institutional reform, aimed at raising standards in general and at the same time reducing gaps in educational attainment between individuals of differing social origins. A movement can thus be set in train towards a new kind of social order in which individuals' access to more or less advantaged positions is above all determined by their degree of achievement within the educational system. The envisaged end state is what could be described as *an education-based meritocracy*.[4]

In short, given that rising inequality is the problem, the promotion of social mobility, and primarily through education, has been seized upon as the political solution of choice.

In the British case, the degree of continuity, within an otherwise rapidly changing political landscape, of governmental preoccupation with social mobility is especially striking. Under the New Labour administrations of 1997 to 2010, under the Conservative and Liberal Democrat coalition that ruled from 2010 to 2015 and again under the Conservatives since 2015, increasing social mobility has been presented as a policy priority. The importance of achieving a more mobile society, and the role to be played in this by education, has been repeatedly emphasised in leading ministerial speeches – those of Tony Blair, Gordon Brown, Nick Clegg, David Cameron and Theresa May being in fact more or less interchangeable in this regard. Over the same period official reports and 'strategy documents' on social mobility and its promotion, with a strong emphasis on education, have regularly appeared, often prompting parallel statements from parties in opposition. And issues relating to mobility have been the concern of various parliamentary committees and groups and other official bodies, perhaps the most notable being the Social Mobility Commission, established in 2010. This commission presents annual

---

[4] The idea of an education-based meritocracy was introduced by Michael Young in his celebrated satirical dystopia, *The Rise of the Meritocracy* (1958). Young became increasingly angry with politicians for ignoring the obvious point of his book and upholding meritocracy as an ideal to be pursued (see, for example, *The Guardian*, 29 June 2001). His fundamental objection to meritocracy was that 'It is hard indeed in a society that makes so much of merit to be judged as having none. No underclass has ever been left as morally naked as that.'

reports to Parliament with extensive policy recommendations and also publishes research papers.[5]

Now it might be thought that for social mobility to become a matter of such political prominence would be welcome to sociologists working in this field. Unfortunately, though, a disturbing situation has in fact emerged. A widening 'disconnect' has become apparent between sociological research on mobility – its conceptual and methodological approaches and empirical findings – and the discussion of mobility in political and policy circles. It was perhaps only to be expected that as issues of mobility became more politicised, research findings would be increasingly treated with some partiality – that is, in being 'cherry-picked' in order to support particular party positions and disregarded or denied where inconvenient. And this kind of practice can indeed be readily documented, as will subsequently be seen. But what is of far greater concern is that while in some of the more substantial official reports referred to above attempts have been made – even if not always successfully – to get to grips with the results of relevant research, little comparable effort is apparent in political speeches on social mobility or indeed in the various policy programmes that have been put forward. Rather, a basic lack of understanding of the results of this research and of their wider implications is all too evident. In consequence, much confusion has arisen in the way in which issues of social mobility are represented and policy objectives conceived and pursued; confusion – for the most part uncorrected or even amplified in the media – that then naturally extends into the discussion of these issues in the wider public domain.[6]

---

[5] The main governmental reports are Aldridge (2001), Cabinet Office (2008), HM Government (2009a, 2011, 2012, 2017). Major party statements are Conservative Party (2008) and Liberal Democrats (2009). Other reports have been produced by an All-Party Parliamentary Group on Social Mobility and by a House of Lords Select Committee on Social Mobility. In addition to the Social Mobility Commission referred to in the text (up to 2015 known as the Social Mobility and Child Poverty Commission), other official bodies that have been active in the field include the Panel on Fair Access to the Professions (see HM Government, 2009b) and the Social Mobility Transparency Board, which was in existence from 2012 to 2016, and of which one of us (JHG), was a member. For further details of official involvement in and discourse on issues concerning social mobility, see Payne (2017: ch. 3) and Atherton (2017: ch. 3).

[6] A complicating factor has been the entry of economists into the field of social mobility research – although with a more or less exclusive focus on *income* mobility. A pioneering study on income mobility by Atkinson, Maynard and

At the root of the problem is the fact that social mobility, however viewed, is a highly complex phenomenon – far more so than might at first appear. An understanding of it does therefore demand a serious engagement with the extensive research that has been carried out, and this in turn requires some knowledge of the methodology of this research and, in particular, *of the concepts and related techniques of quantitative data analysis* that are applied. In other words, a basic degree of numeracy and a capacity to think quantitatively are called for, and these are attributes that often appear to be lacking, or even sometimes to be scarcely welcome, in political circles.

In this book our main aim is to provide readers who have a general, non-specialist interest in social mobility with an introduction to, and guidance through, what has been learnt about social mobility in Britain from recent sociological research, and in particular from research projects in which we have ourselves been involved. At the same time, we seek to show where, and why, political and policy discussion of social mobility falls short of taking adequate account of this research. To anticipate, we may say that in this regard two recurrent themes will be the following: first, the failure, in considering levels and determinants of social mobility, to distinguish, correctly and consistently, between what sociologists refer to as absolute and relative rates; and, second, and relatedly, the inadequate understanding of what must be involved if education is to be the key means of increasing mobility and if the goal of an education-based meritocracy is to be realised – leaving aside all normative questions of whether or not this is a goal that should be pursued. We hope that, in the interests of more coherent political argument and more evidence-based policy, we will be able to contribute something to overcoming the disconnect between research and politics that we will demonstrate, or that we will, at very least, be able to bring about a greater critical awareness of its existence.

Trinder (1983) had for long no follow-up in Britain, but since the end of the 1990s some further research has been undertaken. And although this research is still far less extensive than that undertaken by sociologists, economists have gained generally closer relationships with, and seemingly greater influence on, government departments and other official bodies, including the Social Mobility Commission, than have sociologists. This in part reflects economists' long-standing involvement in governmental policy making but also perhaps an official tendency to view economists as more 'amenable' than sociologists, and to regard treating mobility in terms of income as politically safer than treating it in terms of social class, as sociologists prefer to do (see further Chapter 1).

In the remainder of this introductory chapter we indicate the bases and range of the research on which we will draw, and the approach we will take in presenting the findings that emerge; we also indicate some limitations that arise. We conclude by briefly outlining the overall structure of the book.

As earlier noted, a major advance in social mobility research was made when partial studies of various kinds were superseded by ones based on representative samples of national populations. In Britain, the LSE study of 1949 that pioneered this approach was followed up by one of a basically similar design undertaken from Nuffield College, Oxford in 1972, covering England and Wales, and by a parallel study carried out in Scotland. It has subsequently been possible to make further nationally representative cross-sectional analyses of mobility rates and patterns, although of a more limited kind, using data from social surveys designed in other research contexts or from official general purpose surveys.[7]

However, it is a fortunate fact that in Britain, more so than in most other countries, the opportunity exists to develop the population approach to mobility research in a further way of major importance: that is, through using the datasets of *birth cohort studies* – in the development of which Britain could again claim to have played a leading role. These are studies that collect information on children born into a population at the same time – usually, that is, in the same year – and that aim to follow these 'cohort members' throughout their entire lives: first, by means of interviews with their parents, and possibly also with teachers, so as to obtain detailed information on their family backgrounds and early personal and academic development, and then, as members move into adulthood, by means of interviewing them directly, at regular intervals, so as to obtain information on different aspects of their social lives, including their later educational careers and their employment and occupational histories.

While cross-sectional surveys, if repeated in the same form, allow rates and patterns of social mobility in a population to be compared across historical periods, birth cohort studies enable a further 'over-time' perspective on mobility to be gained. They allow one to see how

---

[7] The LSE study is reported on in Glass ed. (1954) and the Nuffield study in Goldthorpe (1980/1987). Later analyses include those of Goldthorpe and Mills (2004, 2008), Paterson and Ianelli (2007), Li and Devine (2011) and Buscha and Sturgis (2017).

individuals' experience of mobility – or immobility – unfolds in the course of their lives, and to trace the social processes that are involved in the contexts of the family, the educational system and the labour market. Moreover, where, as in Britain, a *series* of cohort studies has been undertaken, it becomes possible for the two over-time perspectives to be combined. By comparing men and women at similar life-course stages in successive cohorts, one can investigate both the extent of any historical changes in levels and patterns of mobility and their determinants and at the same time see how any such changes find expression in the progress of individual lives.

Because of the major advantages offered by such cohort studies, the research on social mobility in Britain that we have ourselves undertaken has been based for the most part on their datasets and, specifically, on those of the three earliest cohort studies. The first of these started out from a sample of children born in Britain in one week in 1946 and has been followed by studies covering all children born in one week in 1958 and all children born in one week in 1970.[8] The datasets of these studies are in the public domain, but we have carried out further extensive data preparation work in order to ensure the greatest possible degree of cross-cohort comparability in the key variables of interest to us.

In the case of the 1958 cohort, a supplementary project was undertaken in 2008 – that is, when cohort members were age 50 – in which a specially selected sample of 220 men and women were interviewed at length on different aspects of their current social lives but were also asked to give their own accounts of their life histories. At various points in this book there are display boxes containing brief case studies that are based on these accounts – primarily in order to illustrate not 'typical' but rather some of the less common and familiar trajectories of mobility or immobility that our quantitative analyses reveal.[9]

---

[8] A further cohort study was launched in 2000 but its members are still not sufficiently advanced in their lives for anything to be usefully said about their social mobility. For a wide-ranging account of the British cohort studies, see Pearson (2016). Full details of the 1946, 1958 and 1970 studies are given, respectively, in Wadsworth et al. (2006), Power and Elliott (2006) and Elliott and Shepherd (2006).

[9] For full details of the project, see Elliott et al. (2010). It should be noted that we use case studies derived from this project to illustrate results reported in Chapters 8 and 9, even though the analyses of these chapters are in fact based on

While the 1946, 1958 and 1970 birth cohort studies are our main data sources, we also at times draw on the datasets of other longitudinal studies of somewhat different design and on those of surveys of a cross-sectional character. All these sources have of course been exploited by other sociologists with interests in mobility, and we seek wherever possible to relate our own findings to theirs and to account for those instances – fortunately few – in which some degree of inconsistency or contradiction might appear to arise.[10]

We should further add that although our focus is on social mobility in Britain, it may often be relevant to view the British case against the background of the extensive research that has by now been carried out into social mobility in other modern societies. We therefore quite often include notes on how far our findings for Britain match up with those for other countries. It is, as it turns out, similarities rather than differences that are most in evidence. However, in this connection we can scarcely avoid the question, much discussed in political and policy circles, of whether on a comparative view Britain has to be regarded as a low mobility society. This is a question that we take up on the basis of a newly formed comparative dataset, and it proves to be one in regard to which the disconnect between political discussion and the findings of sociological research is again rather dramatically apparent.

Having indicated the nature and extent of the data sources on which the research we will review is based, we need next to give some explanation of the way in which we will seek to present the results of this research. As we earlier observed, social mobility is a highly complex phenomenon, and its understanding, beyond a very preliminary stage, requires a methodology that is adequate to this complexity. That which has developed over recent decades is essentially based on the quantitative analysis of large-scale, population-level data *through the application of multivariate statistical models*. What these models serve to do, at least as we would apply them, is bring out regularities that exist in

only the 1970 cohort. In all cases some details have been altered in order to prevent any possibility of identification.

[10] With all birth cohort studies the problem of missing data is exacerbated by cohort attrition – i.e. by cohort members at some point dropping out of the study, although they may later return. To mitigate this problem we have worked for the most part with a dataset in which missing data are replaced through a statistical technique known as multiple imputation. This may appear as a form of statistical black magic, but for further discussion see Kuha (2013).

associations between variables of interest that would otherwise remain irretrievably buried within datasets: for example, and most obviously in mobility research, regularities in the association existing between individuals' social origins and their social destinations. Further, though, we can also examine how far this association varies between men and women or between birth cohorts or between men and women in different cohorts. And, further still, we can analyse the associations existing between individuals' social origins and their educational attainment and then between their educational attainment and their social destinations, and again in relation to other variables such as gender or birth cohort – and so on. The complexities of social mobility, and in turn of the important sociopolitical issues to which they give rise, can, we believe, only be satisfactorily treated through such statistical modelling, demanding though this may be. There are no shortcuts.

From this standpoint, we do, though, have to recognise the following problem. In papers on social mobility published in academic journals the statistical models applied would be formally presented and the results obtained from their application would be given in a highly detailed way, so as to allow readers to make their own professional judgments as to the reliability and validity of the analyses involved. But we are aiming at a more general readership with, we must suppose, a limited knowledge of, and very likely a still more limited interest in, more technical statistical issues. We have, therefore, to follow a much simplified approach. We aim to concentrate on what we take to be the most salient findings that emerge from our analyses, and as far as possible present these findings in a graphical form so that the messages they contain are directly apparent. Further, where resort to a tabular presentation cannot be avoided, we try not to confront readers with a large array of numbers but again seek to indicate the findings that are of main substantive importance. This approach, we would stress, *does* simplify – and in some cases, it might be thought, unduly so; there is certainly a good deal that readers will have in effect to take on trust. However, virtually all the results that we present have been previously reported in papers in academic journals with the full complement of technical information, and for readers who would wish to have a more detailed account of the procedures we have followed, we provide the relevant references.

We must finally note certain limitations of the research that provides the main basis of our book. These mainly derive from the fact that, because of our concern to provide an account of social mobility within British society at large, we are not in a position to consider mobility in regard to relatively small groupings, such as, say, elites of various kinds or ethnic or other minorities. This is essentially a matter of numbers. Although the cohort studies on which we chiefly rely each cover several thousand men and women, this is not nearly enough to allow any reliable analyses to be undertaken of mobility relating to groupings that amount, at most, to only a few per cent of the total population. For such analyses to be possible, either extremely large samples have to be exploited – far larger than would be practicable with a cohort study requiring repeated interviewing – or specialised samples have to be drawn.

By following such approaches, research has in fact been carried out into what are taken to be distinctive issues associated with the recruitment of elites or the social mobility of ethnic minorities. This research is of evident interest and the issues pursued have their own importance. But we would in fact regard analyses of mobility of this kind as being best understood if placed in the wider context of research that relates to the society as a whole. Otherwise, the danger would appear to arise of excessive claims being made.

For example, it has been suggested that in present-day Britain the intergenerational exclusiveness of certain elites is so extreme that it could be seen as a matter of greater concern than inequalities in mobility chances existing within the rest of the population. As we will seek to show later, this is a questionable argument in that, once the full extent of the latter inequalities is recognised, it is far from clear that any major discontinuity between 'elite' and 'mass' mobility does actually exist. Again, there has been a tendency to exaggerate the degree to which the social mobility – or immobility – of members of ethnic minorities gives rise to special problems. In fact, the research that has most adequately addressed this question indicates that the rates and patterns of mobility of members of different ethnic groupings, and especially where individuals who are at least 'second generation' are considered, do, to a very large extent, conform with those that are found in the majority population.[11]

One further limitation our book may be thought to have is that in general the most recent analyses we report refer to the experience of

[11] See Li and Heath (2016).

members of the 1970 birth cohort by the time they reached their late thirties. In other words our analyses do not in the main extend beyond the end of the first decade of the twenty-first century. However, it has to be recognised that social mobility has always to be studied, as it were, through a rear-view mirror. For reasons that will become apparent, one cannot have a reliable understanding of the mobility of men and women until they have reached at least a mid-life stage, and thus in the instances in which we do take into account the experience of those born closer to the end of twentieth century, our conclusions are necessarily subject to various qualifications. We would in fact see it as an advantage that, in drawing on the three cohort studies that we have referred to, we can extend our analyses a good way *back* in time and thus be able to view mobility rates and patterns and the social processes underlying them in a relatively long-term historical perspective.

Our book is structured on the following lines. In Chapter 1 we explain why we wish to take *social class* – rather than, say, income or some other aspect of social advantage and disadvantage – as the context for the study of mobility. We set out how we conceptualise social class and how we make our concept of class operational in the research on which we subsequently report, and present a range of evidence to indicate why we believe it is especially revealing to consider mobility as it occurs between different class positions.

In Chapters 2, 3 and 4 we are concerned with analysing rates and patterns of intergenerational class mobility in Britain, and with tracing trends in these rates and patterns over the period from the mid twentieth to the early twenty-first century. Crucial here is the distinction to which we have already referred – and the significance of which we seek to make fully apparent – between absolute and relative mobility rates. The issues on which we focus are those of whether, over the period we cover, Britain has become a more or less mobile and a more or less fluid or 'open' society, and the extent and at least the more immediate sources of the inequalities in class mobility chances that are revealed.

In Chapter 5 we move on to the question of the role of education in class mobility. We aim to make clear what is required, if education is to promote mobility, in terms of changes in existing associations between individuals' social origins and their educational attainment and in turn between their educational attainment and the class destinations at which they eventually arrive. And we also seek to bring out the importance, in these respects, of how educational attainment is itself conceptualised and measured – that is, in absolute or in relative terms. Chapters 6, 7, 8 and 9 are then all concerned with a more detailed examination of the issues raised in Chapter 5. How far do social origins condition educational attainment in such a way as to lead to inequalities of opportunity and thus a wastage of talent? How far in an emerging postindustrial society are the chances of upward mobility in the course of working life declining, so that education obtained before entry into the labour market becomes increasingly class destiny? How far do individuals' social origins still influence the class destinations they eventually reach independently of their educational attainment: that is, through 'glass floors' that protect those from more advantaged origins against downward mobility and 'glass ceilings' that prevent those from less advantaged origins from achieving upward mobility? And how far does further education in the course of working life – lifelong learning – either provide opportunities for individuals to compensate for low levels of initial educational attainment, or, rather, build on higher levels and thus, from an intergenerational perspective, operate less as a source of mobility than of immobility?

In Chapter 10 we return to questions of levels of absolute and relative class mobility, but in a cross-national, comparative context. As indicated earlier, we consider how far Britain can be regarded as a low mobility society, and further what more general conclusions about the future of social mobility in Britain are suggested by comparative analyses.

Finally, in Chapter 11 we summarise the main findings that emerge from the research we have reviewed; we indicate again the various ways in which a disconnect is apparent between these findings and the political discussion of social mobility; and we try to give some indication of how this discussion might be reoriented, with a greater respect for empirical evidence, and of the implications for policy that would follow.

1 | *Social Class as the Context of Social Mobility*

Social mobility is the movement of individuals over time between different social positions. Insofar as positions are taken to be in some way more or less advantaged, mobility can be characterised as being upward or downward in direction: that is, as being from a less to a more advantaged position or vice versa. To this extent, the understanding of social mobility in the social sciences is on much the same lines as it is in everyday life. However, where questions arise concerning actual rates, patterns and trends of mobility, and the systematic collection and analysis of relevant data have to be undertaken, it is necessary for social scientists to think about mobility in ways that are conceptually more explicit and precise than those that serve for less demanding purposes.

First and foremost, it is essential that the *context* of mobility – that is, the positions between which mobility is seen as occurring – should be clearly specified. Within the social sciences there are in fact significant differences in this regard. Sociologists, who, as indicated in the Introduction, have thus far carried out the greater part of research into social mobility, tend to focus on mobility between social strata, as characterised, for example, in terms of social class. In contrast, economists, among whom a sustained interest in social mobility is, at least in Britain, a relatively recent development, focus on mobility in terms of income – that is, on the mobility of individuals between different levels within the overall income distribution.

In this book we will, as sociologists, be concerned primarily with social class mobility: that is, with mobility between different class positions. The main aims of this chapter are therefore to set out the rationale for this approach and the advantages that we believe stem from it, and further to indicate how we conceptualise social class and how this conceptual understanding is made operational in the main body of research that we will subsequently discuss.

Where one is dealing with social mobility between positions that are more or less advantaged, or, in other words, unequal, it is important to recognise that social inequality can be expressed in two different forms: what may be called *attributional* inequality and *relational* inequality. Attributional inequality arises simply insofar as individuals have, as an attribute, more or less of something that is socially valued. Inequality in income or in wealth would be prime examples. Relational inequality, in contrast, arises where the positions of a more or less advantaged kind that individuals hold derive from certain social relations in which they are involved. Class inequality, as we would understand it, is relational. More specifically, we take class positions as deriving from the social relations in which individuals are involved *in labour markets and workplaces*: that is, from what we will refer to as their *employment relations*. While individuals' class positions are in this way associated with their income levels, they are also associated, via differences in their employment relations, with various other aspects of their incomes: in particular, as we will show in some detail, with income security or insecurity, with short-term income stability or instability and with longer-term income prospects.

We might add here that another form of relational inequality that we treat as distinct from, and only imperfectly correlated with, class is that of social status. In popular discourse, 'class' and 'status' are often used more or less synonymously. But sociologists would see the relational basis of status as lying not in labour markets and workplaces but rather in differential association in the more intimate aspects of social life – status equals are those who eat together and sleep together – and also in participation in, and perhaps exclusion from, distinctive lifestyles. Class and status are thus qualitatively different forms of social stratification. Some sociologists have in fact studied social mobility in terms of status rather than class, and although we will concentrate on social class mobility, we will at various points indicate how this may be influenced by social status.[1]

---

[1] For more on the distinction between class and status, see Chan and Goldthorpe (2004, 2007). Sociologists have also treated mobility in terms of what is referred to as socioeconomic status – in effect, on the basis of occupations scaled in some way according to the average earnings and educational levels of the individuals holding them. However, both the concept of socioeconomic status and its measurement have become subject to increasing criticism (see Bukodi, Dex and

We would argue that in general inequality that is embedded in social relations is at least as *consequential* in individuals' lives as is attributional inequality; and further that, so far as economic life is concerned, social class provides a fuller and more revealing context for the study of social mobility than does income. Again, this is a matter to which we will return at various points subsequently. However, two issues arise that may be taken up at once.

First, it is sometimes held that treating mobility in terms of income is preferable to treating it in terms of class because 'everybody knows' what income is, whereas the concept of social class is vague or contested. In response, we would observe that in the study of income mobility major problems in conceptualisation and making concepts operational are in fact encountered. For example, there are many forms of income, but the work on income mobility that has been carried out by economists has for the most part been limited to just one form: that is, to 'labour income' or earnings. Income from other sources, such as, say, investments, has only rather rarely been taken into account. Moreover, while economists would evidently wish to think of mobility in regard not simply to current income or earnings but rather to 'permanent income' or 'lifetime earnings', these more ambitious concepts have not so far been effectively implemented in empirical research. At most, what has been measured is income or earnings averaged over a number of years in order to iron out transitional variation.[2]

Second, serious difficulties are encountered in obtaining reliable data on income mobility. In social surveys there is an unusually high rate of non-response to questions on income, even in the form only of earnings. And where intergenerational mobility is being studied a yet greater problem arises in that survey respondents cannot be expected to recall – or even to have known – the level of their parents' incomes when they were growing up. Attempts that have been made to 'impute' parents' incomes from information obtained from children on their

Goldthorpe, 2011), and would appear best avoided, at all events in mobility research.
[2] For penetrating reviews of the methodological problems involved in studying income mobility, written by economists, see Jäntti and Jenkins (2015) and Winship (2017).

parents' education and occupation are scarcely adequate.[3] The only
data on income mobility of high reliability are in fact those derived
either from birth cohort or other longitudinal studies focused on this
question or from cumulated taxation records or other forms of income
registration through which the incomes of children and their parents
can be linked. It has to be recognised that, as of now, *no such data exist
for Britain*; and the study of income mobility can therefore make little
progress.[4]

None of the foregoing should of course be taken to imply that the
analysis of social mobility in terms of class is free of conceptual and
data issues. Such issues do indeed present themselves, and it is to these
that we now turn.

It is certainly the case that social class has been conceptualised in
many different ways. Indeed, a large and disputatious literature on the
matter has developed since the controversies over Marxist class analysis of the earlier twentieth century. The arguments that have arisen,
and that continue, are, however, ones for the most part conducted at a
quite abstract level or, at best, with only a loose articulation with
empirical research, and we do not seek here to enter into them. The

---

[3] Imputing an entire variable is a quite different proposition from using imputation
to deal with missing cases on variables, as we have done (see Introduction, n. 10
above). Jerrim et al. (2016) show how estimates of income mobility based on the
imputed incomes of parents are highly dependent on, and consequently can vary
significantly with, the imputation models that are used. In the Social Mobility
Commission's Annual Report for 2016, intergenerational earnings mobility
tables are given a prominent place without it being indicated where parental
earnings have been imputed rather than actually observed (Social Mobility
Commission, 2016: tables 02 and 03); the imputation then turns out to be based
on a very limited and thus quite unreliable model (Friedman, Laurison and
Macmillan, 2017: 8). Such tables could be thought as likely to mislead as to
inform.

[4] In the 1958 and 1970 birth cohort studies referred to in the Introduction some
information is available on cohort members' family incomes when they were age
16 and their own earnings in their adult lives. However, the extent of missing
data is disturbing, the questions asked on family income differ significantly from
one cohort to the other, and the self-employed have to be excluded from
consideration because of the known unreliability of the income information they
provide. Despite the valiant efforts economists have made to overcome these
problems, the results they obtain on intergenerational income mobility remain
open to doubt (see further Chapter 3 below). And still more doubtful are the
efforts that have been made by some economists to infer future income mobility
from the relation between parental income and children's educational attainment,
which rest on a range of question-begging assumptions.

conceptualisation of class that we adopt is one that has by now some wide acceptance in sociology, and also, increasingly, in official statistics, and chiefly for the following reasons. It has a clear theoretical basis; it can be effectively made operational for research purposes; and, perhaps most importantly, when applied in research it has been found to give consistent and revealing results. The ultimate test of any conceptual approach has to lie in the empirical findings that it makes possible.

As we have already indicated, we take class positions as deriving from the relations in which individuals are involved in labour markets and workplaces or, that is, from their employment relations. As understood in this way, class positions are differentiated at two levels. At the most basic level, they are differentiated in terms of *employment status*: employers, the self-employed and employees have clearly different positions in labour markets and workplaces.[5] Employers buy and control the labour of employees, the self-employed sell their own labour to customers or clients, and employees sell their labour to, and accept the control of, employers or their agents. However, in the case of employees, who in modern economies make up the large majority of the economically active population, a further level of differentiation is required. In this regard, what is taken as crucial is the form of the *employment contracts*, considered in regard to both their explicit and implicit elements, under which employees work.

At one extreme of this differentiation, one can identify a contract that is in effect a 'spot' contract for labour: that is, a contract that entails a certain amount of labour being exchanged for a certain amount of pay, and that, even if perhaps recurrent, does not suppose any commitment by employer or employee to the future of the relationship. Contracts of this kind have traditionally applied in the case of 'day labourers' or other casual workers, and today find their most extreme expression in increasingly used zero-hours contracts, under which workers are simply on call for employers who have no obligation to employ them for any fixed amount of time. Further, though, the employment relations of large numbers of other workers in jobs of a manual or entirely routine non-manual kind have always

---

[5] Employment status is a term used in official statistics in relation to differences of the kind referred to in the text. It has no connection with the concept of social status as previously discussed in this chapter.

approximated this basic form of labour contract. Payment is through wages that are directly related to amount of work done on the basis of piece rates or of hourly, daily or shift rates together with overtime rates; and no greater degree of continuity of employment is implied beyond that provided for by minimum legal requirements concerning dismissal and redundancy.

Contracts of the kind in question in effect serve as far as possible to *commodify* labour: that is, to enable it to be bought like any other commodity regardless of its human embodiment. Such contracts have obvious attractions for employers in increasing 'flexibility' and reducing economic risk – by in effect transferring it to their employees. But at the same time they represent an efficient form of contract only in the case of certain types of work: that is, work that is easily monitored as regards worker effort and quality of output and that calls for only relatively low-level, unspecialised and widely available capacities and skills.

This latter point is best brought out by considering the form of employment contract that can be taken as standing at the opposite extreme to a spot contract. This entails what might be called a 'service relationship' and is found in its most developed form in the case of higher-level managerial and professional employees. Managers are engaged to exercise delegated authority, and professionals to exercise specialised knowledge and expertise, on behalf of their employers; it is therefore of advantage to employers if these employees are motivated to act consistently in the interests of the employing organisation and to adapt and develop their abilities and skills over time in its particular context. Thus, what is in these circumstances appropriate is a contract that goes beyond simply a recurrent 'money for effort' bargain and implies an exchange between employer and employee of a relatively diffuse and long-term kind. Employees 'render service' to their employer – and if necessary in excess of any formally contracted requirements – in return for 'compensation' which comprises a fixed salary together usually with a range of fringe benefits and, in addition, important *prospective* elements: for example, regular salary incre-ments, expectations of continuity of employment or at least of employ-ability and, above all, relatively well-defined promotion and career opportunities. That is to say, the employment contract is aimed at creating a general and forward-looking employee commitment to organisational goals by establishing a clear connection between such commitment and the employee's economic security and advancement.

What could be regarded as modified versions of both the basic labour contract and the service relationship are also in wide operation. Thus, on the one hand, workers who are paid on a wage basis but who are in more skilled occupations often have a greater degree of security of employment than less skilled wage-workers, as through 'last in, first out' agreements, and perhaps also some possibility of promotion, say to supervisory positions; while, on the other hand, employees in the lower levels of the managerial and professional salariat may enjoy the advantages of a service relationship only in a limited form. In addition, various 'mixed' forms of employment contract, involving some kind of compromise between the logics of the labour contract and service relationship, can be identified. Typically, these are found with occupations that, in terms of the capacities and skills they require and the responsibilities they entail, lie in between those of managers and professionals and of essentially routine workers. Thus, employees in such occupations – mainly lower administrative, technical or supervisory occupations – may be salaried yet have few promotion opportunities, and with any overtime working or other extra-contractual contributions being compensated for by generally relaxed time-keeping arrangements, 'time off in lieu' or *ex gratia* payments, and also perhaps through admission at the workplace to 'staff' status and facilities.[6]

What in the present context is of importance is that, in the case of employees, *type of occupation can be taken as a fairly reliable indicator of prevailing employment relations*, and occupation can thus be used, along with employment status, as a basis for identifying class positions as defined in terms of employment relations.

It is in fact in this way that the particular class schema that will most frequently figure in the chapters that follow has been constructed: that is, the National Statistics Socio-Economic Classification (NS-SEC) which from 2001 became the main social classification in use in British official statistics, in succession to the Registrar-General's Social Classes which, as originally formulated, dated back to 1911.

---

[6] The theory behind the differentiation of the class positions of employees according to forms of employment contract does in fact derive essentially from developments in economics, in particular organisational, personnel and transaction-cost economics (Goldthorpe, 2007: vol. II, ch. 5; McGovern et al., 2007: ch. 3). This being the case, the apparent reluctance of economists to utilise the concept of class – even when it would appear more relevant to their concerns than that of income – is puzzling.

Figure 1.1 shows the derivation, in terms of employment relations, of the seven-class version of NS-SEC, which is that in most common use, and this version is then set out in Table 1.1.[7] In Figure 1.1 and Table 1.1 we take the liberty of relabelling Class 3, officially 'Intermediate', as 'Ancillary professional and administrative' so as to give a more specific idea of its coverage. Table 1.1 also shows for each class some representative present-day occupations, although it should be recognised that other occupations would be more representative insofar as the classification is applied to earlier periods – as it is in effect when applied to parental generations in mobility analyses.

It may be noted that in the seven-class version of NS-SEC a number of 'collapses' of categories of a more extended version of the classification are implied. Thus, Class 1 includes, in addition to higher managerial and professional employees, both 'large' employers – that is, those with twenty-five or more employees (who are in fact predominantly owners of only medium-size, unincorporated concerns) – and also self-employed professionals. This is because, in most available datasets, the number of such employers and self-employed professionals is too small to allow for separate analysis; and further because distinctions between employers and managers, on the one hand, and between self-employed and employee professionals, on the other, may not be easily made or in any event involve legal or fiscal considerations rather than being of any great sociological significance. Further, Class 4 brings together both small employers – those with less than twenty-five employees – and also own-account workers without employees. This is chiefly because of difficulties that arise in distinguishing in the case of small concerns between employees proper and 'family

---

[7] In the development of NS-SEC, a crucial role was played by analyses, drawing on data collected through the Labour Force Survey, that sought to test the 'construct validity' of the classification: that is, the validity of inferring employment relations from data on employment status and occupation. These analyses produced generally satisfactory results, although the need was emphasised for regular revisions of the official classification of occupations and in turn for the rebasing of NS-SEC to reflect changes in employment relations (Rose and Pevalin, eds., 2003; Rose, Pevalin and O'Reilly 2005; ONS, 2005). Such rebasing is now in fact in progress in preparation for the 2021 Census, and is aimed at taking account of the growth of temporary employment contracts, portfolio working and bogus self-employment. Some further modifications may also be necessary in consequence of ongoing technological change (Williams, 2017b). But for the period with which we are concerned, NS-SEC in its present form can be regarded as an appropriate classification.

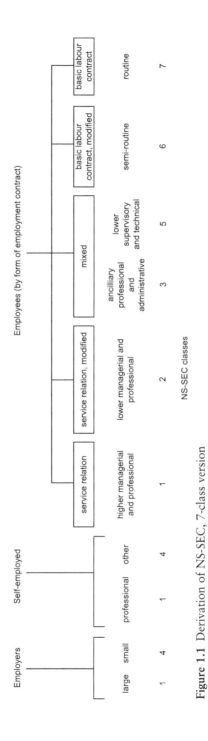

Figure 1.1 Derivation of NS-SEC, 7-class version

Table 1.1 *NS-SEC 7-class version and representative occupations*[a]

Class	Description	Representative occupations
Class 1	Higher managers and professionals	General managers in large companies and organisations, higher-grade civil servants and local government officials, architects, lawyers; medical practitioners, professional engineers, scientists, university teachers
Class 2	Lower managers and professionals	General managers in small companies and organisations, site managers, office managers, workshop managers, lower-grade civil servants and local government officers, librarians, nurses, physiotherapists, school teachers, social workers, surveyors
Class 3	Ancillary professional and administrative	Computer maintenance staff, draughtspersons, library assistants, nursery nurses, paramedical staff, cashiers, clerical workers, data processing operators, personal assistants, secretaries
Class 4	Small employers and own account workers	Garage proprietors, builders, café proprietors, craftsmen, market traders, publicans, shopkeepers
Class 5	Lower supervisory and technical occupations	Foremen, site and works supervisors, auto engineers, heating engineers, instrument technicians, laboratory technicians, printers, tool- and pattern-makers, TV and video engineers
Class 6	Semi-routine occupations	Care assistants, caretakers and housekeepers, chefs and cooks, chemical process workers, crane drivers, factory machinists, fitters, postal workers, receptionists, sales assistants, store controllers and despatchers, traffic wardens
Class 7	Routine occupations	Bus and van drivers, construction site and other labourers, craftsmen's mates, food process workers, counter and bar staff, house and office cleaners, kitchen assistants, packers and fillers, porters and attendants, refuse collectors, warehouse workers

Note (a) Hierarchical divisions are indicated by dashed lines

workers': that is, workers who may not be paid regular wages but share in some way in the proceeds of the business.

In understanding NS-SEC, and analyses of social mobility that are based on it, there are two points in particular that need to be kept in mind. The first is that NS-SEC does not relate in any direct way to the particular nature or content of the work done in different occupations – only indirectly insofar as different kinds of work tasks and roles are associated with different forms of employment contract.[8] One consequence of this is that NS-SEC, unlike the Registrar General's Social Classes and other earlier social classifications in both official and academic use, does not embody any systematic manual/non-manual distinction – as is brought out in Table 1.1.

The second point is that the seven NS-SEC classes as presented in Table 1.1 should not be regarded as completely ordered. In particular, while Class 4 positions, those of small employers and own account workers, are clearly differentiated from the employee positions of Classes 3 and 5, it would be difficult to claim that these positions are, overall, more or less advantaged. Although, then, mobility between Class 3 or Class 5, on the one hand, and Class 4, on the other, would certainly involve a change in employment relations and thus class position, this could be better regarded as 'horizontal' rather than as upward or downward mobility. And much the same could be said about mobility between Classes 3 and 5 themselves. In what follows we therefore treat as upward or downward mobility only that which occurs across the five 'hierarchical' divisions of NS-SEC, as are indicated by the dashed lines in Table 1.1. We will also refer to Classes 1 and 2 taken together as the salariat and to Classes 6 and 7 taken together as the working class.

---

[8] This point is missed by economists (e.g. Blanden, Gregg and Machin, 2005a), who argue that an occupation-based classification, such as NS-SEC, is unsuitable for the study of intergenerational class mobility since over time the occupational composition of classes will change. While such change does indeed occur, as noted earlier, it is not of relevance provided that employment relations in the occupations included within a class remain the same. Thus, four or five decades ago representative occupations in Classes 6 and 7 of NS-SEC would certainly be different from those given in Table 1.1: coal miners, iron and steel workers, shipyard workers, dockers, textiles workers and bus conductors could well figure. But what is important is that essentially the same employment relations could be taken to be in operation – i.e. those of wage-workers under something closely resembling the basic form of labour contract.

In the research we subsequently discuss, it is NS-SEC that chiefly serves to implement our concept of class and that in turn provides the basis for analyses of mobility between different class positions. What remains for us to do now is to set out the grounds on which we believe that we thus have, for the historical period that concerns us, a context for the study of social mobility that is distinctively revealing. This entails showing the various ways in which different class positions, as we would define them, confer advantage or impose disadvantage, in particular of an economic kind, on the individual men and women who hold them, and in turn exert a major influence on their life-chances.

We earlier claimed that as well as individuals' class positions being associated with their income levels, they are also associated with their income (in)security, their short-term income (in)stability and their longer-term income prospects. We aim now to provide the basis for these claims.

The impact of class on income security comes about primarily from the strong association that exists between class, understood in terms of employment relations, and the risk of job loss and unemployment. Various studies from the 1970s onwards have clearly revealed that these risks are greatest for those whose employment relations most closely approximate the basic labour contract – that is, where no long-term commitment exists between employer and employee, even of an implicit kind – and these findings can be fully confirmed by research, based on NS-SEC, for the early twentieth-first century.[9]

In Figure 1.2 we show, using data from the Labour Force Survey for 2014, the relative risks of men and women being unemployed by the class of their last employment. Class effects, following the hierarchical divisions of NS-SEC, are clearly revealed. While there is some overlap of the confidence intervals around our point estimates

---

[9] For earlier work, see White (1991) and Gallie et al. (1998). The most important previous analysis based on NS-SEC is Elias and McKnight (2003) but see also Goldthorpe and McKnight (2006) and Chan and Goldthorpe (2007). Using what could be regarded as a European version of NS-SEC, Lucchini and Schizzerotto (2010) provide a revealing comparative analysis of the impact of class on unemployment in Austria, Denmark, Italy and the UK. And it is of further interest that in the two latter studies cited, educational qualifications are included as a control variable without this seriously modifying the association between class and the risk of unemployment.

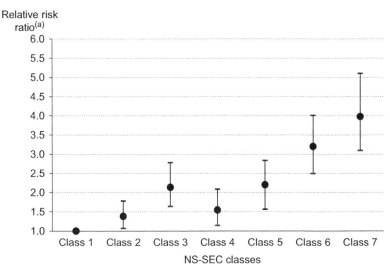

Note

(a) Based on a statistical model which includes gender, age, marital status and
    number of dependent children

Source: Labour Force Survey, 2014, January–March

Figure 1.2 Relative risk of being unemployed by class position of last employment, Class 1 as reference, with 95% confidence intervals

so far as the intermediate classes are concerned, clear contrasts still
emerge between the salariat and the working class.[10] At the extreme,
the risk of being found in unemployment for individuals whose last
employment was in Class 7 – where labour is most completely
commodified – is estimated as four times greater than the corresponding risk for those last employed in Class 1 positions.[11] As regards

[10] Confidence intervals as shown here, and in subsequent figures in the book,
   indicate the range within which we would expect the true value to have a 95 per
   cent chance of occurring. We do not, however, show confidence intervals in
   cases where they are very small and so have no bearing on the interpretation of
   the point estimates.

[11] Another possible source of income insecurity is employment on the basis of a
   temporary contract. While such contracts have become generally more common
   in the recent past, a close link with class exists. Further analyses of Labour Force
   Survey data that we have undertaken reveal that they are significantly more
   often found among men and women in the entirely routine occupations of Class
   7 than among those in occupations comprised by other classes.

the rather low relative risk of unemployment that is indicated for the small employers and own-account workers of Class 4, it should be kept in mind that in their case *under*employment can also be a serious threat to income security.

The association between class and short-term income stability or instability again derives from differences in employment relations: that is, from typical differences in methods of payment. Where, under employment relations approximating the basic labour contract, payment is in the form of wages determined by piece rates or, more commonly today, by time rates of some kind plus overtime and shift premia, it can only be expected that earnings will be subject to more short-term variation than where a fixed, usually annual, salary is paid; and previous research has established that this is indeed the case.[12] There is evidence that of late 'payment for performance' systems have become more extensively applied, and in such a way that class differences might be thought to have been reduced. However, insofar as with managerial or professional employees a variable pay element is introduced, it has to be noted that this is most likely to come in the form of performance payments – bonuses, commission and so forth – that are *additional to* basic salary.

In Figure 1.3 we show, again using Labour Force Survey data for 2014, the importance of variable components of earnings by class for men of employee status (the results for women are on much the same pattern). Class differences are evident. Overtime pay, shift premia and piece rates amount to around 14 per cent of the earnings of men in Classes 5, 6 and 7 but are of slight importance for men in Classes 1 and 2, while bonuses and commission payments count for little among men in any class other than Classes 1 and 2. In the case of men in Class 1 these forms of payment amount to over 10 per cent of their average earnings. Where earnings have significant variable components and are also at a low average level, as especially with employees in Classes 6 and 7, serious difficulties are then likely to arise both in the management of day-to-day family budgets and in any kind of longer-term financial planning. Figure 1.3 does not cover the small employers and own-account workers of Class 4 but from other research it emerges, not surprisingly, that their incomes too are liable

[12] See Goldthorpe and McKnight (2006).

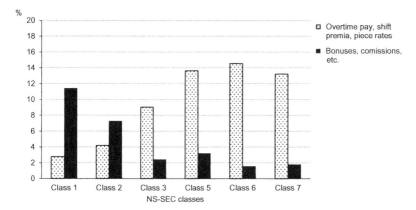

Source: Labour Force Survey, 2014, January–March

Figure 1.3 Variable components of average gross weekly earnings, men in full-time employment

to significant fluctuation and that maintaining 'custom' or the 'flow of work' are common concerns.[13]

Finally, the association between class and income prospects is perhaps that of greatest significance. Under the basic employment contract, or employment relations that approximate to it, there is little reason why earnings should increase with time in employment, except perhaps over a fairly short initial period during which workers acquire such training and experience as may be necessary in the jobs typically involved. In contrast, it is part of the logic of a service relationship that relatively well-defined opportunities for economic advancement, through salary increases and career progression, should exist in order to encourage and reward employees' continuing commitment to organisational goals. What follows is that within different classes clearly different 'age–earnings curves' are created.

In Figures 1.4 and 1.5 we show such curves for men and women of employee status based on recent data, which in fact are essentially the same as those that have been found in earlier analyses extending back to the 1970s. As can be seen, with men and women in Classes 6 and 7, earnings increase – relatively slowly – with age up to around

[13] See Scase and Goffee (1980, 1982) and Boden and Corden (1994). The earnings of workers on zero-hour contracts are of course also likely to be subject to much instability. For an analysis of zero-hour contracts as an emergent special case of the basic labour contract, see Williams and Koumenta (2016).

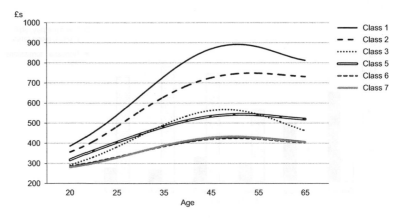

Source: Annual Survey of Hours and Earnings, 2014

Figure 1.4 Median gross weekly earnings by social class and age, full-time male employees

age 35 and then tend to level out, whereas with men and women in Classes 1 and 2, earnings rise far more sharply, and until around age 50: that is to say, up to this age earnings inequalities between the salariat and the working class steadily widen over the life course. The curves for men and women in Classes 3 and 5 lie in intermediate positions.[14]

Two additional points regarding the relationship between class and income might be made here. First, despite the stability over time of class differences in age–earnings curves, it has been suggested that as earnings inequalities in Britain widened from the mid 1970s earnings differences *between* occupations and in turn between classes decreased, while earnings differences *within* occupations, and classes, increased. However, this view is not borne out by the most detailed empirical research that has been undertaken. To the contrary, what this

[14] For earlier results, see Goldthorpe and McKnight (2006) and also the work of Phelps-Brown (1977), a member of a generation of labour economists who readily recognised the fact, and the significance, of occupational differences in age–earnings curves. It should be understood that the curves shown are not based on individual 'biographical' data but, as indicated, on medians by age. The downturns in the curves for Class 1 after age 50 are most likely the result of semi-retirement; and the downturn in the curve for Class 3 for men from around age 40 onwards reflects the fact, we suspect, that men who have not achieved upward mobility from this class by this age are in some way negatively selected.

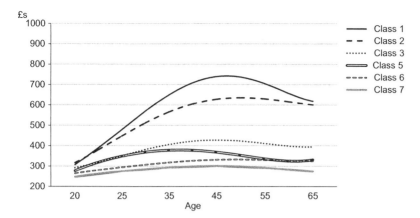

Source: Annual Survey of Hours and Earnings, 2014

Figure 1.5 Median gross weekly earnings by social class and age, full-time female employees

shows is that widening earnings inequality has been in large part occupation-based. It has resulted from widening differences in average earnings between occupations and, further, from the 'earnings polarisation' of the occupational structure. Occupations with an intermediate range of earnings have contracted, while both low-paying and high-paying occupations have expanded. And this same pattern of change is then replicated at the level of social classes.[15]

Second, recognition of class-specific age–earnings curves serves in another way to bring out the limitations of representing economic inequality simply in terms of current earnings. What can be inferred from the curves shown in Figures 1.4 and 1.5 is that individuals who are found at any one time at a similar level within the overall earnings distribution may well be, in terms of age and class, quite heterogeneous. Especially with men, the lower to middle levels of the earnings distribution are likely to comprise managers and professionals at the start of their careers, together, say, with somewhat older clerical and sales workers and technicians, and also semi-routine or routine

[15] See Williams (2013, 2017a). The main exception to this general finding that should be recognised comes with the marked increase in income inequality within Class 1, associated mainly with the rise of so-called 'super-managers' (Piketty, 2015: ch. 9), who, however, represent only a very small minority – probably less than 1 per cent – of all those in this class.

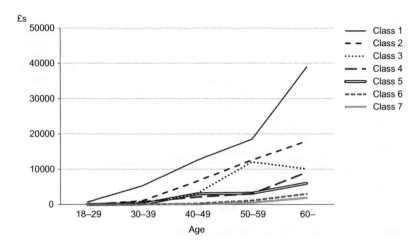

£s

Source: British Household Panel Survey, 2000; using variables constructed by
Banks, Smith and Wakefield (2002)

Figure 1.6 Household median net financial wealth by social class and age of
head of household

wage-workers who are at their earnings peak. In other words, individuals are being grouped together in income bands who, as regards their
income security and stability, as well as their income prospects, could
be said to be living in significantly different economic worlds.

Finally, moving on from the association between class position and the
different aspects of income that we have considered, it is also relevant to
take up a matter on which, so far, rather little information has been
produced: that is, the association between class and wealth. In Figure 1.6
we show estimates of households' median net financial wealth – defined
as savings plus investments minus debts – by social class and age group of
head of household. The distinctive situation of households headed by
members of Class 1 is apparent, and especially on account of the 'surge'
in their wealth that occurs in later life – as a result, one may suppose, of
accumulating income but also of bequests from those similarly advantaged in the previous generation. The gap in wealth between, on the one
hand, Class 1 – and to a lesser extent Class 2 – households and, on the
other hand, Class 5, 6 and 7 households is especially notable; again, a
clear indication of different economic worlds.

The foregoing are, then, the grounds on which we would argue that
social class provides a more comprehensive basis than does earnings,

or even income considered more generally, for displaying the prevailing form and pattern of economic advantage and disadvantage, and in turn for the analysis of social mobility insofar as the degree of intergenerational transmission of such advantage and disadvantage is concerned.

In recent times it has been claimed, in some academic as well as, more frequently, in political and media circles, that Britain is no longer a 'class society'.[16] It might therefore appear appropriate for us to add something more concerning the still wider consequences of class than those we have so far shown for individuals' life-chances. In the chapters that follow, we will in fact have much to say about how individuals' class origins influence their levels of educational attainment and in turn their opportunities in labour markets. For now, therefore, we will limit ourselves to showing how class directly conditions individuals' lives in one other different, but crucial, respect: that is, via their risks of mortality or, in other words, their life-chances in a quite literal sense.

In Figure 1.7 we graph age-standardised mortality rates by NS-SEC classes for men and women aged 25–64. The differences that are revealed are striking, and especially notable is that which shows up between men in Class 1 and in Class 7. It is difficult to think of any way in which class inequalities could be more starkly expressed than in what amounts to a substantial disparity in allotted lifetimes.

It is of course the case that the causal pathways underlying the association between class and mortality are complex, and other factors, such as income, social status and education, are known to be involved. Nonetheless, strong evidence exists of social, psychological and physiological processes that do causally connect class with the risk of premature death: that is, ones operating in part through the damaging effects on health of the adverse physical conditions of some forms of wage-work but, more generally, through the increased stress, resulting from subordination, 'effort–reward imbalance' and, above all, economic insecurity, that are associated with the employment relations of more disadvantaged class positions.[17] It is with mortality

---

[16] Among academic works, see, e.g., Bauman (1982), Beck (1992), Giddens (1994). The arguments advanced are largely 'data free'.

[17] See the extensive literature on these issues referred to in White et al. (2007), one of the first and still most detailed analyses of mortality differences carried out on the basis of NS-SEC, and in particular the work cited of epidemiologists such as Davey-Smith and Siegrist and their associates.

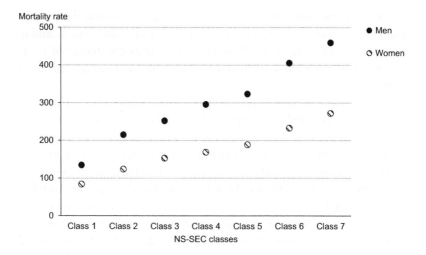

Source: Office for National Statistics (2013)

Figure 1.7 Age-standardised mortality rates per 100,000 population aged 25 to 64 by social class, England and Wales, 2008–10

statistics that any attempt to represent present-day Britain as a classless society can be most obviously and effectively confronted.

One last issue on which we should comment in this chapter is that of the consequences for individuals not of social class itself but, rather, of the actual experience of class mobility. This is relevant because, from the pioneering work of Sorokin onwards, the question has been raised of the effects of mobility on individuals' social lives and psychological states. Sorokin himself regarded mobility as being in fact 'dissociative', separating individuals from their families and communities of origin and thus often leading to isolation, loneliness and personal distress. And in British sociology there has been a long-standing concern with the social and psychological costs of upward mobility in particular – with, as one author has put it, 'the price of the ticket'. In turn, it has been queried whether equalising opportunities and raising levels of mobility should be so unequivocally taken as prime policy objectives.[18]

[18] See Sorokin (1959: 515–24). The phrase 'the price of the ticket' is taken from Friedman (2014, 2016). For arguments to the effect that a more 'holistic' approach to social mobility is needed, and that the idea of 'success' should be re-evaluated, see Atherton (2017).

However, what has to be noted is that claims of the negative effects of upward class mobility, although rather insistently repeated, are not well grounded at all. They derive almost entirely from small-scale qualitative studies – or even 'auto-ethnographies' – the reliability and representativeness of which have to be regarded as highly questionable. There can be little doubt that the individual experience of mobility is highly variable. But large-scale research based on population samples, while able to accommodate this variability, has rather consistently supported what has been called the 'mid-way' hypothesis: that is, the hypothesis that on most outcomes of interest, including social relations and psychological well-being, mobile individuals lie somewhere in between the average for their class of origin and that for their class of destination. Given, then, that men and women in more advantaged class positions do report higher levels of both social participation and general life satisfaction than those in less advantaged positions – as well as certainly enjoying better physical and mental health – individuals who are upwardly mobile can be regarded as, overall, tending to benefit in these regards, rather than suffering costs.[19]

It does of course also follow that it is downward rather than upward class mobility that is more likely to be damaging. And this is important since, as will become apparent as this book proceeds, both the actuality and also the perceived threat of downward mobility are in various ways crucially involved in the class mobility trends and processes in operation in British society today.

---

[19] For an extensive review of the field and for new research findings on class mobility and individual well-being in British society, based on a nationally representative sample, which leads to a forceful critique of the work of Friedman as cited in the previous note, see Chan (2018).

2 | Class Mobility in Absolute Terms: The End of the Golden Age

In this chapter we focus on social class mobility as considered in *absolute* as opposed to *relative* terms. This is a quite crucial distinction, and a great deal of the confusion in discussion of social mobility in political and policy circles to which we referred in the Introduction arises from its neglect or misunderstanding. We must therefore try to make the distinction clear and to bring out its significance, although we may be able to achieve this fully only as the book proceeds.

Absolute class mobility can in itself be readily understood. It refers simply to the proportions of individuals moving between different class positions, and, as will be seen, it can be adequately measured simply as percentages in one form or another. What is, however, important to recognise is that absolute rates are conditioned by two different, and essentially independent, factors: first, by the structure, and changes in the structure, of the class positions between which mobility occurs; and, second, by relative rates of class mobility. In other words, the class structure and relative rates together imply absolute rates:

$$\text{class structure} + \text{relative rates} => \text{absolute rates}$$

How relative rates are conceptualised and measured is a more difficult matter, and will be explained in some detail in the next chapter. For the moment, it may be sufficient to think of relative rates as ones that *compare the chances* of individuals of different class origins being found in different class destinations, and that thus reflect social processes which, as they operate within the class structure, generate the absolute rates that are actually observed. The class structure sets the context of class mobility; relative rates determine how, within this context, absolute rates are realised.

In what follows we will start our analyses of the level, pattern and trend of absolute rates by tracing the development of the class structure over the historical period of interest to us. But since relative rates are also involved, we will reach a point at which, in order to sustain the argument that we seek to develop regarding absolute rates, we will need to anticipate one of our main findings on relative rates – asking readers to take this finding on trust until we can set out in detail how we arrive at it.

In establishing the development of the class structure, we would ideally wish to do this on the basis of NS-SEC, which, as we have stated, is the classification on which we will chiefly rely in our analyses of mobility. However, the historical sources on which we have to draw are official, primarily Census, statistics, and NS-SEC came into operation in official statistics only in 2001. Before then a variety of other social classifications were in use which, while also being based, like NS-SEC, primarily on employment status and occupation, cannot be straightforwardly mapped on to NS-SEC. To gain some idea of the way in which the British class structure has changed over the last half-century or more, we have therefore to try as far as possible to harmonise, in relation to NS-SEC, data deriving from a range of sources that are not entirely comparable. The results we arrive at, as displayed in Figure 2.1, have then to be regarded as no more than approximate at a detailed level. Nonetheless, the overall picture that is provided is one that can be taken as reliable enough for our purposes.

What is shown in Figure 2.1, in graphical form, are our best estimates of how the class distributions of economically active men and women would have appeared, according to a somewhat collapsed version of NS-SEC, at the census years of 1951, 1971, 1991 and 2011.

In the case of men, it can be seen that the shapes of the distributions steadily change from a clearly pyramidal form in 1951 to a more rectangular one in 2011. In 1951 the wage-earning working class, as represented by NS-SEC Classes 6 and 7, was predominant, accounting for well over half the active male population. In contrast, the managerial and professional salariat, as represented by Classes 1 and 2, accounted for little more than a tenth. But over the period covered the working class contracts and the salariat expands, and especially rapidly between 1951 and 1991. Thus, by 2011 the working class is reduced to less than a third of the active male population while the salariat comprises around two-fifths. The three intermediate classes, NS-SEC Classes 3, 4 and 5, remain more stable in size, although some slight decline is indicated in the proportion of men in Class 3, that of employees in ancillary professional and administrative occupations.

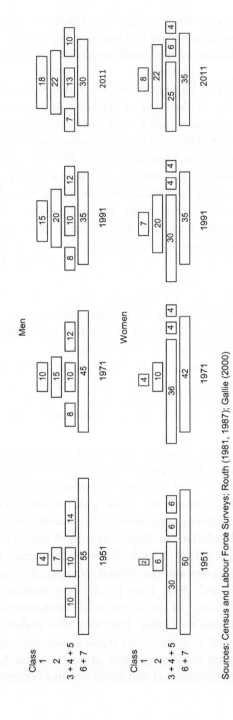

Figure 2.1 Class distributions (%) of economically active population, 1951–2011

Sources: Census and Labour Force Surveys; Routh (1981, 1987); Gallie (2000)

In the case of women, the distributions change for the most part in the same way as with men, even if somewhat more slowly, and in particular the increase in the proportion in the higher-level managerial and professional positions of NS-SEC Class 1 is less marked. The one major difference from men comes with NS-SEC Class 3 which between 1951 and 1971 expanded so as to account for over a third of the active female population but then contracted so as to account for only a quarter by 2011 – a reflection chiefly of the rise and fall of the office secretary and typist.

A class structure developing on the lines shown in Figure 2.1 can in fact be regarded as a quite characteristic feature of societies making the transition from industrialism to postindustrialism – a transition driven by technological advance and rising productivity, the sectoral shift from extractive and manufacturing industries to services, and the growth of governmental and corporate administrative hierarchies. In the British case, the changes in question might, however, be seen as somewhat accentuated – as much by political as economic influences – in two respects: first, as regards the expansion of the managerial and professional salariat by the creation and development of the welfare state in the postwar decades; and, second, as regards the decline of the working class, by the speed and extent of the deindustrialisation of the 1980s and 1990s.[1]

It is, then, in this structural context that we have to situate the analyses that follow in this chapter. As will become apparent, in understanding levels, patterns and trends of absolute intergenerational class mobility, *it is the changing shape of the class structure that is all-important.*

In order to bring out this point most clearly, we have in fact to go back to a period before that covered by the birth cohort studies which, as we have indicated, provide the basis for most of the research that we will discuss. This earlier period is covered by the Nuffield mobility

---

[1] It has been widely argued that in postindustrial societies the class structure tends to be 'hollowed out', with declining numbers being found in classes intermediate between the managerial and professional salariat and the lower stratum of the wage-earning working class. If the distributions of men and women shown in Figure 2.1 are taken together, support for this argument can in fact be seen. It is, however, at the same time important to note that often in this regard attention has centred on employees, and there has been a neglect of the self-employed and small employers whose numbers have of late tended generally to increase (see Arum and Müller eds., 2004).

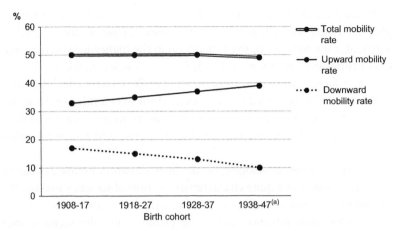

Note

(a) Rate adjusted to allow for young age in 1972 – i.e. between age 25 and 34 – on the basis of life-course changes in the class positions of men in the 1928–37 cohort

Source: Goldthorpe (1980/1987)

Figure 2.2 Total mobility rates and upward and downward components, men born 1908–1947, interviewed in 1972

study of 1972 that was referred to in the Introduction, and Figure 2.2 is derived from results obtained in this study. What Figure 2.2 shows is the *total mobility rate*, and its upward and downward components, for four cohorts, or, to be more precise, for four 'quasi-cohorts', or age groups, of men who were born in the ten-year periods indicated.[2] The total mobility rate, in intergenerational perspective, is simply the proportion – percentage – of individuals who, at some age or, as here, at some time are found in a different class to that in which they originated. In the Nuffield study class origins were determined by the class of

---

[2] When with a mobility survey of cross-sectional design, as in the case of the Nuffield study, the aim is to investigate changes in mobility, it is common practice to divide up the sample into individuals born in successive periods and to treat these groupings as if they were birth cohorts. The limitation of this practice is that at the time of the survey, when respondents' class positions are established, those in a series of such 'quasi-cohorts' will be of differing age. Care has then to be taken (see note to Figure 2.2) with younger persons, since class position can often change in the early stages of working life. Only around the late 30s does the probability of changes in employment that imply changes in class position tend to fall away (see Bukodi and Goldthorpe, 2009, 2011a). With data relating to the life courses of true birth cohorts, the possibility arises – which we consistently exploit – of comparing members of successive cohorts *at the same age*.

men's fathers, or other 'family head', during their early adolescence. In order to maintain sufficiently large numbers in the analyses underlying Figure 2.2, only three, hierarchically ordered, classes are distinguished, broadly corresponding to NS-SEC Classes 1 and 2, the managerial and professional salariat, Classes 3, 4 and 5, the 'intermediate' classes, and Classes 6 and 7, the wage-earning working class. It is then by reference to these three ordered classes that the upward and downward components of the total mobility rate are calculated.

There are two main points that should be noted from Figure 2.2. First, the total mobility rate remains remarkably constant across the four cohorts at close to 50 per cent: that is to say, half the men in each cohort alike were, when interviewed in 1972, found in a different class from that in which they originated. Second, though, the upward and downward components of the total mobility rate show clear trends, the upward mobility component steadily rising across the cohorts and the downward mobility component falling. Thus, among men born 1908–17 around a third had experienced upward mobility – that is, from working-class origins to intermediate classes or to the professional and managerial salariat or from intermediate class origins to the salariat – and around a sixth had experienced mobility in the reverse direction. But among men born 1938–47 the proportion who were upwardly mobile rises to two-fifths and the proportion who were downwardly mobile falls to only a tenth.

Against the background of these earlier findings we may now consider comparable results relating to the later twentieth and early twenty-first centuries that come from our own analyses: that is, from analyses based on the datasets of the three cohort studies referred to in the Introduction that cover men and women born in 1946, 1958 and 1970, but supplemented for present purposes by data for a further cohort of men and women born 1980–4 that we have derived from the UK Household Longitudinal Study.[3]

Figure 2.3 shows total mobility rates and their upward and downward components for men in these four cohorts. Cohort members' class origins are determined in the same way as in Figure 2.2.[4]

---

[3] For a full account of the research drawn on in the text, see Bukodi et al. (2015) and for further commentary Goldthorpe (2016).

[4] With the 1958 and 1970 cohorts it is possible to investigate the effects of taking the mother's class also into account, in various ways, in determining cohort members' class origins. Results we obtain indicate that this in fact makes rather

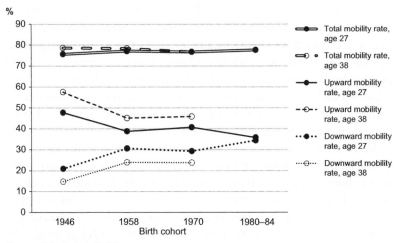

Source: Bukodi et al. (2015)

Figure 2.3 Total mobility rate and upward and downward components, men born in 1946, 1958 and 1970 at ages 27 and 38, and born 1980–4 at age 27

However, their own class positions are taken not at a particular time but rather at two ages – namely, at around age 27 and at age 38. This is so because the age range 24–30 is the oldest for which we have information on the class positions of members of the 1980–4 cohort, and 38 is the oldest age at which we have information on the class positions of members of the 1970 cohort. One further difference is that in Figure 2.3 mobility is treated according to the standard seven-class version of NS-SEC, as shown in Table 1.1. However, since, as was earlier noted, Classes 3, 4 and 5 are not regarded as ordered, mobility between these classes is regarded as 'horizontal' and, although included in the total rate, is not itself shown in the figure. The upward and downward components of the total rate refer to mobility across the five hierarchical divisions of NS-SEC as indicated by the dashed lines in Table 1.1.

It may be observed that in Figure 2.3 the total mobility rate, at around 80 per cent, appears higher than in Figure 2.2. But this is only to be expected since in using NS-SEC we create more classes – seven rather than just three – between which mobility can occur. Thus, no

little difference to estimates of the overall strength and pattern of the association between origins and destinations.

real change in total mobility need be supposed. What is more important to note is that, whether we consider men at around age 27 or at age 38, the total mobility rate is, again as in Figure 2.2, essentially stable across the cohorts. However, the really striking feature of Figure 2.3, when set in comparison with Figure 2.2, is the differences that are shown up in the trends in the upward and downward components of the total rate. *These are now the reverse of those that were previously seen.* It is the downward component that is increasing and the upward component that is decreasing. Thus, while men in the 1946 birth cohort were at age 27 about twice as likely, and at age 38 almost three times more likely, to have experienced upward rather than downward mobility, these differences narrow considerably in later cohorts. And indeed for men in the 1980–4 cohort at around age 27 the chances of having been upwardly or downwardly mobile are more or less equal.[5] It is true that some improvement in the situation of these men could be expected by the time they reach age 38, since a tendency exists for upward class mobility to prevail over downward in the course of earlier working life, and this is indeed apparent from Figure 2.3 itself in that the upward mobility rate is always higher and the downward mobility rate lower at age 38 than at age 27. Nonetheless, the big picture that emerges from the figure would seem clear enough. During the later twentieth century and into the twenty-first century the experience of upward mobility has become less frequent in men's lives and that of downward mobility more frequent.

In Figure 2.4 we show comparable results for women. A number of differences with our findings for men can be seen, although none is of great magnitude. First, the total mobility rate for women tends to increase somewhat across the cohorts, from a little under to a little over 80 per cent – for reasons that will emerge in the following chapter. Second, as regards the upward and downward components of the total rate, the differences that appear between the graphs for women at age 27 and at age 38 are less than with men, indicating that the tendency

---

[5] The fact that men in the 1958 cohort appear as falling 'below trend' as regards decreasing upward mobility and 'above trend' as regards increasing downward mobility can be explained by the adverse effects on the working lives of these men of the highly unfavourable labour market conditions prevailing in the early 1980s: i.e. at the time of, or shortly after, their entry into employment. See further Bukodi and Goldthorpe (2011a).

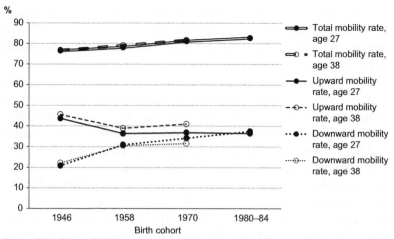

Source: Bukodi et al. (2015)

Figure 2.4 Total mobility rate and upward and downward components, women born in 1946, 1958 and 1970 at ages 27 and 38, and born 1980–4 at age 27

for upward mobility to be more common than downward during earlier working life is less marked for women. Third, the decline in upward mobility between the 1946 and 1958 cohorts levels out across both the 1970 and the 1980–4 cohorts rather than continuing between these cohorts, as it does with men. But, fourth, the rise in downward mobility, at least when women's class positions are taken at age 38, is more continuous than with men. It thus turns out that the overall outcome for women is essentially the same as for men: across the four birth cohorts, women's experience of upward mobility becomes less frequent and that of downward mobility more frequent, and to much the same extent as with men.[6]

---

[6] Indications that the trends in the upward and downward components of total mobility among men shown in Figure 2.2 had at all events levelled out, if not actually reversed, can be found in earlier research based on cross-sectional surveys (e.g. Mills and Payne, 1989; Goldthorpe and Mills, 2004, 2008; Paterson and Ianelli, 2007) and also on the Office of National Statistics Longitudinal Study dataset, which comprises a 1 per cent sample of linked census records from 1971 (Buscha and Sturgis, 2017). In the case of women, earlier work appears less often to have anticipated the reversal in trends in upward and downward mobility that our inclusion of relatively recent birth cohorts serves to bring out.

How, then, is this reversal of trends in the upward and downward components of the total mobility rate to be explained? The middle decades of the twentieth century, during which social ascent so clearly predominated over social descent, have been described, with the benefit of hindsight, as the golden age of social mobility in Britain. Why, we have to ask, has this golden age come to an end?

The key to the answer lies in Figure 2.1. The expansion of the managerial and professional salariat and the contraction of the working class that is shown in this figure carry an important implication. They mean that in the second half of the twentieth century, *the distribution of the class origins* of men and women also began to change substantially. Steadily more started out in life from relatively advantaged class positions and fewer from relatively disadvantaged positions. For example, between the 1946 and 1980–4 cohorts the proportion of men and women originating in Classes 1 and 2 tripled, from 13 to 39 per cent, while the proportion originating in Classes 6 and 7 halved, from 54 to 26 per cent. In other words, across our birth cohorts the number of individuals 'at risk' of being downwardly mobile in terms of social class, as we would treat it, steadily increases and the number 'at risk' of – or, that is, having the possibility of – being upwardly mobile steadily decreases. And we can in fact say that it is this change in itself that almost entirely accounts for the increasing component of downward mobility in the total mobility rate and the decreasing component of upward mobility.[7]

It is in order to justify this claim that, as we forewarned at the start of the chapter, we have to anticipate one of our principal findings regarding relative rates of class mobility. This is that across our birth cohorts relative rates – with one rather special exception – *remain constant or at most merely fluctuate in a trendless fashion*. In the present context, all that needs to be understood is that, in being

---

[7] Given that upward and downward mobility are determined according to the fivefold hierarchical division of NS-SEC, it is obviously the case that it is not only mobility from Class 1 or 2 origins to lower classes that contributes to downward mobility, nor mobility from Class 6 or 7 origins to higher classes that contributes to upward mobility. But it is in fact mobility of these kinds that preponderantly lies behind the changes in the upward and downward components of the total mobility rate we have described.

themselves essentially *un*changing, relative rates can contribute little to the changes in absolute rates that we have demonstrated. It then follows that in accounting for the contrast that is revealed between Figure 2.2, on the one hand, and Figures 2.3 and 2.4, on the other, *it is the evolving class structure that must be seen as the crucial driving force.* And the further implication is that the structural change that underlay the golden age – the rapid growth of the salariat, creating ever more 'room at the top' – proves to have, from the standpoint of the present, its darker side. With relative chances of mobility remaining more or less unaltered, an expanded salariat, entailing an increased number of individuals who are at risk of downward mobility, can only result in a rise in the numbers who do actually move down the class hierarchy – that is, from among the children of those men and women who previously benefited from increasing upward mobility into the salariat or from increasing immobility within it.

Upwardly mobile father, downwardly mobile son – 1

Basil

Basil's father was upwardly mobile, rising from modest social origins to a position of professional eminence. Basil was brought up in a highly cultured home and attended a private school, but his main interests were sport and music rather than academic work. After getting very poor grades at A level – 'I'm not the brightest spark' – he left school and joined a firm of accountants. His brothers all went on to university and Basil feels 'a huge pang ... at not being more a part of that' and also fears that he was something of a disappointment to his parents.

   Basil tried to make a career in accountancy but failed the exams for 'chartered' status. He then joined a large catering firm, working chiefly as a buyer. He has subsequently stayed in the same firm and has 'slowly' made some progress, though not to a managerial level. Opportunities were restricted after the 1980s recession and he is not ambitious: 'I wouldn't fall over anybody to get to the top.' He remains very interested in sport and especially in music, to which he increasingly devotes himself in a semi-professional capacity.

   He lives with his wife in a suburban cul-de-sac of 'tightly packed' houses with small gardens.

Upwardly mobile father, downwardly mobile son – 2

Eric

Eric's father pursued a successful career as a professional engineer and, when Eric was a small child, accepted a highly paid position abroad. A little later his wife and Eric followed. However, within a year the marriage had broken up and Eric and his mother returned to Britain. Eric did well at school, got decent A levels, and decided that he wanted to become a lawyer. He was not attracted to the idea of going to university but entered a solicitor's office as a trainee legal executive.

Eric eventually qualified for this position, moved to a City firm on quite a high salary, and seemed set for a successful legal career. But in the early 1990s he was unexpectedly made redundant. He lost his mortgage, had other debts, and was declared bankrupt. He worked for a time as a barman – 'just as a fun job' – then as a security guard and in a call centre before finding another legal position. However, in 2008 he was again made redundant. This time he left the City, moved to a small flat in a coastal area to be near where his mother lives, and now works as a bouncer in a night club – 'I'm a very big guy.'

After a failed marriage, he has come out as gay. Although he says that he is now enjoying life more in being free of the stress of working in the City, he has continuing psychological problems that he puts down in part to the loss of his career.

How, then, do the findings on absolute mobility rates we have reported relate to the political discussion of social mobility that has become of increasing prominence in today's Britain? We suggested in the Introduction that the concern that has developed across the political spectrum in a growing number of western societies with social mobility and equality of opportunity has to be seen in the context of a widening inequality of condition. But what has to be added is that in Britain this concern has been further strengthened on the basis of a claim that over the recent past *social mobility has actually been in decline* – a claim that has then developed into a widely accepted 'factoid'. This situation is primarily the result of the entry of economists into the field of mobility research. For insofar as the claim of declining mobility has any evidential basis, it lies in just one piece of research carried out by a group of economists on which they first reported in a paper published in 2004.[8]

Economists sought to show, using data from the 1958 and 1970 birth cohort studies (see Chapter 1, n. 4), that between these two cohorts a decrease occurred in intergenerational *income* mobility. We will say more about this research itself in the following chapter since it has in fact to be seen as referring essentially to relative rather than absolute mobility. What is here chiefly relevant is the extraordinary degree of political impact the research achieved. Acceptance of a problem of declining mobility proved highly attractive both to New Labour, in power at the time, and likewise to the then opposition parties and to the governments that they subsequently formed. Reinforcement could in this way be given to the political strategy, favoured in one form or another by all parties, that gave priority to the creation of a greater equality of opportunity, primarily through educational policy, over measures in some way aimed at countering widening inequalities of condition more directly.

However, because the economists' work was so readily taken to serve political purposes – but in part too because they themselves failed to make it sufficiently clear that their analyses centred on relative rather than absolute mobility – the findings they presented were not only widely discussed but also widely misinterpreted and their implications much exaggerated. Indeed, as growing political interest in mobility fuelled media commentary, what can only be described as a spiral of hyperbole set in. The report that some decline in income mobility had occurred between two birth cohorts, just twelve years apart, became transmuted into claims that social mobility had 'plummeted', was 'at its lowest level ever recorded' or had even 'ground to a halt'. And while commentators for the most part showed no understanding of whether it was in fact absolute or relative mobility that was at issue, it would seem evident enough from the views they expressed that it was, inappropriately, mobility in absolute terms that they had in mind.[9]

---

[8] Blanden et al. (2004).

[9] For further discussion of the sources and extent of the impact of the economists' work and of the increasingly extreme versions of its findings that emerged in the media, see Goldthorpe (2013). The authors themselves became concerned by such misrepresentations (see House of Commons Select Committee on Children, Schools and Families, Oral Evidence, 23 January 2008), and it has also been acknowledged (Blanden and Machin, 2007: 18) that 'the oft-cited finding of a fall

In the light of our own findings, the reception of the economists' work can therefore be only regarded as unfortunate, and in two ways. First, assuming the focus is on absolute mobility, then, at least if mobility is treated in terms of social class rather than income, a concern with declining mobility is simply misplaced. *There is no evidence whatever of such a decline*, and over a much longer period than that considered by the economists. Men and women who were born in the 1980s are no less likely to have moved to different class positions to those of their parents than men and women who were born at any time earlier in the twentieth century. The total mobility rate appears to be highly stable.[10]

Second, though, and more seriously, while a preoccupation with supposedly declining mobility has built up, what our findings would point to as the real mobility problem in present-day Britain as regards absolute rates has been very largely overlooked: that is, the reversal of trends in the upward and downward components of the total rate, so that the experience of downward mobility is becoming almost as common as that of upward mobility. And likewise overlooked has then been the crucial part played by class structural change in producing this reversal – as also in producing the previous far more benign pattern of mobility of the golden age.

It might perhaps be thought that the increase in downward mobility that we have revealed is not of major importance in that individuals' relative risks of such mobility have – like other relative rates, as we will show – remained little changed. But the greater numbers becoming downwardly mobile, simply as the result of the greater numbers at risk of so doing, could appear of larger potential significance from a societal point of view. As was observed at the end of Chapter 1, insofar as the experience of mobility carries negative consequences, these would seem more likely to occur with social descent than with social

in intergenerational mobility between the 1958 and 1970 cohorts appears to have been an episode caused by the particular circumstances of the time' rather than indicative of any longer-term trend. Nonetheless, the idea of mobility in decline still persists in official reports (see e.g. Social Mobility Commission, 2016: iv) and among the commentariat (see e.g. Peston, 2017).

[10] Because of the lack of adequate data, little attempt has been made in Britain to investigate income mobility in absolute terms – i.e. how the (real) incomes of men and women compare with those of their parents. In the US several studies have been made but with no clear consensus as yet emerging. See Winship (2017).

ascent. And the possibility of a growing body of men and women who have failed to maintain the more advantaged class positions of their parents becoming associated with rising sociopolitical disaffection, in whatever form this might be expressed, is one that can scarcely be disregarded.

At all events, what remains clear enough is that, while attracting remarkably little attention, a situation has come about that is quite new in modern British history. Young people who are at the present time entering the labour market are, collectively, facing less favourable mobility prospects than did their parents – or their grandparents. Moreover, although the salariat appears still to be growing, it has from the 1990s, as Figure 2.1 brings out, grown far less rapidly than previously. Unless, therefore, this slowdown is countered, it can only be expected that the balance of upward and downward mobility will tend to become yet more unfavourable than it is at present. And the only way in which this balance could be moved back towards something like that which prevailed in the golden age of mobility would be through another marked expansion of positions at the higher levels of the class structure. To repeat, this situation has attracted little political attention and insofar as any recognition of it has been apparent, few policy responses have followed. However, an intervention made by Gordon Brown during his time as prime minister – and in part, it would seem as a reaction to work by sociologists – is of interest and calls for comment.[11]

Brown's argument was that, in the context of the emerging global economy, the idea that some 'ceiling' might come to exist on the number of high-level jobs, 'thus imposing a limit to the ambitions of the many', has become outdated. If, through educational expansion and reform, Britain can produce a labour force that is 'globally competitive', then jobs requiring high expertise and skill can be pulled into the national economy from all around the world, and there will, therefore, 'be almost no limits to aspirations for upward mobility'. Perhaps the most obvious difficulty with this argument – that Brown in part recognised though did not adequately address – is that in any global competition for attracting 'top-end' jobs, Britain must be at an evident disadvantage in relation to newly industrialising countries, in Asia especially, that are able to provide highly qualified personnel at a

[11] Gordon Brown, *The Observer*, 10 February 2008.

much lower cost. Indeed, in what has been aptly called the 'global auction' that now operates in this regard, the weak position of Britain, along with other western societies, could be seen as constituting in itself a major problem, and one that could indeed lead to the slowing expansion of the higher levels of the class structure that is already in evidence ending in a complete stall.[12]

Moreover, a related, yet deeper, difficulty underlying the Brown scenario is the extreme 'supply-side' assumptions on which it rests. What is supposed is that if, by the development of its educational system, Britain can demonstrate that it has an appropriately qualified labour force, this supply will simply create its own demand, so that higher-level class positions and in turn opportunities for upward mobility will multiply.[13] This can be taken as a prime expression of the wide political consensus that exists, as we have already remarked, in seeing educational policy as central to all attempts at increasing social mobility. However, the role played by education in processes of mobility is an issue on which the disconnect between sociological research and thinking in political circles becomes apparent in many respects – as will emerge in later chapters. In the present connection, what has to be observed is that while there are no market or other mechanisms that readily bring into equilibrium the general level and distribution of educational qualifications in the labour force and the structure of demand in the labour market, the empirical evidence would strongly suggest that *it is easier for supply to adapt to demand than vice versa.*

The example of the golden age is itself instructive in this regard. When, following the Second World War, the expansion of the managerial and professional salariat began, Britain did not, by the standards of other economically advanced societies, have an educational system that was all that highly developed at its secondary and tertiary levels. But this did not prevent the expansion of managerial and

---

[12] On 'the global auction', see Brown, Lauder and Ashton (2011).

[13] Having read a paper by Goldthorpe and Jackson (2007), in which class structural effects on mobility were emphasised, a close political associate of Gordon Brown did in fact enquire of the authors if they had ever heard of Say's Law. The reference is to an argument advanced by the French political economist, J.-B. Say (1767–1832), which is often, but rather misleadingly, summarised as 'supply creates its own demand'. Say himself appears never to have used the phrase.

professional employment from going ahead – together with the steady increase in upward mobility that was thus generated. Results from the Nuffield mobility study are again revealing. They show that of men born between 1908 and 1947 who by 1972 had gained access to the managerial component of the salariat only one in twenty had a degree and *over two-fifths had no formal qualifications at all*. These men had in fact mostly risen to managerial positions over the course of their working lives, regardless of their lack of 'credentials', and, one has to suppose, primarily on the basis of their demonstrated ability to do well in jobs that needed filling. Moreover, even among men found in professional occupations only one in five had a degree, with most of the remainder having entered into professional employment not through qualifications gained within the mainstream of the educational system but through what were in effect professional apprenticeships and examinations taken in the course of working life under the auspices of a great diversity of 'qualifying associations'. In other words, it was demand that mattered; and while anything above secondary level qualifications obtained before entering the labour market virtually guaranteed an eventual managerial or professional position, such positions could be, and very frequently were, accessed via other routes.[14]

It might be thought that by the present day a high level of formal qualifications at labour market entry has become a more important requirement for positions within the salariat as the result of what economists refer to as 'skill-biased technological change' and the growth of the 'knowledge economy'. How far this is so is an issue to which we will return later in Chapter 7. But what is more relevant to observe here is that while throughout the twentieth century demand ran ahead of, or at all events readily accommodated, the supply of highly qualified individuals, even as this supply increased, it is by no means clear that this continues to be the case. A concern has of late become apparent in Britain, as in a number of other advanced societies,

---

[14] See Goldthorpe (1982: table 2) and on the importance of access to the professions via qualifying associations, Millerson (1964). It may be added that very questionable supply-side assumptions also underlie the Leitch Review of Skills (Leitch, 2006), which are challenged in analyses subsequently made by the Chartered Institute of Personnel and Development (2015). These show *inter alia* that across European countries the relationship between the employment share of graduates and the growth of high-skilled occupational groups is, if anything, *negative*.

regarding the possibility of *over*qualification in the labour market: that is, the possibility, in direct contradiction of the Brown scenario, of the supply of the highly qualified outstripping demand for them. And it is, for example, relevant to note that in Britain today the idea – and, more importantly, the reality – of the 'graduate job' would seem to be fast fading away, with many graduates now entering occupations that in previous generations would have been largely filled by non-graduates.[15]

As regards the future shape of the class structure, and thus of the pattern of absolute rates of mobility within it, forecasting is extremely difficult, and this should be clearly acknowledged. It could well be that the developments that created mobility's golden age will come to be seen as a historical 'one-off' from the standpoint of a subsequent period in which change in the class structure is relatively slow and limited, at least so far as any upgrading is concerned. But what can be said is that *if* any return towards the conditions of the golden age does prove possible, this is unlikely to be through the effects of educational policy in the context of the global labour market. Policies will rather be needed – as we will discuss further in the concluding chapter – in quite different areas, such as industrial strategy and the advancement of the range and quality of social and other public services: that is, policies directed by a particular vision of economic and social development, rather than simply of economic growth, that can ensure that within the national economy fewer men and women are confined to low-grade wage work while increased demand and opportunity are created at higher levels of employment for those who have come through the educational system with appropriate trained capacity and expertise.

---

[15] On the twentieth-century situation, see Bukodi and Goldthorpe (2011b). On more recent changes in graduate employment, see again the report of the Chartered Institute of Personnel and Development (2015). An early recognition of the possibility of overqualification in the British labour market can be found in Wolf (2002: chs. 1, 6 esp.) and see further the discussion in Chapter 5.

3 | Class Mobility in Relative Terms: Resistance to Change

In this chapter we move on to consider intergenerational class mobility in relative rather than in absolute terms. We noted at the start of the previous chapter that by absolute class mobility is meant mobility as it can be directly observed as individuals move from one class position to another, and we showed how absolute mobility rates can be expressed in a fairly straightforward way through percentages. We also noted – somewhat cryptically – that relative mobility rates compare the chances of individuals of different class origins being found in different class destinations and reflect social processes creating inequalities in mobility chances that, as they operate within the class structure, generate absolute rates. We now need to expand on this statement: that is, we need to explain more fully the concept of relative mobility, to show how this concept is made operational in research, and to bring out the possible interrelations that can exist between changes in the class structure, in relative rates and, in turn, in absolute rates.

Relative rates of intergenerational class mobility are intended to capture what sociologists refer to as the 'endogenous mobility regime': that is, the total pattern of individuals' relative chances of moving intergenerationally between different class positions when these chances are considered *net of* all changes in the class structure. This is in fact equivalent to saying, as will emerge, that relative rates capture the strength of the *inherent association* – of the inherent 'stickiness' – that exists between the class positions of parents and their children, whatever may be happening to the class structure. Sociologists take the strength of this inherent association as indicating the degree of *social fluidity* that prevails within the class structure: a strong association implies low fluidity, a weak association, high fluidity. It is, then, relative rather than absolute rates of mobility that are of prime relevance in regard to questions of how 'open' a society is or of the degree of equality of opportunity that exists within it.

Table 3.1 *The odds ratio for Omega*

	Class of destination		
Class of origin	a	b	Odds
a	F_{aa}	F_{ab}	ratio
			F_{aa} / F_{ab}
b	F_{ba}	F_{bb}	F_{ba} / F_{bb}

In measuring relative mobility rates, a key role is played by a statistic known as an *odds ratio*. Imagine a society – we may call it Omega since Ω is the symbol often used for the odds ratio – that has only two classes, Class *a* and Class *b*. We can construct a hypothetical mobility table for Omega, on the lines shown on the left-hand side of Table 3.1, in which individuals' class origins are cross-classified against their class destinations and F stands for frequency. Thus, F_{aa} is the number of individuals originating in Class *a* who are found in Class *a*, F_{ab} is the number originating in Class *a* who are found in Class *b*, and so on. The corresponding odds ratio will then be calculated as is shown on the right-hand side of Table 3.1.

What this odds ratio tells us is the chance of someone originating in Class *a* being found in Class *a* (F_{aa}) rather than in Class b (F_{ab}) *relative to* the chance of someone originating in Class *b* being found in Class a (F_{ba}) rather than in Class b (F_{bb}). If these chances were to be equal, then the odds ratio would obviously work out as 1, and this would mean that *no association* exists between individuals' class origins and their class destinations. Someone originating in Class *a* has exactly the same chance of being found in Class *a* rather than in Class *b* as someone originating in Class *b*. In this case fluidity would be at its maximum level: or a state of 'perfect mobility' would prevail. Conversely, the more unequal the relative chances, the further the odds ratio would rise above 1, and the stronger would be the association between class origins and destinations and the lower the level of fluidity.[1]

As said above, relative rates of class mobility concern mobility treated independently of class structural change; and it is the crucially

---

[1] It would of course be possible for an odds ratio to fall below 1 but this would then imply a *negative* association between class origins and destinations.

Table 3.2 *Class mobility in Omega; results from three successive surveys*

	Survey 1			Survey 2			Survey 3		
	Class of destination			Class of destination			Class of destination		
Class of origin	a	b	Total	a	b	Total	a	b	Total
a	120	80	200	240	60	300	120	180	300
b	80	720	800	160	540	700	280	420	700
Total	200	800	1000	400	600	1000	400	600	1000
Total mobility (%)			16			22			46
Upward mobility (%)			8			16			28
Downward mobility (%)			8			6			18
Odds ratio			13.5			13.5			1.0

valuable property of odds ratios that they allow this to be done. To illustrate, we may stay with our imaginary society of Omega and consider results obtained from three successive mobility surveys carried out in this society. The first and second surveys were separated by years in which significant class structural change occurred, with Class *a* expanding and Class *b* contracting, and the second and third surveys were separated by years of class structural stability but in which a social revolution took place, leading to Class *a*, previously the superior class, losing the distinctive privileges that it had held over Class *b*. The results of the surveys, each of which was based on a random sample of 1,000 individuals drawn from Omega's population, are shown in the three mobility tables that are brought together in Table 3.2.

At the time of the first survey, as can be seen from the marginal distributions of the mobility table, Class *a* was much smaller than Class *b*. The total mobility rate was rather limited at 16 per cent (80 + 80/1000) with this rate being then equally divided into 8 per cent of the total sample who were upwardly mobile from Class *b* to

Class *a* and 8 per cent moving in the reverse direction. Also at this stage in its history Omega could not be regarded as a very fluid society. As can further be seen, the odds ratio, following the formula given in Table 3.1, works out at 13.5: that is to say, the chances of someone originating in Class *a* being found in Class *a* rather than in Class *b* were thirteen and a half times greater than the chances of someone originating in Class *b* being found in Class *a* rather than in Class *b*.

By the time of the second survey, the marginal distributions of the mobility table show that Class *a* has expanded and Class *b* contracted. The total mobility rate has now increased to 22 per cent (160 + 60/ 1000), with the upward component rising to 16 per cent while the downward component falls to only 6 per cent. Between the first two surveys, one might say, Omega enjoyed, as a result of the expansion of Class *a* – more room at the top – its own golden age of mobility, like that of Britain in the mid twentieth century in which social ascent became far more widely experienced that social descent. But did Omega at the same time become a more fluid society? In fact, it did not. Despite all the other changes, the odds ratio, again using the formula of Table 3.1, remains exactly as it was before at 13.5. The level of social fluidity is unaltered.

The third survey comes after the egalitarian revolution. The class structure has not changed further from the time of the second survey: the marginal distributions of the tables for the second and third surveys are identical. But the total mobility rate has increased substantially, up to 46 per cent (280 + 180/1000), with the upward component rising from 16 to 28 per cent and the downward component also rising from 6 to 18 per cent. Given the stability of the class structure, these changes have then to be attributed entirely to the change in the odds ratio which, it can be seen, has been reduced, as a result of the revolution, from 13.5 down to 1: that is, down to a level indicating *no* association between individuals' class of origin and their class of destination – a state of perfect mobility has been created.

For our present purposes, the important point that this imaginary example brings out is the following. Relative mobility rates, as expressed through odds ratios, can remain unaltered even while class structural change is having a major effect on absolute rates – the total mobility rate and its upward and downward components. But if a change in relative rates does occur, this will necessarily influence absolute rates – upward and downward alike – and even in the context of a stable class structure.[2]

In providing a way of capturing relative mobility chances, independently of structural effects, odds ratios play an essential role in the analysis of social mobility. But a difficulty does arise. If one need distinguish only two classes, as in the case of Omega, then there is only one odds ratio to be calculated, as we have shown. However, where more than two classes are distinguished, the number of odds ratios that is calculable rises rapidly with the number of classes. There is an odds ratio for every possible pair of classes of origin taken together with every possible pair of classes of destination. Thus, when we base our analyses of mobility on tables in the same form as those shown for Omega in Table 3.2 but using the seven NS-SEC classes, there are (7 x 6)/2 pairs of classes of origin to be taken together with (7 x 6)/2 pairs of classes of destination or, in all, 21^2 = 441 odds ratios involved.

We cannot therefore proceed simply by the inspection of odds ratios but have to resort to statistical models: that is, to models that make statements about odds ratios – all of the odds ratios of interest in a particular case – which models and the statements they embody can then be tested against the relevant empirical data. In examining relative rates of class mobility across the birth cohorts with which we are concerned, we apply three such models that can be specified as follows.

Model 1: *The independence model.* This model states that in mobility tables for men and women in our birth cohorts all odds ratios are equal to 1. That is, just as in post-revolutionary Omega, there is no association between class origins and destinations – they are

---

[2] What is crucial about odds ratios in this regard is that they are – to use the technical phrase – 'margin insensitive' measures of association. So with mobility tables like those of Table 3.2, the odds ratio will be insensitive to – i.e. will be unaltered by – any changes in the marginal distributions resulting from a row or column of the table being multiplied by a (non-zero) constant. The mobility table for Survey 2 is in fact derived from that for Survey 1 by multiplying the left-hand column by 2, so as to increase Class *a*, and the right-hand column by 0.75, so as to decrease Class *b*, and the odds ratio is thus left unchanged. In the mobility table for Survey 3 an odds ratio of 1, implying no association between class origins and destinations, is obtained by deriving each cell value from the marginal distributions of the table alone: i.e. by setting each cell value equal to the product of its corresponding row and column marginal values divided by the total N of 1000.

independent of each other – and perfect mobility prevails. We would not in fact expect this model to apply in any real society but it can serve as a useful baseline.

Model 2: *The constant association (CA) model*. This model – sometimes also referred to as the constant social fluidity model – states that there is an association between class origins and destinations but that all the odds ratios expressing this association *are constant over time* – in our case, across the birth cohorts that we distinguish. That is, just as in pre-revolutionary Omega between the first and second surveys, the level of social fluidity remains unaltered, regardless of any changes that may be occurring in the class structure.

Model 3: *The uniform difference (UNIDIFF) model*. This model states that there is an association between class origins and destinations but that over time – in our case, from one cohort to another – the odds ratios expressing this association *all change by some common multiplicative factor*, the parameter for which is labelled as β. That is to say, from one cohort to another all odds ratios, depending on the direction of change in the value of β, either increase or decrease to the same extent, so that social fluidity within the class structure, rather than being constant, is either systematically falling or systematically rising.[3]

How, then, do these models fare when we set them against our mobility data? We organise these data in the form of mobility tables, like those shown for Omega in Table 3.2, but using the seven NS-SEC classes as presented in Table 1.1, and then fit each of the three models to the data in turn. We focus here on results for men and women – treated separately – in the 1946, 1958 and 1970 birth cohorts. With

---

[3] In statistical terminology, Models 1 and 2 are loglinear models and Model 3 is a logmultiplicative model. Formal presentations of these models can be found in Bukodi et al. (2015). As noted in the Introduction, it is now generally recognised that the analysis of social mobility requires the application of statistical models rather than the calculation of various ad hoc indices directly from the data. Unfortunately, some British sociologists writing on mobility still wish to resort to such indices, which reflect the *combined* effects of structure and relative chances (see e.g. Payne, 2017: 134–6, 176–8). But whatever descriptive value these indices may have, given the class structure at a particular point in time, the confounding of effects involved means that they are of little value analytically – as, for example, in understanding *change* in either absolute or relative rates.

these cohorts we can determine class destinations at age 38, by around which age it is known that the probability of changes in occupation involving changes in class position falls away, whereas in earlier working life, as was previously noted, class positions are less stable, due mainly to upward worklife mobility.

We have in fact already anticipated the main outcome of our analyses in our discussion of absolute mobility rates in the previous chapter: that is, that across the cohorts *little directional change in relative rates occurs* – with then the implication that we wished to stress that changes in absolute rates have to be seen as essentially driven by class structural effects. However, we need now to spell out in some detail how we reach this conclusion regarding relative rates, and also to elaborate on the particular exception to it to which we also referred.[4]

To begin with men, we discover, not surprisingly, that Model 1, the independence model, does not give at all a good fit to the mobility tables for the three cohorts. Under this model, 15 per cent of all men in these cohorts would be misclassified – that is, would be placed in different cells of the mobility table to those in which they are actually found. We can then say that most of the odds ratios calculable within the tables do differ significantly from 1. For men in Britain over the period covered mobility was certainly not 'perfect'. However, when with Model 2, the CA model, we allow for an association between individuals' class origins and their class destinations but require that this association is at the same level in the tables for all three cohorts, we obtain a quite satisfactory fit to the data. Now only 4 per cent of all cases in the tables are misclassified and this lack of fit is not statistically significant: that is to say, one cannot safely rule out the possibility that all 441 corresponding odds ratios underlying the tables for the three cohorts are in fact the same – or, in other words, that constant social fluidity prevails. Moreover, if we go on to apply Model 3, the UNIDIFF model, envisaging some uniform increase or decrease in odds ratios from one cohort to another, we find that this gives no significant improvement over the CA model in its fit to the data.

---

[4] For further details of the research reported on in the following paragraphs, see Bukodi et al. (2015) and, specifically in regard to women, Bukodi et al. (2017).

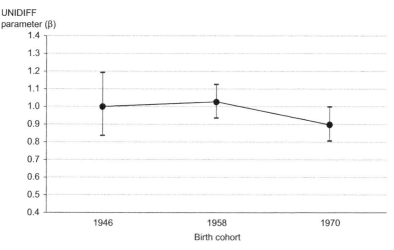

UNIDIFF
parameter (β)

Birth cohort

Source: Bukodi et al. (2015)

Figure 3.1 UNIDIFF parameters for 1946, 1958 and 1970 cohorts, men at age 38, with 95% confidence intervals

In Figure 3.1 we plot the β parameters that are returned with the UNIDIFF model: that is, the factors by which, under the model, odds ratios should increase or decrease from cohort to cohort. It can be seen that, taking the 1946 cohort as reference, a very slight increase between this cohort and the 1958 cohort is suggested – all odds ratios are to be multiplied by something just a little over 1; but this is followed by a somewhat larger decrease between the 1958 and the 1970 cohorts. There is, then, no sign here of any consistent directional change. And what it is more important is that the confidence intervals shown around the point estimates substantially overlap, thus indicating in another way that a conclusion of 'no change' in fluidity within the class structure is that which can best be drawn.

Turning to women, we find that, as with men, the independence model is far from fitting the data of the mobility tables we have constructed: 12 per cent of all individual cases are misclassified. But, also as with men, the CA model does provide an acceptable fit, by conventional statistical criteria, and again reduces the proportion of cases misclassified to 4 per cent. To this extent, no gender differences are apparent. However, when we move on to apply the UNIDIFF model, we obtain a somewhat surprising result. Despite the CA model being an acceptable one, the UNIDIFF model still significantly

UNIDIFF
parameter (β)

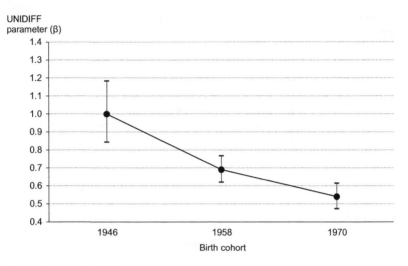

Source: Bukodi et al. (2015)

Figure 3.2 UNIDIFF parameters for 1946, 1958 and 1970 cohorts, women at age 38, with 95% confidence intervals

improves on it, with now only 3 per cent of cases being misclassified. And, further, if, as shown in Figure 3.2, we plot the β parameters that are returned, we see that these decrease steadily across the cohorts and that there is no overlap of the confidence intervals. While we should not exaggerate the magnitude of the change that is involved here, some increase in fluidity among the women represented in our three cohorts has to be recognised.

The gender difference that in this way emerges is of obvious interest, and we would like to know how it comes about. One explanation that has been suggested for possibly increasing fluidity among women, but not among men, is that women move into part-time work more often than men, and thus become more exposed to what has been called 'perverse fluidity': that is, fluidity that results from constraints rather than from opportunity. When women become part-timers, as, say, for family reasons, it is known that, because of the limited range of jobs available to them, they have often to take up employment that implies downward mobility relative to their earlier full-time employment. And insofar as this downward worklife mobility is such as *also* to imply downward mobility intergenerationally, then, with the growing numbers of women working part-time, this could lead to a weakening in the association between class origins and destinations – or, that is, to an increase in fluidity – becoming apparent among women at large.[5]

As an initial test of this explanation, we have divided the women in each of our cohorts into those who have and have not been in part-time work for a period of at least six months' duration – the 'part-timers' as opposed to the 'full-timers'. We have then repeated our previous modelling sequence on mobility tables for these two groups of women taken separately. The result is clear. The UNIDIFF model is preferred and an increase in fluidity is revealed *only among the part-timers*: that is, in their case we can essentially replicate Figure 3.2. Among the full-timers, and even among those who have had periods of absence from the labour market, the UNIDIFF model gives no improvement in fit on the CA model: that is, in their case we can essentially replicate Figure 3.1 for men. We can therefore say that the increase in fluidity that shows up among women is not general but is indeed confined to those who have had some experience of part-time work.

However, it does not necessarily follow from this that it actually is part-time work, and the downward worklife mobility to which it may lead, that generates the increasing fluidity among part-timers in inter-generational perspective. And if we go on to identify, from their detailed work histories, those part-timers who have in fact followed 'perverse fluidity' paths – that is, whose downward worklife mobility has also entailed downward intergenerational mobility – it turns out, first, that they are rather few in number, in fact less than 10 per cent of all part-timers, and, second, that the increase in fluidity is still clearly present among the majority of part-timers who have *not* followed such paths. Perverse fluidity cannot, then, be a satisfactory explanation for the general increase in fluidity among women who have worked part-time; and in turn the possibility is raised that an explanation has to be sought 'further back', so to speak, in the life-courses of these women.

In pursuing this possibility we do in fact obtain findings that are illuminating. Eventual part-timers, we discover, do not differ from full-timers in their class origins – they are just as likely to come from more advantaged as from less advantaged families; nor in the two later cohorts do they have consistently lower educational qualifications than

---

[5] An early version of the perverse fluidity explanation is given in Goldthorpe and Mills (2004). For evidence on the association between women's part-time working and downward worklife mobility, see Connolly and Gregory (2008), Dex, Ward and Joshi (2008) and Dex and Bukodi (2012).

full-timers at the time of entering the labour market. However, where they do differ is *in the level at which they enter*. They are significantly more likely than women who subsequently work only full-time to enter the labour market in wage-earning jobs falling into NS-SEC Classes 6 and 7, and even if at this point, as is the case with the large majority, they are working full-time.

What is therefore suggested is that those women who become part-timers *tend to have from the start a different orientation to work* to those who remain full-timers; one, it may be suggested, that entails giving priority – if initially, perhaps, in only an anticipatory way – to marriage or partnership and to family life. Thus, where these women come from more advantaged class backgrounds, they are in effect not seeking to exploit their advantages as fully as they probably could *in the context of their own working lives*. And since the numbers of women from Class 1 and 2 origins who eventually move into part-time work is steadily increasing across our cohorts, it would appear that it is the cumulative effects of the life-course choices made by these women, rather than the effects of part-time working itself, that pro-duces the weakening in the association between class origins and destinations that we find among part-timers.[6]

One further point may be added that confirms but at the same time qualifies the foregoing. Part-timers who come from managerial and professional families in Classes 1 and 2 do still appear to draw benefit from their advantaged backgrounds *in the marriage market* even if they do not seek to do so in the labour market. In the case of women of Class 1 and 2 origins who are themselves in Class 1 or 2 positions, there is little difference between part-timers and full-timers in the class distributions of their husbands or partners. But with women of Class 1 and 2 origins who are in Class 6 and 7 positions, part-timers are

---

[6] This explanation of increasing fluidity among women is in line with arguments advanced by Hakim (2000, 2004) to the effect that women's orientations to work are highly heterogeneous and probably becoming more so. However, we would not wish to follow Hakim in seeing this as reflecting no more than the expression of different 'preferences'. As critics of Hakim have pointed out (e.g. McRae, 2003; Kangas and Rostgaard, 2007), preferences are formed in particular social contexts; and under different institutional arrangements – regarding child care provision, maternity (and paternity) leave, flexible working hours etc. – women's orientations to work could also be quite different. At the same time, though, the possibility of 'free choice by equal-but-different men and women' (Charles, 2011: 367) should not be precluded.

clearly more likely than full-timers to have husbands or partners in positions within the managerial and professional salariat. It thus follows that the increase in social fluidity that is apparent among women when only their own class positions are considered will be of significantly reduced impact on the level of fluidity overall if it is the conjugal family rather than the individual that is taken as the unit of analysis.[7]

Women's part-time work and downward mobility – 1

Bronwen

Bronwen was born into a professional family but when she was three her mother died. Her father remarried and she never developed a close relationship with her stepmother. She got decent O levels but decided not to stay on at school to do A levels. After leaving she worked in a series of junior office jobs.

She married young and on the birth of her first child, when she was 23, left work and went abroad with her husband who was starting on a managerial career. After two years, they returned but her husband, who has risen to become a senior executive in a multinational manufacturing firm, always had to spend a lot of time away, travelling around Europe. So 'home life', especially looking after eventually three children, and now her invalid stepmother, has always been 'first priority'.

Eventually, Bronwen did go back to work but only part-time – 'never full-time' – in various routine clerical jobs. She says she did not have a career 'because I chose not to'. Work is 'just somewhere I go... and then come home – it doesn't have any effect'. But she says she has no regrets. She enjoys a 'very comfortable' standard of living, with an ideal house, a full leisure life and frequent holidays.

---

[7] In the 1970 cohort 52 per cent of women of Class 1 and 2 origins who were working part-time in the semi-routine or routine wage-earning jobs of Classes 6 and 7 were paired with men in Class 1 or 2 positions as compared with only 28 per cent of such women who were working full-time in Class 6 or 7 jobs (see further Bukodi et al., 2017).

Women's part-time work and downward mobility – 2

Donna

Donna grew up in what she describes as a middle-class business family: 'we never seemed short of money'. At school she was 'about average'. When she was 16 a wealthy aunt offered to take her on a world tour so she left school and was away for six months. On her return, she did not know what to do, except that she did not want to go back to school. She had some thoughts of becoming a beautician but eventually worked as a receptionist and in various routine office jobs. She says 'I never had a career', but she is unsure about whether she ever wanted one.

When she was 23 she married and had two daughters in quick succession. Her husband is an executive in an IT firm and often has to travel away from home. So Donna brought up the children more or less single-handed. By the time they were of secondary school age, her father had developed dementia and then later her mother got cancer. So for several years Donna was completely preoccupied with family responsibilities. Now both her father and mother are dead and her daughters, though still living at home, are quite independent: 'I scarcely see them.' While she again works part-tine in a customer service centre – 'just 20 hours a week' – she is at something of a loss to know what to do with the rest of her time: 'I'm left with this big gap.'

Donna appreciates the fact that she has 'a nice house and money in the bank'. But while her husband enjoys an active social life, centring around golf and watching football, these things don't interest her, and she is finding it difficult to renew her own social and leisure life: 'I can't say I'm a happy person at the moment.'

To sum up, our analyses of relative rates of intergenerational class mobility, as measured by odds ratios, indicate that no change of any major or systematic kind has occurred over the historical period that our birth cohorts cover. Britain is far from being a society of perfect mobility – individuals' class destinations are significantly associated with their class origins – and, more importantly, *the strength of this association shows a high degree of temporal stability.* Among men and among women who have not taken up part-time employment – that is, among a substantial majority of the economically active population – relative rates, indicating the level of social fluidity within the class structure, are more or less unchanging. And that we come to such a conclusion should not in fact be regarded as especially surprising. It is essentially the same conclusion as that which has emerged from a series of previous studies of class mobility in Britain based on cross-sectional surveys of the population and dating back to the Nuffield study of 1972.[8] In exploiting the possibility of cross-cohort comparisons, our work serves primarily to confirm these earlier results from a different perspective, and to show that a situation of largely constant social fluidity has extended from the twentieth into the twenty-first century.

We may now go on to consider the significance of our findings on relative rates in the context of the discussion of social mobility in political and policy circles, just as we did in the case of our findings on absolute rates. Again, it is the disconnect that is striking. Most obviously, the results we have obtained contradict in a further way the prevailing idea of mobility in decline. We find no evidence of relative rates becoming more unequal, or, that is, of the association between class origins and destinations strengthening, and of absolute mobility being in this way increasingly restricted. Insofar as there is any exception to our general conclusion of unchanging relative rates, it goes, as we have seen, in the opposite direction: that is, more equal relative rates, implying greater social fluidity, are apparent among women who have worked part-time.

We noted in the previous chapter that the one – and only – piece of research that has actually indicated declining mobility in Britain is that carried out by a group of economists concerned with income mobility: specifically, with the association between the earnings of members of

---

[8] See, for example, Goldthorpe (1980/1987), Goldthorpe and Mills (2004, 2008), Paterson and Ianelli (2007). Buscha and Sturgis (2017), on the basis of their work on the ONS Longitudinal Study referred to in Chapter 2, n. 6, obtain results that contrast yet more sharply with those of Blanden et al. than do our own. They find evidence of some *increase* in fluidity among men and women between cohorts born in the late 1950s and late 1960s (cf. Figure 3.1 above), although this increase is not maintained between the latter cohort and subsequent ones, and was in any event very slight when individuals were considered at age 40–46 rather than at an earlier age. We might add here that if we take individuals' class destinations at age 27 and on this basis bring the 1980–4 birth cohort into our analyses, we also find, for men and women alike, that the UNIDIFF model improves on the CA model and that its parameters indicate increasing fluidity. However, whether this reflects some emerging long-term trend must remain open to doubt until analyses can be made of the mobility of members of this cohort when they have reached a later age.

the 1958 and 1970 birth cohorts at age 33–34 and their family incomes when they were aged 16. This association is found to strengthen from the earlier to the later cohort. However, although, as earlier described, this research achieved great political and media impact, it has by now attracted critical questioning on a number of grounds. For our present purposes, the following points are of main relevance. First, and to revert to what was said in Chapter 1, the data available for the analysis of income mobility in Britain – including data from the cohort studies – are not of high quality, and any results deriving from these data have to be seen as subject to a wide margin of error. Second, although there is no reason why research on income and class mobility should necessarily lead to similar conclusions, other – less publicised – research on relative income mobility, while also subject to data problems, has produced results that are clearly more in line with those on class mobility in showing no directional change.[9] And third, and again to go back to the argument of Chapter 1, there are good grounds for claiming, both in the case of the 1958 and 1970 cohorts and more generally, that the association between origins and destinations is *stronger* when mobility is treated in terms of class than it is when treated in terms of income, or, in other words, the intergenerational transmission of economic advantage and disadvantage is more comprehensively captured through a focus on class.[10]

We would therefore again have to see the economists' work, or at all events the reception it received, as serving largely to misdirect attention so far as the political and wider public understanding of current issues

[9] See Ermisch and Francesconi (2004) and Nicoletti and Ermisch (2007). Economists involved in the research referred to in the text have subsequently claimed that the findings of these studies are consistent with their own conclusions, but this is not correct. Nicoletti and Ermisch (2007: figs. 1 and 2) show that for cohorts in their study born between 1961 and 1972 the correlation between fathers' earning and sons' earnings remained stable or actually decreased.

[10] See, for Britain, Cox, Jackson and Lu (2009), Erikson and Goldthorpe (2010) and Goldthorpe (2013); and for Sweden, where far better quality income data are available, Erikson (2016). The association shown by the economists between family income and children's earnings in the 1958 cohort is remarkably weak, and must give rise to doubts about the reliability of the family income variable in particular. Yet a version of this variable is still being used in further analyses of income mobility, again claiming a decline (Belfield et al., 2017). For what we would regard as a balanced assessment of the debate between economists and sociologists on this issue – written by economists – see Jäntti and Jenkins (2015: section 5.3).

of social mobility is concerned. As a corrective to the preoccupation with 'mobility in decline', what we would wish to bring out is the significance of the finding that, although mobility as considered in terms of relative as well as absolute rates has not in fact decreased, *neither is there any evidence that it has shown a steady and general tendency to increase, and over a period extending back to at least the middle of the last century.*

To begin with, it is worth repeating that it is this finding of constant social fluidity that underpins the central argument of Chapter 2: that the crucial changes observed in absolute mobility rates – the reversal in trend of the upward and downward components of the total rate – have to be seen as almost exclusively the result of class structural change. Thus, if we were to redraw Figures 2.3 and 2.4 on the basis not of our actual data but of the mobility tables that would be predicted under the CA model, when all odds ratios would be the same across cohorts by construction, *the graphs would be indistinguishable from those we have presented* – except that the slight increase shown in Figure 2.4 in the total mobility rate for women, which we can now see as reflecting the increase in fluidity among part-timers, would not be picked up. And in turn the further argument of Chapter 2 is reinforced: that any policy initiatives that might be taken to try to move back from the present pattern of absolute mobility rates towards that of the golden age, in which social ascent predominated over social descent, will need to be ones focused not on making relative rates more equal but rather on regenerating the upgrading of the class structure.

Moreover, the significance of the finding of a long-term constancy in the level of social fluidity is heightened when two further considerations are taken into account, as we will here simply flag up before going on to more extensive discussion in subsequent chapters.

First, the inequality involved in relative rates of class mobility, as well as being persistent, is also in certain respects quite extreme. What is important in this regard is not that British society falls short of exhibiting perfect mobility – which could be thought a rather implausible and, in any event, perhaps not altogether desirable state.[11] It is, rather, that prevailing departures from perfect mobility, although overall highly variable in their extent, are in the case of some mobility transitions so large as to be difficult to reconcile with any notion of

[11] On the question 'Would perfect mobility be perfect?', see Swift (2004).

equality of opportunity. Our research, as we will show in the next chapter, allows us to make better estimates of the extent of inequalities in individuals' relative chances of mobility or immobility than have been possible in previous work, and also to trace their pattern within the class structure and how this pattern is formed.

Second, it has to be recognised that the period over which relative rates of class mobility have remained little altered is one in which repeated efforts have in fact been made to bring about a greater equality of opportunity, *primarily through policies of educational expansion and reform.* And, as we have observed, politicians from all parties continue to regard educational policy as key in regard to this objective. But, in the light of findings of the kind we have reported, the question is obviously raised, even if politicians themselves fight shy of it, of why educational policy has over so many decades had so little apparent effect on relative rates of mobility – so little effect in weakening the association between class origins and destinations and in making Britain a supposedly more 'open' society in the form of an education-based meritocracy. In the chapters that form the second part of this book we will elaborate on this question and draw on the results of our research to try to provide an answer.

In conclusion of the present chapter, however, we need to make one further observation as essential background to what is to follow. In any attempt at understanding the long-term constancy of relative rates of mobility, in the face of policy interventions aimed at reducing the inequalities they entail, it is important to see this constancy – or what we might refer to as the stability of the endogenous mobility regime – not as some impersonal 'social fact' but rather as the outcome of *a powerful resistance to change* stemming from the actions of individuals whose interests lie in the status quo.

In this regard, it has always to be kept in mind that the effects of changes in relative rates, unlike the effects of class structural change, necessarily impact on upward and downward mobility *in the same way and to the same extent.* Thus – as is well illustrated in the case of post-revolutionary Omega (see again Table 3.2) – if relative mobility rates become more equal, then, assuming no class structural change, upward mobility will increase *but so too, and in similar measure, will down-ward mobility.* Or, to put the matter another way, if the net association between the class positions of parents and their children is weakened, the chances of children moving down the class hierarchy intergenerationally must, overall, increase in exactly the same degree as their chances of moving up. In this sense, relative mobility chances amount to a zero-sum game – a fact that politicians deploying the easy rhetoric of 'greater opportunity for all' either do not grasp or at all events would rather not acknowledge. When politicians speak of 'mobility' they have in fact almost invariably to be understood as referring to mobility upwards: downward mobility is a taboo topic.[12]

What is, however, important to recognise is that, as against the mathematical symmetry of changes in relative rates, there has to be set a psychological *a*symmetry. There is by now a substantial body of psychological research on the issue of 'loss aversion' that reveals a general human tendency to subjectively experience losses more intensely than gains, even if, objectively, they are of the same value. You are more displeased if you lose a £20 note in the street than pleased if you find one: losing what you once had, and perhaps felt entitled to, is especially disturbing.[13] In the light of this research, it has then to be expected that a still stronger motivation will exist *to avoid downward mobility* – to avoid losing a relatively advantaged class position – than to achieve upward mobility. And, further, the resources of those families and individuals who have most to lose through downward mobility will, in the nature of the case, tend to be greater than those of families and individuals who have most to gain through upward mobility. Taken together, then, the high priority that is likely to be given to avoiding *déclassement* on the part of those faced with this possibility and their capacity to protect themselves – or their

[12] At a Cabinet Office seminar on social mobility held a little while before the 2001 general election, several sociologists present managed finally to get across the point that equalising relative mobility rates implied a zero-sum game, whereupon one of Prime Minister Blair's senior political advisors strongly objected 'But Tony can't possibly go to the country on a platform of increasing downward mobility!' The advisor was, however, still somewhat confused. What has to be understood – and what, it has to be admitted, *some* sociologists still fail to see (e.g. Saunders, 2010: 27–30) – is that the idea of a zero-sum game *applies only to relative and not to absolute mobility*. Thus, as we have shown, during the golden age, rates of upward mobility into the salariat increased without rates of downward mobility from salariat origins likewise increasing – because, that is, of the steady expansion of the salariat.

[13] See, for example, Kahneman (2011: ch. 26 esp.). Kahneman regards loss aversion as involving 'a failure of rationality'. But while this is evidently true in relation to 'content blind' norms of rationality deriving from principles of logic and probability and to which economists tend to adhere, it is far less so from the standpoint of 'rationality for mortals' (Gigerenzer, 2008).

children – against it have to be seen as creating a large potential for resistance to any attempts at widening opportunity, in the sense of equalising mobility chances, whether through educational policy or otherwise.

It is in this regard instructive that in the one instance we have found of relative rates in fact becoming more equal – that is, among women part-timers – it would appear that this trend results from growing numbers of women from more advantaged class backgrounds in effect *opting* to become downwardly mobile intergenerationally by declining opportunities in the labour market – if not in the marriage market – that their class origins and educational attainment would probably have made available to them. But, in general, it has to be accepted that policies aimed at reducing inequalities in relative mobility chances will not be costless to the members of families who hold more advantaged class positions; and that, rather than showing a merely passive acceptance, these families can be expected to apply their superior resources, economic and otherwise, in all available ways in order to counter or circumvent such policies.

4 | The Pattern of Social Fluidity within the Class Structure: Hierarchy, Inheritance and Status Effects

In the previous chapter we have shown that over a period extending back at least to the middle of the last century there has been little change in relative rates of class mobility in British society. Or, in other words, little change has occurred in the level of social fluidity within the class structure as expressed by the strength of the association between the class positions of children and their parents when considered net of all structural change. The only exception arises in the rather special case of relative rates becoming more equal among women who at some point have worked part-time. In the present chapter we move on to consider a number of questions that arise. First, given the essentially stable *level* of social fluidity, so far as the large majority of the active population is concerned, what is the *pattern* of this fluidity within the class structure and how is this pattern created? Second, is this pattern itself stable over time? Third, is this pattern and its degree of stability the same for men and for those women who when in employment have only worked full-time? And, finally, and most consequentially, what are the implications of the patterning of social fluidity for the likelihood of different mobility transitions being made and in turn for issues of equality of opportunity?[1]

When considering possible trends in the level of social fluidity, we observed that because relative mobility rates are captured by a very large number of different odds ratios, it is necessary to proceed by formulating statistical models that make statements about all odds ratios of interest and by then seeing how well these models can

---

[1] We do not seek to address a comparable set of questions in the case of women who have worked part-time since we know that in their case the level of fluidity has in fact increased, so that in certain respects at least the pattern of fluidity cannot have remained stable – and also must be, or have become, different from that applying in the case of men and of women who have only worked full-time. To investigate in further detail the changes that have occurred would require more data on part-timers than we have presently available.

71

reproduce the empirical data. The same applies in treating the pattern of social fluidity.

In the light of theoretical arguments that have successfully guided previous research,[2] we envisage a model according to which the pattern of social fluidity within the class structure is created by three different kinds of effect: those of *class hierarchy*, *class inheritance* and *status affinity*. We now explain these effects in turn.[3]

Hierarchy Effects. Hierarchy effects are ones that *limit mobility* between classes as a result of differences in the advantages or disadvantages that are associated with them as classes of origin – in terms of family economic, social and cultural resources; and of differences in the barriers that exist to their attainment as classes of destination – in terms of required skills, qualifications or capital. We noted in Chapter 1 that the seven NS-SEC classes we use in our analyses of mobility cannot be regarded as entirely hierarchically ordered but that, as was indicated in Table 1.1, four lines of hierarchical division can be drawn, with Classes 3, 4 and 5 being for this purpose placed at the same level (these were the divisions we previously used in Chapter 2 in order to define upward and downward as distinct from 'horizontal' mobility). Correspondingly, in our model we include four class hierarchy effects, labelled as HI1, HI2, HI3 and HI4, that relate, as is shown in Table 4.1, to cells of the mobility table that involve the crossing of one, two, three or all four of the hierarchical divisions. These effects, as can be seen, are intended to operate cumulatively with the hierarchical range of the mobility transitions that are involved.

Inheritance Effects. Inheritance effects are ones that *promote immobility* and thus, like hierarchy effects, also limit mobility. This occurs, on the one hand, as a result of the distinctive motivations and opportunities that individuals may have for remaining in the same class as that in which they originated, as, say, through family occupational traditions or the direct intergenerational transmission of family businesses or capital; and, on the other hand, as a result of distinctive constraints that may exist on individuals' mobility away from their class of origin, as, say, through restricted employment possibilities in local labour markets. Inheritance effects thus apply only in cells on the main diagonal of the mobility table – that is, in those cells indicating immobility – and in our model

---

[2] See in particular Erikson and Goldthorpe (1992: chs. 4 and 5).
[3] For full technical details of the model – known as a topological model – that we go on to describe, see Bukodi, Goldthorpe and Kuha (2017).

Table 4.1 *Hierarchy effects for the 7 x 7 mobility table*

Class of origin	Class of destination						
	Class 1	Class 2	Class 3	Class 4	Class 5	Class 6	Class 7
Class 1		HI1	HI1 HI2	HI1 HI2	HI1 HI2	HI1 HI2 HI3	HI1 HI2 HI3 HI4
Class 2	HI1		HI1	HI1	HI1	HI1 HI2	HI1 HI2 HI3
Class 3	HI1 HI2	HI1			HI1	HI1	HI1 HI2
Class 4	HI1 HI2	HI1			HI1	HI1	HI1 HI2
Class 5	HI1 HI2	HI1	HI1	HI1		HI1	HI1 HI2
Class 6	HI1 HI2 HI3	HI1 HI2	HI1	HI1	HI1		HI1
Class 7	HI1 HI2 HI3 HI4	HI1 HI2 HI3	HI1 HI2	HI1 HI2	HI1 HI2	HI1	

we include two such effects, labelled as IN1 and IN2. As shown in Table 4.2, in which inheritance effects are included along with hierarchy effects, IN1 applies in all diagonal cells and is intended to capture a general propensity for class inheritance, while IN2 applies, additionally, in the cells indicating immobility in Class 1 and in Class 4. In the case of Class 4, that of small employers and own-account workers, the possibility clearly exists of 'going concerns' or amounts of capital being passed on from parents to children. In the case of Class 1, while this largely comprises (higher-level) salaried managers and professionals, it also includes, as was earlier noted, a small number of large employers and independent professionals and also a probably larger number of managers and professionals whose employment status is somewhat ambiguous in that, as well as receiving a salary, they participate to some extent in business or practice profits. Thus, the possibility again arises of class immobility being maintained via direct inheritance and also perhaps through privileged intergenerational access to high level positions.

Status Affinity Effects. We explained in Chapter 1 that while our focus is on class and class mobility, we recognise social status as the basis of a further form of stratification that we may need at some points to take into account. The main line of status division in British society has for long been, and still remains, that between what might be called the 'white-collar' and 'blue-collar' worlds. This can be shown to be the main division that runs through the structure of more intimate social relations, such as close friendship and marriage or partnership.[4] We thus introduce status affinity effects into our model as ones that *promote class mobility* in that they in part offset hierarchy effects insofar as mobility occurs *only within* either the white-collar or blue-collar worlds. Although the NS-SEC classes do not map perfectly on to status divisions, Classes 1, 2 and 3 can be regarded as being very largely within the white-collar world, and Classes 5, 6 and 7 very largely within the blue-collar world. Correspondingly, as shown in Table 4.3, which includes status affinity effects along with hierarchy and inheritance effects, a white-collar status affinity effect, AF1, is taken to apply in all cells indicating mobility between any two of the former three classes, and a blue-collar status affinity effect, AF2, in all cells indicating mobility between any two of the latter three classes. What this means is, for example, that under our model we would

---

[4] This is evident from the status scale, based on the occupational structure of close friendship, developed by Chan and Goldthorpe (2004).

Table 4.2 *Inheritance effects for the 7 x 7 mobility table*

Class of origin	Class of destination						
	Class 1	Class 2	Class 3	Class 4	Class 5	Class 6	Class 7
Class 1	**IN1 IN2**	HI1	HI1 HI2	HI1 HI2	HI1 HI2	HI1 HI2 HI3	HI1 HI2 HI3 HI4
Class 2	HI1	**IN1**	HI1	HI1	HI1	HI1 HI2	HI1 HI2 HI3
Class 3	HI1 HI2	HI1	**IN1**			HI1	HI1 HI2
Class 4	HI1 HI2	HI1		**IN1 IN2**		HI1	HI1 HI2
Class 5	HI1 HI2	HI1			**IN1**	HI1	HI1 HI2
Class 6	HI1 HI2 HI3	HI1 HI2	HI1	HI1	HI1	**IN1**	HI1
Class 7	HI1 HI2 HI3 HI4	HI1 HI2 HI3	HI1 HI2	HI1 HI2	HI1 HI2	HI1	**IN**

Table 4.3 *Status affinity effects for the 7 x 7 mobility table*

Class of origin	Class of destination						
	Class 1	Class 2	Class 3	Class 4	Class 5	Class 6	Class 7
Class 1	IN1 IN2	HI1 **AF1**	HI1 HI2 **AF1**	HI1 HI2	HI1 HI2	HI1 HI2 HI3	HI1 HI2 HI3 HI4
Class 2	HI1 **AF1**	IN1	HI1 **AF1**	HI1	HI1	HI1 HI2	HI1 HI2 HI3
Class 3	HI1 HI2 **AF1**	HI1 **AF1**	IN1			HI1	HI1 HI2
Class 4	HI1 HI2	HI1		IN1 IN2		HI1	HI1 HI2
Class 5	HI1 HI2	HI1		IN1	HI1 **AF2**	HI1 HI2 **AF2**	HI1 HI2 **AF2**
Class 6	HI1 HI2 HI3	HI1 HI2	HI1	HI1	HI1 **AF2**	IN1	HI1 **AF2**
Class 7	HI1 HI2 HI3 HI4	HI1 HI2 HI3	HI1 HI2	HI1 HI2	HI1 HI2 **AF2**	HI1 **AF2**	IN1

expect that although Class 3 and Class 5 are placed at the same hierarch-ical level, mobility between Class 3 and Classes 1 or 2 will be more likely, because of white-collar affinity effects, than mobility between Class 5 and Classes 1 or 2; and that mobility between Class 5 and Classes 6 or 7 will be more likely, because of blue-collar affinity effects, than mobility between Class 3 and Classes 6 or 7.

In sum, our model states that the pattern of social fluidity within the British class structure can be captured by the interplay of the class hierarchy, class inheritance and status affinity effects that it comprises – eight effects in all – as these operate in the cells of mobility tables based on the NS-SEC classes. That is to say, the numbers of individuals found in each cell will be determined by these effects, net of the effects of class structural change, and so too therefore will be all the odds ratios in terms of which social fluidity is defined. From Table 4.3, in which the distribution of the effects appears in full, it may be observed that there are six cells – those referring to mobility occurring between any two of the three intermediate classes, Classes 3, 4 and 5 – where none of the effects we distinguish are included. This is because the theoretical ideas underlying our model give no reason to do so, and we therefore suppose that the numbers in these cells will be determined simply in consequence of the effects operating in other cells. How well, we may now ask, does the model succeed in reproducing our empirical data?[5]

To begin with, we can apply the model to mobility tables for men in our 1946, 1958 and 1970 birth cohorts where class destinations can be determined at age 38 – that is, to the same tables we used in our analysis of relative rates of mobility in the previous chapter. If, first of all, we pool the data for all three cohorts, we find that the model does in fact fit the data well by standard tests. Only around 4 per cent of all individual cases are misclassified, and this lack of fit cannot be regarded as statistically significant. Moreover, if we then apply the model with the parameters for the eight effects being allowed to vary from cohort to cohort, we do not in this way achieve any significant improvement in fit. In other words, what is indicated is that, so far as men are concerned, not only is the level of fluidity highly stable over time, as was shown in Chapter 3, *but likewise the pattern of fluidity*. Over the historical period covered by our birth cohorts, the effects of class hierarchy, class

---

[5] Full details of the model fitting leading to the results reported in the following paragraphs are provided in Bukodi, Goldthorpe and Kuha (2017).

inheritance and status affinity would appear to have operated in essentially constant ways in creating this pattern.

Next, we can apply the model to the corresponding mobility tables for women, although limited to those women who have worked only full-time and for whom, as for men, we find no evidence of change over time in the level of fluidity. The results that emerge are in fact the same as for men. With the data pooled across the cohorts, the model fits well, with again only around 4 per cent of all cases being misclassified, and again allowing the effect parameters to vary by cohort produces no significant improvement in fit.

However, while the overall pattern of fluidity can then be regarded as showing long-term stability for men and for women 'full-timers' alike, the further question remains of whether gender differences exist as regards the *strength* of the several effects that are involved. To investigate this possibility, we start by fitting our model to the mobility data pooled across *both* cohorts *and* genders. Once more we obtain a satisfactory fit, pointing to a large degree of commonality in the strength of the effects that prevail. Nonetheless, we do achieve an improvement in fit, of a slight but still significant kind, if we go on to allow the effect parameters to vary by gender. Further light can be thrown on the differences that arise if, as in Figure 4.1, the strengths of the different effect parameters are compared when the model is fitted to men and women separately.

In interpreting Figure 4.1, the following points should be kept in mind. First, hierarchy effects, in limiting mobility, are negative in sign because they depress the numbers in any off-diagonal cell of the mobility table in which they apply. Second, inheritance effects, in promoting *im*mobility, are positive because they raise the numbers in the diagonal cells in which they apply. And, third, status affinity effects are also positive in that they serve to raise mobility by offsetting the negative hierarchy effects in those off-diagonal cells that relate to mobility between classes within the white-collar or blue-collar worlds. What then substantively emerges from Figure 4.1 is that gender differences sufficiently marked to attain statistical significance occur in only two respects, both of which are, however, of some interest.

The largest difference arises with the white-collar status affinity effect, AF1, which is clearly stronger for men than for women. In Figure 4.1 the length of the bars involved indicate that with men this effect is sufficiently large to offset both the HI1 and HI2 effects, while with women it offsets only the HI1 effect. In accounting for this difference, it is relevant to note that there is a tendency for women, even if from more advantaged class

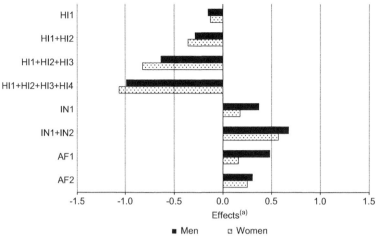

Note

(a) These effects can be understood as those that, in combination, determine the numbers of individuals found in each cell of the 7 x 7 class mobility table to which they apply (Table 4.3)

Source: Bukodi et al. (2017)

Figure 4.1 Hierarchy, inheritance and status affinity effects, men and women 'full-timers'

backgrounds, to be more concentrated than their male counterparts in employment in the *lowest* white-collar status groups – mainly those of routine administrative and clerical workers – and, further, that women are more likely than men to remain in such employment over the course of their working lives (see further Chapter 7).

A somewhat smaller difference is found with the general inheritance effect, IN1, which is also stronger for men than for women. In accounting for this greater propensity for class immobility among men, what would appear chiefly important is that the tendency for men to follow their fathers *in specific occupations* is stronger than the tendency for women to follow their fathers – or indeed their mothers – in this way. In other words, one could say that men appear, whether for better or for worse, to be more caught up than women in family occupational traditions.[6]

By applying our model, we have now answered the first three of the questions from which we started out. So far as men and also women 'full-timers' are concerned, the pattern of fluidity within the

---

[6] This gender difference in the tendency for 'occupational succession' is evident in cross-national studies (see Jonsson et al., 2009; Erikson, Goldthorpe and Hällsten, 2012), and can be clearly shown with our own birth cohort data if we move down to consider mobility at an occupational rather than a class level.

class structure is one that can be adequately captured by class hierarchy, class inheritance and status affinity effects as these apply under our model; for both men and women this pattern proves to be highly stable over the historical period that we cover; and, while certain gender differences can be identified in the strength of effects, what is most notable is the degree of cross-gender commonality that is found. We can then move on to the last question we posed: that of what is implied for the chances of individuals making particular mobility transitions and for inequalities in these chances.

Since our model of social fluidity reproduces to a close approximation the numbers of individuals found in each of the cells of the seven-class mobility tables that we have constructed for men and for women full-timers in the 1946, 1958 and 1970 birth cohorts, it will likewise reproduce all the odds ratios that can be derived from these numbers. There are, it may be recalled, 441 odds ratios implicit in each of these mobility tables – one for every possible pair of the seven origin classes taken together with every possible pair of the seven destination classes. However, for our present purposes, we can concentrate on a particular, quite limited, subset of these odds ratios that is sociologically most readily interpretable and informative: that is, the subset of *symmetrical* odds ratios. An odds ratio is symmetrical where the pair of origin classes involved is *the same* as the pair of destination classes. Thus, an odds ratio giving the chances of an individual originating in Class 1 being found in Class 1 rather than in Class 2 relative to the chances of an individual originating in Class 2 being found in Class 1 rather than in Class 2 is symmetrical, whereas an odds ratio giving the relative chances of individuals originating in Class 1 and in Class 2 being found in, say, Class 5 rather than in Class 7 would not be symmetrical.

Figure 4.2 shows in graphical form the ranges of magnitude of the symmetrical odds ratios – twenty-one in all – that are implied by our seven-class mobility tables. Men and women are treated separately but in each case the data for the three cohorts are pooled – since we know that no significant change occurs across the cohorts. The first entry in the first row of the figure is the symmetrical odds ratio for Class 1 and Class 2, the next entry, that for Class 1 and Class 3 and so on down to the one entry in the last row which is the symmetrical odds ratio for Class 6 and Class 7. The ranges of the magnitudes of the ratios, as derived from our model, are indicated by the depth of shading of the blocks; the deeper the shading, the larger the ratio or, that is, the greater the inequality in the

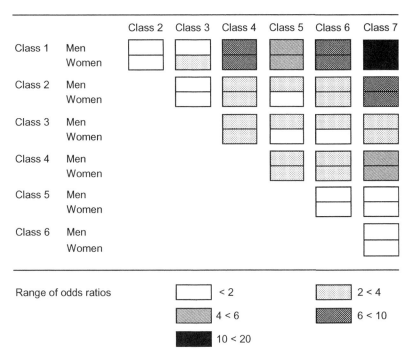

Source: Bukodi et al. (2017)

Figure 4.2 Symmetrical odds ratios under the topological model for men and women 'full-timers'

relative mobility chances that are involved.[7] If we think of Figure 4.2 as, so to speak, mapping a mobility terrain, with the shadings indicating contours, then the following three features are most notable.

First, cells in the top-left and bottom-right corners of the figure form rather 'flat' areas where inequalities in relative mobility chances are quite low, with odds ratios falling for the most part somewhere between 1, which would imply perfect mobility or the absence of any association between class origins and destinations, and 2. These are areas relating to

---

[7] It may be asked why we derive the values of the symmetrical odds ratios from cell values under our model rather than from the values that we actually observe in our mobility tables. The answer is that where a theoretically informed model closely reproduces the empirical data, the values given under the model can be regarded as preferable to those calculated directly from the data in that the latter are likely to contain purely chances perturbations. And of course insofar as the model *is* a well-fitting one, the differences that arise will in any case be very slight.

mobility that falls within either the white-collar world of Classes 1, 2 and 3 or the blue-collar world of Classes 5, 6 and 7. Thus, for example, one could say that the chances of someone originating in Class 1, the higher salariat, being found in Class 1 rather than in Class 2, the lower salariat, are not more than twice as great as the same chances for someone originating in Class 2, and an analogous statement could be made as regards the relative chances of mobility between Class 6 and Class 7, the higher and lower strata of the working class. The high fluidity that prevails in the cases in question results from such hierarchical barriers as arise being in large part offset by the white-collar and blue-collar status affinity effects that are included in our model (see Tables 4.1 and 4.3), and the – rather small – departures from perfect mobility that still occur are brought about primarily by the general class inheritance effect.

Second, in cells in the middle areas of Figure 4.2, relating to all mobility transitions occurring between origins and destinations in Class 2, in the three intermediate classes, Classes 3, 4, 5, and in Class 6, the inequalities become steeper, with the symmetrical odds ratios now in the main falling within the range of 2 to 5. This reduced fluidity derives from two main sources: mobility between, on the one hand, Classes 2 and 3, and on the other, Classes 5 and 6, entails crossing the division between the white- and blue-collar worlds so that hierarchy effects are no longer offset by status affinity effects; and, further, all mobility transitions involving Class 4, that of small employers and own account workers, are affected by the increased propensity for intergenerational immobility in this class that is captured by the additional inheritance effect (see Table 4.2).[8]

Third, in the cells relating to mobility transitions involving Class 1 and Class 7 that run along the top and down the right-hand side of Figure 4.2, apart from those in the flat corners previously discussed, inequalities rise again and sharply so. This is the result of successive hierarchical effects coming into play and also the additional inheritance effect that applies with Class 1 as well as with Class 4 (see, again, Tables 4.1 and 4.2). The symmetrical odds ratios indicating inequalities in relative chances of mobility between Class 1 and Classes 4 or 5 and between Classes 2 or 4 and Class 7 lie, with one exception, in the

---

[8] As earlier noted, it is a shortcoming of the studies of income mobility that have been made in Britain that they leave small employers and the self-employed out of account because of the unreliability of their reporting of their incomes. But individuals falling into NS-SEC Class 4 now account for between 10 and 15 per cent of the active population, and of late self-employment would appear to be steadily on the increase, even discounting its more bogus forms.

range of 5 to 10, while those indicating such inequalities between Class 1 and Classes 6 or 7 are still higher, in the range of 10 to 20. For men, the ratio for mobility between Class 1 and Class 7 works out in fact at exactly 20: that is to say, the chances of a man originating in Class 1 being found in Class 1 rather than in Class 7 are estimated as being twenty times greater than the chances of a man originating in Class 7 being found in Class 1 rather than in Class 7. Mobility transitions made between the classes in question here are very much 'against the odds'.[9]

Upward mobility against the odds – 1

Harold

Harold's father was a bricklayer, working on building sites, and his mother an office cleaner, so as he was growing up 'there wasn't a lot of money around'. However, his parents were quite strict and placed a strong emphasis on good manners and 'respectability'. They could not afford holidays, and, when a child, Harold spent his summers helping out on his grandfather's smallholding.

Harold was always 'quite academic' and won a place at a grammar school. He did well in all examinations and went on to university where he obtained a good first degree in physics. He then moved to another university to take a Ph.D and, on completing this, was offered a research position in a physics laboratory. However, he decided to become a science teacher.

He has made a very successful professional career, becoming Head of Science in a high-ranking school, and has the possibility of a school headship now open to him. His wife is also a teacher. They have known each other since their schooldays together and, Harold says, 'she is really, really my very best friend' and his main source of support. They have no children and so live in an apartment in a pleasant suburb of a large city. But they are 'Mediterranean enthusiasts', for the sun and food, spend all their holidays in a villa on the Italian coast, and think that they may eventually retire there.

---

[9] The inequalities in relative mobility chances reported here are clearly greater than those found in previous studies covering in part at least the same historical period (e.g. Goldthorpe and Jackson, 2007; Li and Devine, 2011). This would appear to be the result of NS-SEC providing a more accurate and reliable instrument for determining class positions than the classifications previously in use. See further Bukodi et al. (2015).

Upward mobility against the odds – 2

Gordon

Gordon grew up in a large working-class family living on the top floor of a tenement building: 'lino on the floors and coal fires'. He did well at school, always being top of his class, and got good O levels in a range of 'applied' subjects. But when he was 16 his father died so Gordon, who says that by this time he had become 'a bit of a tear-away' and a member of a street gang, decided to leave school to earn some money. He started training as a surveyor, but this did not work out well, and he switched to an apprenticeship in carpentry.

On completing his apprenticeship, Gordon married, and he and his wife decided to join with an older brother who had set up his own construction firm. Gordon took on managerial responsibilities from the start. The firm became highly successful until, following some misfortunes in the late 1980s, it failed and went into receivership. However, after a few years, Gordon and his brother rebuilt the business and, after his brother died, Gordon took over full control, again with his wife as his main assistant: 'She has been my best friend, my pal, ever since we met ... We are together 24/7.'

The firm is now in good shape, with some thirty employees on the books and a steady flow of work coming in. Gordon and his wife have been able to send their children to private schools and have a large house in a 'village-like' suburb. They work hard but go away on 'weekend breaks' every month.

As might be expected from what has been said earlier, the gender differences that show up in Figure 4.2 are not great. There is, overall, a tendency for symmetrical odds ratios to be lower for women than for men, which is chiefly because, as was noted, the general class inheritance effect is weaker for women. But the particular differences that arise in this way are sufficiently large to reach statistical significance in only three cases: that is, with the ratios indicating relative mobility chances between Class 2 and Class 5 and between Class 3 and Classes 5 and 6. As Figure 4.2 shows, for women these ratios all fall into the lowest range that we distinguish. There is one contrary instance where the ratio for women is higher than that for men. This occurs with relative mobility chances between Class 1 and Class 3, resulting, again as was previously discussed, from women benefiting less than men from the white-collar status affinity effect so that hierarchical barriers to mobility within the white-collar world are stronger in their case. At the extremes, gender differences are slight.

Upward mobility against the odds – 3

Carol

Carol's father was a bus driver. Her family was always short of money, even for food. Her father gave her brothers encouragement in their education but less so Carol: 'he believed that a woman's place was in the home'. Carol was in fact doing well enough in secondary school to be a university applicant but 'rebelled' and left at age 17. Between then and age 26, while in a series of routine jobs, she had two failed marriages and was left as a single mother with two children. She also agreed to be foster parent to a relative's child, since she enjoyed 'mothering'.

In this situation Carol decided to try to resume her education and get to university as a mature student. She was accepted but found that she was not eligible for any grants. She therefore took a degree in social work on a part-time basis, while continuing to look after her own children and doing more fostering in order to support herself financially. She says of her education: 'I did it all arse upwards.'

After completing her degree, she became a social worker, then moved into social work management, and eventually became a senior manager in charge of children's services for a large regional authority. She now works independently as a consultant. As well as having gained 'complete financial security', she also has a more stable personal life with a third husband. They feel they will both be able to retire at 55. They presently live in a 'gated' community but are having a new house built for them in the countryside. They enjoy golf, skiing and travelling the world on holiday.

What, then, are the implications of our findings on the pattern of fluidity existing within the British class structure when set in relation to current political discussion of social mobility?

An initial point to be made is that our finding of an essential stability in the pattern as well as in the level of social fluidity across a period of more than half a century clearly reinforces the idea we introduced at the end of the last chapter: that of an endogenous mobility regime that is powerfully resistant to change. The effects on social fluidity of class hierarchy, class inheritance and status affinities persist over time in what can only be regarded as a rather remarkable fashion. We can therefore reassert that the abiding concern in political circles with change in social mobility – that is, with a supposed decline – is misdirected. *The focus of attention should be not on change, in any direction, but, to the contrary, on its absence.*

Further, the results we have reported call into question two, not entirely consistent, claims that are often made or at least implied: first, that relative mobility chances in Britain are in all respects of a very unequal kind; and second, that a quite distinctive problem arises with inequalities in access to certain elite groupings – as mediated, say, through the influence of exclusive schools, 'Oxbridge' and metropolitan social networks.[10] The conclusions to which our findings would point are, first, that some very wide *variation* exists in the degree of inequality of chances that are involved in different mobility transitions; but, second, that this variation is, in a rather systematic way, *continuous* rather than discontinuous.

On the one hand, our model of the prevailing pattern of social fluidity reveals that as regards certain mobility transitions a situation not widely divergent from that of perfect mobility does in fact prevail: that is, most importantly, in the case of mobility within the white-collar world of Classes 1, 2 and 3 – especially for men – and likewise within the blue-collar world of Classes 5, 6 and 7. The barriers to mobility in these regions of the class structure are not high, and it is in this connection relevant to recall that, as shown in Chapter 2, the total, absolute mobility rate in Britain, based on the seven NS-SEC classes, appears stable over time at around 80 per cent: that is, on this basis four out of five

---

[10] The Social Mobility Commission, for example, in its annual reports has tended to take a generally undifferentiated view of inequalities in mobility chances among the population at large, while at the same time apparently regarding elite mobility as a special case (see e.g. Social Mobility and Child Poverty Commission, 2014). In the academic context, sociologists associated with the Great British Class Survey have argued that the data from this survey, even if unsuitable for the study of mobility at a population level because of its lack of representativeness, can still be a reliable source for treating what are taken to be largely separate but now crucial issues of elite mobility. See Savage (2015), but also, the cogent critique by Mills (2015) of both the conceptual and empirical bases of the studies undertaken.

individuals are found in adult life in a different class to that in which they originated. To be sure, much of the mobility in question here is of only a short-range kind, but this is not to say that it should be discounted. In the light of the evidence on the extent of class inequalities that was presented in Chapter 1, mobility, whether upward or downward, between, say, Class 1 and Class 3 or Class 5 and Class 7 could scarcely be regarded as inconsequential. Our results in this regard do, incidentally, undermine suggestions that odds ratios are a statistic favoured by sociologists who are ideologically committed to the view of extreme inequality of opportunity in British society – because the quite unrealistic base of 1 serves to make all actual odds ratios appear excessive.[11] However, for some mobility transitions odds ratios not far removed from 1 can in fact be shown to occur, so that comparisons made with the higher odds ratios arising with other transitions are entirely appropriate.

On the other hand, as the range of mobility extends so that the white-collar–blue-collar division is crossed and hierarchy effects come increasingly into play, the odds ratios that emerge from our model do indicate that inequalities in relative mobility chances progressively widen to a rather extreme degree. And in view of this, it becomes open to some doubt whether a focus on elite groupings – unless of a very specialised and minoritarian kind – is likely to reveal inequalities that are of a quite different order of magnitude. At all events, recent research on elite mobility has not produced results that would lend any very compelling support for this possibility. The important point may be that the inequalities in mobility chances that arise in the case of elite groupings do not imply a step change from those indicated by the odds ratios reaching up to 20 that we have reported – *and that refer to mobility between classes covering quite substantial sections of the population.* At the present time Class 1 accounts for around 10 per cent of all economically active individuals and Class 7 for upwards of 15 per cent.[12] A preoccupation with inequalities in access to elites may

---

[11] See, for example, Saunders (2010: 26–32) and Payne (2017: 177).

[12] The Social Mobility and Child Poverty Commission's study of elite mobility in Britain (2014) covered only a limited range of – somewhat arbitrarily defined – elites, analysed recruitment only in terms of school and university attended, with no reference to class origins, and made no attempt to determine statistically the extent to which the elites considered were more exclusive than higher level managerial and professional occupations in general. Reeves et al. (2017), focusing on individuals included in *Who's Who* – approximately 0.05 per cent of the total adult population – also have no data on class origins but do calculate

therefore lead to an undue disregard of restrictions on intergenerational class mobility that, while perhaps not all that less severe, *are far more extensive*, and that could, for this reason, be regarded as being, if anything, of greater concern from the normative standpoint of equality of opportunity.[13]

Finally, and most importantly, the results emerging from Figure 4.2 point to serious difficulties with the widely accepted political argument, or at least assumption, that promoting social mobility is the most effective response to the present-day problem of increasing inequalities of condition. Through seeking to increase equality of opportunity, and thus social mobility, it is supposed, inequalities of condition can be given greater meritocratic legitimation. However, what is indicated by our analyses of the pattern of relative mobility rates is that this strategy is highly questionable in that equality of opportunity, and its expression via social mobility, *appears to be systematically compromised by inequalities of condition*. The class hierarchy and inheritance effects that are included in our model serve, in the ways explained at the start of the chapter, to capture such inequalities. And what the model then shows is that it is where these effects are most limited that relative mobility chances are most equal, and social fluidity is at its highest level, while as these effects come into fuller operation, relative mobility chances become increasingly disparate – to a point at which any conception of equality of opportunity becomes difficult to sustain.

some odds ratios in relation to type of school attended. Thus, for the period 2001 to 2016, men and women who had been at Headmasters' and Headmistresses' Conference schools – which account for around 2.5 per cent of all children in secondary education – were, as compared to others, thirty-five times more likely to become included, rather than not included, in *Who's Who*. While no direct comparison can of course be made with our odds ratios relating class origins to class destinations, no sharp discontinuity in chances is suggested so far as mobility between Classes 1 and 7 is concerned, and especially in view of evidence presented by Laurison and Friedman (2016) indicating that odds ratios referring to mobility chances between only the 'traditional' professions within Class 1 and Class 7 could go well above the 20 mark.

[13] Reeves (2017) is a forceful critique of the preoccupation in current American social and political commentary with the most advantaged 0.1 or 1.0 per cent of the population, to the neglect of what would appear to be a steadily widening gap between the 'upper middle class' – defined as some 20 per cent of all Americans – and the rest of the population in terms of material living standards, quality of life and intergenerational mobility chances.

It is in this regard that the disconnect that exists between the discussion of social mobility in political and related policy contexts and what has been learnt from sociological research is perhaps most fundamental. In the numerous reports and official or quasi-official policy documents dealing with mobility that we referred to in the Introduction, very little mention can be found of the possibility that, rather than greater equality of opportunity being a means of offsetting greater inequality of condition, it will only be achieved if the reduction of the latter is itself a primary policy objective. This issue becomes of particular importance in regard to socially grounded inequalities in educational attainment. For reducing such educational inequalities is seen as crucial to increasing equality of opportunity and thus levels of mobility – as being in effect *the key way in which the link between inequality of condition and inequality of opportunity can be broken.* In the chapters that follow we turn our attention to the role education has actually played in mobility, and specifically in class mobility, in British society over the decades since the Second World War; and we ask how far here too a gap exists between the assumptions and beliefs that are built into prevailing political and policy discourse and the evidence of sociological research.

5 | Education and Social Mobility: The OED Triangle

We noted in the Introduction that as well as a broad political consensus existing on the need to increase social mobility, it is also generally supposed that in achieving this goal it is educational policy that is of crucial importance. This supposition is built into all the ministerial speeches and governmental policy statements on mobility that we referred to, into the series of annual reports and policy recommendations that have been made by the Social Mobility Commission, and also into the programmes of various 'third sector' organisations concerned with social mobility.[1] In Chapter 2, in focusing on absolute class mobility, we examined the argument that it is primarily through educational expansion and reform that absolute mobility rates can be brought back closer to the pattern prevailing in the golden age when upward movement predominated over downward: that is, by building up a highly qualified labour force that will then pull in 'top-end' jobs to Britain from all parts of the global economy. We gave reasons for regarding this argument as unrealistic. In the present chapter our focus moves to the role of education in regard to relative rates of class mobility: that is, to the question of how far through education a significant reduction can be achieved in the inequalities – in some instances, as we have seen, the very marked inequalities – that exist in these rates, so that a new, more 'open' mobility regime can be brought into being, and one that can make some claim to meritocratic legitimation.

On the face of it, the idea that education plays a major role in social mobility might appear quite obvious. And, as will subsequently emerge, there is indeed ample evidence that in present-day Britain educational attainment is a major, even if not always an overriding,

---

[1] For example, attached to the logo of the Sutton Trust is the phrase 'Improving social mobility through education' and the Social Mobility Foundation describes its main aim as being that of providing support in their educational careers for young people from low-income backgrounds.

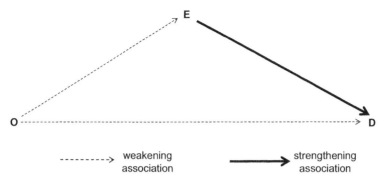

Figure 5.1 The OED triangle: requirements for education to create greater social fluidity

factor in determining *who* is mobile or immobile – that is, *which individuals*. But what has then to be further recognised – though it is in fact widely overlooked – is that it in no way follows automatically from this that education will be of similar importance in determining *the amount of mobility within society at large*. It is essential here to make the distinction between the individual and the societal levels of analysis. This is because education can serve to promote mobility at the societal level, through creating a greater equality of relative mobility chances or, that is, greater social fluidity, *only if* a number of conditions are met.

In treating the often rather complex issues that arise in this regard, sociologists refer to what is known as 'the OED triangle': that is, the triangle of associations that exists between individuals' social origins (O), their educational attainment (E) and their eventual social destinations (D). If education is to play the role in increasing mobility that is generally envisaged for it in current political discourse, what is necessary is that the associations within the OED triangle should change over time on a particular pattern. This pattern is shown in Figure 5.1.

As is indicated, the OE association has to weaken. As a result of policies of educational expansion and reform aimed at widening equality of opportunity, differences in individuals' levels of educational attainment related to their social origins should diminish. At the same time, the ED association has to strengthen. Educational attainment has, through the decisions made by employers, to be the key determinant of individuals' social destinations. And, finally, the 'direct' OD association – that which is not mediated through education – should, like the OE association, also weaken (or at all events not strengthen so as to offset the changes in the OE and ED associations). *Given* these conditions, the overall association between origins and destinations will then itself weaken and social fluidity will increase. Under models such as those discussed in the two previous chapters, all the odds ratios underlying intergenerational mobility tables that express inequalities in relative mobility chances will tend to move closer to 1 – the value implying perfect mobility.

It might be added that among theorists of postindustrial society writing in the later twentieth century from a broadly 'liberal' position, the view was widely held that changes within the OED triangle on the lines shown in Figure 5.1 were readily predictable if not indeed already under way. On the one hand, the demand for an increasingly better educated and trained labour force, stemming from technological and economic advance, would, in conjunction with democratic pressures for greater equality of opportunity, ensure that the appropriate pro-gressive development of educational systems took place. And, on the other hand, employing organisations would, as a requirement of their operating efficiency, have to base their recruitment procedures increas-ingly on formal educational qualifications rather than on any other criteria. The postindustrial society, it was claimed, was 'in its logic' an education-based meritocracy.[2]

However, one may ask how far, at least in the British case, this liberal scenario has been borne out, and in turn how far support is given to the politically prevalent idea that education is the key driver of mobility at the societal level. In Figure 5.2 another version of the OED triangle is shown that reflects the findings of a substantial body of sociological research in Britain covering the period since the Second World War and in which origins and destinations have been treated primarily in terms of social class.

The following points emerge. First, so far as the OE association is concerned, the most comprehensive studies have in fact revealed a tendency for inequalities in educational attainment related to class origins to narrow, even if only slightly and mainly at lower educational levels. In this respect, therefore, the liberal view can claim at least some

[2] The phrase comes from the work of the best-known theorist of postindustrial society, the American sociologist Daniel Bell (1972, 1973).

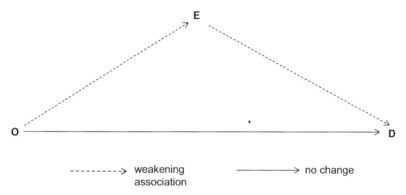

Figure 5.2 The OED triangle: typical results from sociological research

degree of confirmation: Figure 5.2 replicates Figure 5.1. But, second, a very different situation arises with the ED association. It has been quite regularly found that this association, as indicated in Figure 5.2, *also weakens* rather than strengthening as in Figure 5.1. And, third, studies of the direct OD association have detected no consistent weakening or strengthening.[3] The upshot, then, is that from the research findings represented in Figure 5.2 no firm conclusion can be drawn as regards the overall OD association. What is implied is that any equalisation that may have been achieved in educational attainment in relation to class origins has been in some degree or other offset, so far as its

---

[3] On the OE association, the most important papers are Jonsson and Mills (1993), Jonsson, Mills and Müller (1996) and Breen et al. (2009, 2010); on the ED association, Goldthorpe and Mills (2004), Breen and Luijkx (2004b), Jackson, Goldthorpe and Mills (2005) and Goldthorpe and Jackson (2008); and on the direct OD association, Goldthorpe and Mills (2004) and Vandecasteele (2016). A good deal of this research has a comparative, cross-national dimension, and the results reported for Britain for the most part follow the general pattern. But one apparent exception may be noted. Evidence that educational expansion may serve to increase mobility has mainly related to a three-way 'interaction effect' within the OED triangle. It has been found that the OD association is strongest among those with the lowest levels of education and weakest among those with the highest levels. Thus, as the number of individuals attaining higher levels of education increases, so too does social fluidity, simply through a 'compositional' effect (see Breen, 2010). However, our analyses of the birth cohort data reveal that while this interaction effect is present over the early years of a working life, at least in the 1970 cohort, it has disappeared by age 38 (Bukodi and Goldthorpe, 2016). A possible explanation for this British 'exceptionalism' is suggested in Chapter 9, n. 11 below.

potential impact on social fluidity is concerned, *by a decline in the class returns that education brings.*

The explanation for the weakening ED association that has been most often put forward is that of overqualification or 'credentials inflation', and we have already noted in Chapter 2 that there is evidence of such a situation now developing within the British labour force. This was an outcome simply not envisaged by the theorists of postindustrial society, and it is one that has been almost entirely disregarded in attempts to present policies of educational expansion and reform as being of leading importance in raising levels of social mobility.[4] It is true that difficulties arise over what the concept of overqualification actually entails and that, in consequence, estimates made of its extent and trend are open to some dispute. But with the growth of the managerial and professional salariat slowing down (cf. Figure 2.1) while the number of individuals with higher-level educational qualifications steadily rises, *some* change in the relationship between qualifications and class positions would seem scarcely avoidable.

We will return to this matter later in the hope of providing a degree of clarification. For the moment, however, the relevant point remains that, as they stand, the findings represented in Figure 5.2 are indeterminate as regards the question of whether or not in Britain, over recent decades, changes in the associations within the OED triangle have been such as to create greater mobility. For this reason – among others that will become apparent – we have been led to ask whether it might be possible to gain some better understanding of the situation through a reconsideration of the way in which educational attainment, in its relation to social mobility, is conceptualised and measured.

In research of the kind that underlies Figure 5.2 education has for the most part been treated in what might be described as *absolute* terms, and measured according to the number of years of education that individuals have completed or the highest level of educational qualification that they have obtained. This approach would appear appropriate insofar as education is being viewed as a *consumption* good and therefore as an 'absolute' good in the sense that its value to one individual is unlikely to be affected by the extent of its

---

[4] We can find no reference to the possibility of overqualification in any of the series of annual reports of the Social Mobility Commission.

consumption by others. If, for example, by taking a university degree, someone discovers the joy of knowledge and expands their intellectual and cultural horizons, this outcome need be little affected by the number of others who have the same experience. But in analyses of associations within the OED triangle education is in effect being treated not primarily as a consumption good but rather as an *investment good* – that is, in relation to individuals' economic futures in the labour market. And this being so, it could then be thought preferable to treat education not as an absolute but rather as a 'positional' good in the sense that the value of an individual's particular level of educational attainment *will* be directly dependent on the levels of attainment of others. If someone has a university degree, its value in the labour market will be greater if, say, only 10 per cent of everyone in the labour force have degrees than if 40 per cent have degrees.[5] And it would in turn appear appropriate, in analyses of the kind in question, to measure education in positional or, in other words, relative rather than absolute terms: that is, to recognise that what matters in this case is not simply how much education individuals have but how much relative to others and, in particular, relative to those others with whom they will be in most direct labour market competition.

To pursue this issue, we have drawn on the same dataset from the British cohort studies we have used in our analyses of absolute and relative rates of class mobility, and we have examined the OE and the ED sides of the OED triangle with educational qualifications being measured in both absolute and relative terms, so as to be able to see what differences may arise. For the purposes of this comparison, we focus on men in order to avoid difficulties in the interpretation of results that women's more complex employment histories would be likely to cause. But we can see no reason why the conclusions we reach should not in principle apply in the case of women also.

Our absolute measure of individuals' educational qualifications is provided by the eight ordered categories that are shown in Table 5.1, ranging from 'no qualifications' to 'postgraduate qualifications'. However, the rather small size of the 1946 cohort means that in order to maintain adequate numbers in our analyses, we have to collapse the

---

[5] The pioneering and still highly influential work on the distinction between absolute and positional goods is Hirsch (1977). On education as a positional good, see Wolf (2002), an important but, in the prevailing political climate, unduly neglected book.

Table 5.1 *Distribution (%) of male cohort members by highest level of educational qualification (absolute measure)*[a]

	Cohort		
Level of qualification	1946	1958	1970
1. No qualifications	34	21	15
2. Sub-secondary (below O level or GCSE, NVQ1)	5	10	7
Total	39	31	22
3. Lower secondary – low performance (1–4 O level or GCSE passes, NVQ2)	19	21	21
4. Lower secondary – high performance (5+ O level or GCSE passes or 1 A level pass, NVQ 3)	17	18	21
Total	36	39	42
5. Higher secondary (2+ A level passes)	2	4	3
6. Lower tertiary (tertiary sub-degree qualification, NVQ 4)	14	12	15
Total	16	16	17
7. Higher tertiary (degree, NVQ 5, 6)	8	11	15
8. Postgraduate	1	2	4
Total	9	13	19
Total	100	100	100
N	2394	7219	5979

Note (a) All vocational qualifications are either National Vocational Qualifications (NVQs) or are given as their NVQ equivalents
Source: Bukodi and Goldthorpe (2016)

eight categories to four, as is indicated. It can be seen from the distributions given that, as would be expected, there is a tendency for the overall level of qualification to increase across the cohorts. In particular, the proportion of men with no, or only sub-secondary, qualifications falls while the proportion with higher tertiary qualifications rises.

Our relative measure is then derived, as is shown in Table 5.2, from further fourfold collapses of the eight categories of Table 5.1 *but collapses that change from cohort to cohort according to the proportions of cohort members holding the qualifications that the categories comprise,* and with the aim of producing relative categories of as

Table 5.2 *Collapses of eight categories of educational qualifications to produce relative levels*

Level of qualification	Cohort					
	1946	%	1958	%	1970	%
Lowest level	1	34	1,2	31	1,2	22
Next to lowest level	2,3	25	3	20	3	21
Next to highest level	4	17	4,5	22	4,5,6	38
Highest level	5,6,7,8	23	6,7,8	25	7,8	19
Total		100		100		100
N		2394		7219		5979

Source: Bukodi and Goldthorpe (2016)

similar size as possible given the 'lumpiness' of the distributions shown in Table 5.1. In fact, the proportions of men at each relative level range from 17 to 38 per cent, but in seven cases out of the twelve they fall between 20 and 30 per cent.

The changes across the cohorts amount to the following. With the 1946 cohort only men with no qualifications are placed at the lowest relative level but with the 1958 and 1970 cohorts those with no more than sub-secondary qualifications are also placed at this level. With the 1946 cohort the next to lowest level comprises both those with sub-secondary and those with low performance secondary qualifications, while with the 1958 and 1970 cohorts only the latter are at this level. Men with high performance secondary qualifications are at the next to highest level in all three cohorts but also placed at this level are men in the 1958 cohort whose highest qualifications are A levels and men in the 1970 cohort with A levels and tertiary sub-degree qualifications. In turn, the highest relative level comprises with the 1946 cohort all men with A level or higher qualifications, while with the 1958 cohort only men with tertiary qualifications are included, and with the 1970 cohort only men with degree-level qualifications. In short, one could say that as the proportion of cohort members with degrees increases, other qualifications tend to be pushed down the relative levels.[6]

In our analyses of the OE and ED associations, using our four-level absolute and relative measures of qualifications, we treat class origins and class destinations on the basis of the fivefold 'hierarchical' collapse of NS-SEC that is indicated in Table 1.1. We thus have 5 x 4 and 4 x 5 tables that, respectively, cross-classify origins by qualifications and qualifications by destinations for each cohort. We then apply to these tables versions of the same three statistical models we previously applied in investigating possible changes in relative mobility rates: first, the independence model proposing no association and under which all odds ratios underlying the tables are equal to 1; second, the constant association (CA) model proposing an association but one that is unchanging across the cohorts, with all corresponding odds ratios taking the same value; and, third, the uniform difference (UNIDIFF) model proposing an association that, from cohort to cohort, becomes uniformly weaker or stronger, with all odds ratios moving close to or further from 1 by some common factor.

Considering the OE association with our absolute qualifications measure, we find, not surprisingly, that the independence model shows a significant and substantial lack of fit to the data: over 11 per cent of all men are misclassified. That is to say, an association clearly does exist between men's class origins and the level of their educational attainment according to the four categories of Table 5.1. The CA model does then significantly improve on the independence model, misclassifying less than 3 per cent of all cases. But this model still does not give an entirely acceptable fit to the data and it is in turn significantly improved upon by the UNIDIFF model. This misclassifies less than 2 per cent of all cases and the β parameters that are returned – that is, the factors by which the odds ratios expressing the OE association have to be multiplied – are as plotted in the left-hand panel of Figure 5.3. A weakening association is apparent: the point estimates fall across the cohorts and quite sharply so between

---

[6] For the 1958 and 1970 cohorts, men's level of qualification was determined at age 37 but for the 1946 cohort, because of data limitations, at age 26. For full details of the construction of the absolute and relative educational measures and of the analyses discussed in the following paragraphs, including results of robustness checks on the results obtained, see Bukodi and Goldthorpe (2016).

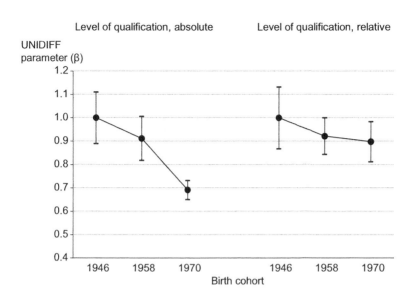

Source: Bukodi and Goldthorpe (2016)

Figure 5.3 Association between class of origin and level of qualification by cohort: UNIDIFF parameters with 95% confidence intervals

the 1958 and 1970 cohorts, in which case no overlap of the confidence intervals occurs. Our results here do therefore serve to confirm those of previous research relating to the OE association, as represented in Figure 5.2.

However, when we repeat the same sequence of modelling but now using our relative measure of qualifications, we have a different outcome. As before, the independence model fits badly, with again over 11 per cent of all men being misclassified; and, also as before, the CA model makes a large improvement, misclassifying only a little over 2 per cent. But what we further find is that now the UNIDIFF model does *not* significantly improve on the CA model. The point estimates of the β parameters, as plotted in the right-hand panel of Figure 5.3, do fall slightly across the cohorts but there are wide overlaps of the confidence intervals around them, so that it is the model of constant association that can most safely be accepted. In other words, the weakening association between men's class origins and their qualifications that shows up when education is measured in absolute terms is not reproduced when qualifications are measured in

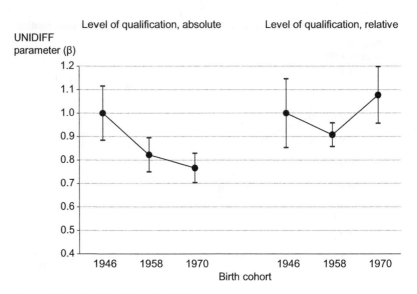

Source: Bukodi and Goldthorpe (2016)

Figure 5.4 Association between level of qualification and class of destination by cohort: UNIDIFF parameters with 95% confidence intervals

relative terms – that is, when education is envisaged as an investment good in regard to individuals' economic futures.

Turning then to the ED association, we follow the same analytical approach as with the OE association except that in our modelling we now control for the OE association on the basis of the results reported above. When we treat the ED association on the basis of our absolute measure of qualifications we find that while the CA model greatly improves on the independence model and does in fact give a statistically acceptable fit to the data, we still obtain a significantly better fit by moving to the UNIDIFF model. And from the β parameters that are returned, as displayed in the left-hand panel of Figure 5.4, it can be seen that it is a weakening association that is shown up, and especially between the 1946 and 1958 cohorts. Thus, just as with the OE association, our results are here in line with those of previous research in which education has been measured in absolute terms: the class returns to educational attainment would appear to be falling.

Again, though, when we work with our relative measure of qualifications a different situation is indicated. The CA model once more gives a big improvement on the independence model but in this case the further improvement made by the UNIDIFF model on the CA model is only marginally significant, and further, as is shown in the right-hand panel of Figure 5.4, the β parameters returned do not indicate any change of a directional kind. There is a possible weakening of the ED association between the 1946 and 1958 cohorts but then a strengthening between the 1958 and 1970 cohorts. If therefore, on the basis of our relative measure, any change at all occurs in the class returns to education, it would be best seen as taking the form simply of rather minor and short-term fluctuation, in response, it could be supposed, to changing labour market conditions. As regards the suggested dip in the ED association for the 1958 cohort, we do in fact know that men in this cohort, and especially those who had been longest in education, entered the labour market at a time of severe recession and high unemployment – the early 1980s – and that this had a lasting negative influence on their occupational careers.[7]

Finally, we may add that in all the analyses undertaken, whether qualifications are treated in absolute or relative terms, no evidence emerges of any change in the direct OD association – that which is not mediated via education. This would appear essentially stable.

From our comparison of changes in the associations within the OED triangle using our two different measures of educational attainment, we can then draw the following conclusion. As well as the relative measure appearing the more appropriate in this context, it leads to results that are open to a far more straightforward interpretation than those obtained using the absolute measure. Rather than having to suppose that some equalisation in educational attainment in relation to class origins is offset, to a greater or lesser extent, by a decline in the class returns to education, and with no change occurring in the direct origins–destination association, we can simply envisage a situation in which *all the associations in the OED triangle are unchanged*, or, at most, change in only limited and directionless ways. And this is of course a conclusion that is entirely consistent with what we have shown in Chapters 3 and 4 concerning the absence of significant change in the case of the men in our cohorts in either the level or the pattern of relative rates of class mobility. In other words, what is again

---

[7] For further details, see Bukodi and Goldthorpe (2011a).

pointed to is the essential stability of the endogenous mobility regime – or, that is, the resistance to change that it offers.

If this interpretation of the empirical evidence is accepted, we are thus brought back to the question, already introduced in the conclusion to Chapter 3, of how it could come about that over a period in which educational expansion and reform have been more or less continuous, a reduction in class-linked inequalities in educational attainment leading to increased social mobility has not been achieved. To pick out only the major developments over the years relevant to our analyses, the Butler Act of 1944 introduced free secondary education for all and raised the school-leaving age from 14 to 15; during the 1960s the selective, tripartite system of secondary education was progressively changed to a comprehensive system in order to prevent 'social segregation' and increase equality of opportunity; following the Robbins Report of 1963 a major expansion of university education occurred with the aim of making this available for all of those 'qualified by ability and attainment'; in 1972 the school-leaving age was raised again, to 16; and from the 1980s a further phase of university expansion began. These developments were associated with a substantial advance in levels of education and qualification within the population at large, as is reflected in Table 5.1. But why did they contribute so little to realising the liberal scenario of steadily rising social fluidity resulting from the creation of an education-based meritocracy?[8]

The explanation we would give starts out from the proposition that employers, on the one hand, and in turn parents and their children, on the other, *do themselves in many contexts view education in relative rather than in absolute terms*. And, from this, the persisting strength of the associations within the OED triangle that

---

[8] It may be noted that in the case of two of the measures referred to in the text, specific evaluations of their impact on social mobility have been made – with negative results. Boliver and Swift (2011) have exploited the fact that children in the 1958 birth cohort passed, in almost equal numbers, through tripartite and comprehensive secondary school systems and, on the basis of a careful comparison, find that the mobility chances of the two sets of children, whether considered in terms of class or income, differed very little. Sturgis and Buscha (2015) have examined the effect of raising the school leaving age in 1972, using the data of the ONS Longitudinal Study, and conclude that while an increase followed in levels of educational attainment among the population at large, no change was discernible in rates of intergenerational mobility in terms of class or social status. Earlier, Halsey (1977) found no evidence that the 1944 Act had served to reduce educational inequalities or thus to promote social mobility.

we have demonstrated when using a relative measure of educational qualifications can be seen to follow.

As regards employers, what may be supposed is that as well as treating educational qualifications as certifying forms of knowledge and skill that are required for particular occupations, they also treat them as indicators, or 'signals', of certain more general attributes of potential employees – such as their self-control, perseverance and capacity to learn; that is, as indicators of individuals' trainability and productivity once in employment. Qualifications understood in this way then serve employers as a means of ranking potential employees in what may be thought of as a 'labour queue', which they will seek to match up to the jobs they have to fill – their 'job queues' – starting with the best qualified of those available and working downwards. In other words, it is the relative aspect of qualifications that counts. If there is an increase in potential employees with higher-level qualifications, so that their number extends further down the labour queue, then, assuming no accommodating change in the state of demand, more of them will be taken on at lower levels in employers' job queues than was previously the case – and with the effect of 'bumping down' in turn all those with inferior qualifications.[9] On an absolute view of qualifications, a weakening of the ED association within the OED triangle will thus show up: class returns to educational attainment will appear to fall and overqualification to be present. But on a relative view – that is, with due account being taken of the changing distribution of qualifications within the labour force – no weakening of the association need occur. Apart from any effects of changes in demand, the same *relative* level within the distribution can still attract the same class returns.[10]

---

[9] There is mounting evidence that in Britain today – following on from the major expansion of the tertiary educational sector in the 1990s – employers are significantly differentiating among graduates, at least in terms of the pay they receive, according not only to their class of degree and field of study but also to the university they attended (Green and Zhou, 2010; Britton et al., 2016). The increasing variance in earnings returns to a degree that has resulted means that the average return becomes less and less informative.

[10] We draw in the foregoing paragraph on work in labour economics guided by what are known as signalling theory and job competition theory, which seem to us far more illuminating in regard to sociologists' empirical findings on associations within the OED triangle than the prevailing orthodoxy of human capital theory. These theories, it may be added, do allow for the existence of overqualification in the sense that certain levels of qualification may become 'devalued' and also in the sense that qualifications may be necessary *to get a*

Insofar, then, as employers do view qualifications relatively, and act accordingly, parents and children, at least to the extent that they see education as an investment good, will be under evident constraint to follow suit. Thus, where attempts are made through public policy to widen and equalise educational opportunities, parents in more advantaged class positions will not be unappreciative of the implications for their own children's life-chances. They may be expected to respond by drawing on their superior resources in order to take 'defensive measures': that is, measures designed to ensure that, in the context of generally rising levels of educational attainment and qualification, their own children retain their competitive edge. And there is indeed no shortage of evidence of such a response in the British case. While resort to the private schools sector has always been favoured by the wealthiest, it is clear that over recent decades a steadily growing number of parents with adequate means have sought to protect their children's relative positions within the state sector in a number of different ways: by paying for high-quality preschool child care, purchasing houses in areas with high-performing state schools, engaging home tutors, and providing their children with a wide range of educationally relevant extra-school activities and experiences. In other words, possibilities for what has been aptly called 'the commodification of opportunity' have been increasingly taken up.[11]

We are now in a position to say more about the political consensus that prevails on the need to increase social mobility and on educational

job that are not necessary *to do the job*. For further discussion, see Goldthorpe (2014).

[11] The idea of 'the commodification of opportunity' comes from the American sociologist, David Grusky. Several studies of parental strategies of the kind in question have been sponsored by the Sutton Trust. Francis and Hutchings (2013) give a good idea of their general spread, and Kirby (2016) focuses on the growth of private tutoring or 'shadow education'. Both studies very probably underestimate the association with parental resources in relying on inadequate measures, such as the Market Research Society social categories or the 'free school meals' proxy for parental income (see further Chapter 6, n. 5). Jerrim (2017a) is a better-grounded investigation and indicates that private tuition plays an important role in providing a 'safety net' for children from better-off families who are in apparent danger of educational underperformance. A further study, Cullinane et al. (2017), reveals how many high-performing state comprehensives are in effect socially selective, partly as a result of the social composition of their catchment areas but also as a result of their admissions procedures which, it appears, more advantaged parents can often successfully 'game'.

policy as being the prime means to this end. As we observed in the Introduction and again at the end of the previous chapter, the concern to promote mobility can be understood as a response to rising economic and social inequality of condition – a response that is seen as politically more manageable and, at least from some points of view, more desirable than attempting to reduce inequality itself. And insofar as a contradiction might be seen to arise between widening opportunity while inequality also widens, it is further supposed that education is the way through which any such contradiction can be overcome. It would be difficult to find a better encapsulation of the thinking here involved than in two famous quotes from the New Labour era: Peter Mandelson's acknowledgement that he was 'intensely relaxed about people getting filthy rich' and Tony Blair's declaration that in seeking 'opportunity for all' his priorities were 'education, education and education'.[12]

However, the results of the research that we have reviewed would strongly suggest that to look to education to break the link between inequality of condition and inequality of opportunity is to ask of it far more than it can alone deliver. What has to be realised is that if educational policy is designed to equalise educational opportunity with the further aim of thus equalising relative rates of mobility, *then the zero-sum game that we have shown to be involved in the latter case is, as it were, simply brought forward.* To the extent that some would benefit from the policy – that is, end up in a better relative position in the qualifications hierarchy – others would correspondingly have to

---

[12] Mandelson was speaking in 1998 to a meeting of US industrialists. He modified his views after the 2008 financial crisis, conceding that more concern had to be shown over rising economic and social inequality resulting from globalisation. Blair apparently first used his priorities phrase in his leader's speech at the Labour Party conference in 1996, but reused it several times later. John Major took the opportunity to respond by saying that these were his priorities too 'but not necessarily in that order'. Lord Adonis (2012) takes Blair's words as the title of his book describing, and proclaiming the success of, the policy of converting state comprehensives into independently managed 'academies', of which he was the chief architect while in the Cabinet Office and then Minister of State for Education from 2005 to 2008. While it is still too early to assess what effects, if any, this policy has had on social mobility, the most detailed evaluation of it to date, by the Education Policy Institute and the LSE (Andrews and Perera, 2017), concludes that its results have been very variable and that 'academies are not a panacea for school improvement'. It is of interest that the Executive Chairman of the EPI is David Laws, who was from 2012 to 2015 Minister for Schools in the coalition government.

lose out. This being the case, and recalling the psychology of loss aversion referred to in Chapter 3, it is only to be expected that a reaction will come from parents in more advantaged positions, and that where policy appears likely to create a situation in which their children's interests are under threat, they will draw on their superior resources so far as is necessary in order to take countervailing action.

We would not wish our position here to be misunderstood. We recognise – indeed we have emphasised – that during the period to which our research relates educational expansion and reform did substantially raise the overall educational level of the British population. Opportunity certainly *has* been widened in the sense that more men and women than ever before have been able to fulfil more ambitious educational aspirations, with both intrinsic benefits for themselves and wider economic and social benefits. And we would further recognise that many educational policy initiatives proposed with the aim of increasing mobility could in fact have positive consequences from a purely educational standpoint: for example, the extension and upgrading of preschool programmes for children from disadvantaged backgrounds, higher-quality vocational education, more transparent admissions procedures to elite universities and wider provision for lifelong learning. But what we would question is whether through educational measures alone a greater equality of opportunity is likely to be created in the sense of a significant reduction in inequality in relative mobility chances. The historical record of the last half-century or more, as we can reconstruct it through our research, makes it difficult to avoid the conclusion that educational policy, directed towards expansion and, for the most part, egalitarian reform, has had very little effect in weakening the association that exists between individuals' class origins and their class destinations.

We cannot of course rule out the possibility that educational policy of some new and more effective design could have a greater societal impact in the future than has been the case in the past. However, an alternative possibility has also to be recognised, and one that seems to us sociologically more plausible: that is, that in any society with a capitalist market economy, a nuclear family system – even if one less stable and thus more complex than previously – and also a liberal democratic polity, a *limit* exists to the extent to which relative mobility chances can be made more equal by means of educational policy on which some broad degree of consensus might be possible, and that, as this limit is approached, any further advances will increasingly require forms of intervention that will be of a politically far more controversial and contested kind.[13]

We will return to and develop this line of argument in Chapter 10, in the context of our analyses of social mobility in Britain in a cross-national comparative perspective, and we will take up some of the wider implications that arise in our concluding chapter. However, in the chapters that directly follow our concern is to draw further on the experience of the men and women in our birth cohorts in order to provide a series of more detailed analyses of the associations that exist within the OED triangle.

---

[13] It should be added that even if educational policy loses its capacity to further reduce inequalities in relative mobility chances, it could of course still serve to *widen* them. Such 'one-way' effects are not uncommon in public policy: to use the old analogy, one may be able to pull on a string without being able to push on it. Certain developments in the recent past that might be thought likely to increase inequalities – though no decisive evidence has as yet been produced – are the reduction in funding for Sure Start, the ending of Educational Maintenance Allowances, and the shift in higher education from free tuition and maintenance grants to tuition fees and student loans.

6 | *Social Origins, Ability and Educational Attainment: Is there a Wastage of Talent?*

If education is to play a major role in increasing social mobility, the association between individuals' social origins and their educational attainment – the OE association within the OED triangle – should weaken. In the previous chapter we showed that if educational attainment is conceptualised and measured in absolute terms, some, albeit slight, weakening in its association with social class origins would appear to have occurred in Britain over the last half-century or so. However, if educational attainment is treated in relative terms, this weakening no longer shows up. In this chapter we aim to investigate the OE association in greater depth. Specifically, we wish to develop our analyses in the two following ways.

On the one hand, while we retain our concern with social class as the context of mobility, we recognise that other aspects of individuals' social origins than their parents' class may be associated with their educational attainment. We will therefore report on analyses of educational inequality in which, in addition to parental class, we also include parental social status and parental education. Parents' class position can serve, on the grounds outlined in Chapter 1, as a good indicator of the economic resources that they have available in order to promote their children's educational success – as, for example, in the ways referred to at the end of the previous chapter. But, further, parents' social status can be seen as indicating their sociocultural resources, the kinds of lifestyle and social networks in which they are involved, and through which information relevant to their children's education may be obtained, useful contacts made and, perhaps, influence exerted. And parents' education can be taken as an indicator of their specifically educational resources: in particular, of their capacity to create a favourable home learning environment for their children and to provide them with informed guidance through the educational system.

In much previous research into social inequalities in educational attainment the assumption has been made, implicitly if not explicitly, that different features of individuals' social origins, as represented by parental characteristics, can in effect serve as 'interchangeable indicators': that is, it matters little which is taken as the basis of analyses since the results obtained will be essentially the same.[1] We believe that this assumption is an invalid one, and will lead to the importance of social origins being significantly underestimated. For while variables such as parental class, status and education will be correlated, the correlations are likely to be far from perfect, and it is therefore necessary to consider how far these different parental characteristics may have *independent* and in turn *cumulative* effects on children's educational performance.

On the other hand, we wish to bring cognitive ability into our analyses, since it has been argued that if such ability is neglected, social origin effects on children's educational attainment are likely to be overestimated. In this regard, a number of contentious issues arise, and we need to make our own starting position clear. We use the term 'cognitive ability' rather than 'intelligence' to try to avoid debates about different types of intelligence and to refer to a general, underlying capacity – referred to by psychologists as the '*g* factor' – that has been shown to be involved in a range of mental processes, such as comprehension, knowledge acquisition, reasoning and problem solving. We then recognise, in the light of a large body of research, that if cognitive ability, thus understood, is measured at a relatively early stage in children's lives, it is quite strongly associated with their subsequent educational attainment, whatever their social origins.[2] For this reason, we believe – and will seek to show – that there is, *for analytical purposes*, advantage in treating cognitive ability independently of social origins in relation to educational attainment.

However, this does not imply that we regard children's cognitive ability as being *in fact* independent of their early life family environments. We would not accept the claim made by some authors that

---

[1] For example, in the annual reports of the Social Mobility Commission results are regularly presented on educational inequalities in relation to parental income, parental class (measured in a variety of ways), parental 'socioeconomic status', parental education, and so on, without any consideration of the differing degree of reliability of these results or of how they might be related to each other.

[2] For results from the 1946, 1958 and 1970 birth cohort studies, see Schoon (2010), and for similar results from a five-year prospective longitudinal study of 70,000 English children, see Deary et al. (2007). There is now growing evidence of a neurological basis for *g* (Burnett, 2016).

what may appear to be inequalities in educational attainment that are socially grounded should rather be understood, in the context of modern educational systems, as primarily, if not entirely, the result of the intergenerational transmission of purely genetic advantage and disadvantage. This claim depends on the supposition that the variance in cognitive ability within a population can be divided, additively, into one part due to environmental effects and another part due to genetic effects – and that the latter part predominates over the former. But this supposition would no longer appear tenable. With a phenotypical trait such as cognitive ability, it is becoming increasingly evident not only that many different genetic variants are involved, and complex gene–gene interactions, but, further, yet more complex processes of *gene–environment interaction* occurring from the womb onwards. Thus, while variation in cognitive ability does have a genetic component – and we would also regard as misguided those who would seek to deny this out of hand – the important point is that this component is not fixed in some once-and-for-all way but is, rather, open to environmental modification in its expression, and especially, it would seem, in the course of early life.[3]

From the foregoing, the key issues to be addressed in this chapter directly derive. To begin with, we examine how far parental class, status and education, *considered separately*, are associated with children's educational attainment when their early life cognitive ability is also included in the analysis, and how far any changes in this regard are apparent over time – that is, across our birth cohorts. Then, we turn to the question of how far children who in early life are at the same level of cognitive ability differ in their eventual educational attainment according to their social origins when parental class, status

---

[3] For statements of hereditarian views, with reference to Britain, see Saunders (1996, 2010) and Marks (2014) – both authors being greatly influenced by the American work of Herrnstein and Murray (1994). The research that calls such views into question is, first, that in the rapidly developing field of epigenetics (Jablonka and Lamb, 2013; Carey, 2012), which focuses on how environmental conditions influence the expression of genes; and, second, that based on the human genome itself. It has so far proved difficult to pin down the genetic basis of any large part of variation in cognitive ability, although it is becoming evident that many different genes are involved. For a general review of relevant literature, see Heckman and Mosso (2014); and for evidence from the 1946 birth cohort of the effects of various aspects of parenting on the formation of cognitive ability, see Byford, Kuh and Richards (2012).

and education are *considered in combination*, and we again look for any changes over time. Insofar as men and women of less advantaged origins fare less well educationally than do men and women of more advantaged origins when cognitive ability is held constant, it may be supposed that there is a wastage of talent – a failure of the educational system to ensure that the academic potential of all individuals is fully realised.[4] And whether or not the extent of any such wastage is reduced across our cohorts – that is, over a period of more or less continuous educational expansion and reform – is a question of obvious relevance in evaluating the realism of the liberal scenario outlined in the previous chapter and of the capacity of educational policy alone to increase equality of opportunity in the face of persisting inequalities of condition.

One other preliminary point to be made is that, given our concern with the realisation of educational potential, we see it as more appropriate to treat education in this chapter as an absolute, consumption good – that is, as one that is of value in itself regardless of how many others share in it – rather than as a positional, investment good in relation to the labour market, and we therefore measure education in absolute rather than relative terms. We in fact focus our analyses on whether or not cohort members reached two key educational 'thresholds'. We consider, first, whether they attained at least *higher-level secondary qualifications* – Level 5 in Table 5.1 – rather than any lower level; and, second, whether they attained *degree-level qualifications* – Level 7 in Table 5.1 – rather than any lower level.

Table 6.1 derives from results we obtain from analyses in which we take together data from the 1946, 1958 and 1970 cohorts and estimate the effects of parental class, status and education, along with those of cognitive ability, on the chances of men and women reaching these two thresholds (with cohort being included as a control variable). Parental class is based on the NS-SEC classes but with Classes 6 and 7, the higher and lower strata of the working class, being collapsed since preliminary analyses showed no significant difference in their effects; parental status is measured on a scale that reflects differential association in the form of the occupational structure of close friendship (see Chapter 4, note 4). In cases where an individual's parents had different

---

[4] We do of course recognise that cognitive ability is only one of many different kinds of talent – but it is one of particular importance in the present context.

Table 6.1 *Effects of cognitive ability and of parental class, status and education on the probability of attaining two educational thresholds*[a]

	Men		Women	
	Higher secondary	Degree	Higher secondary	Degree
Cognitive ability quintile				
first, lowest	− −	− −	− −	−
second	−	−	−	−
third	reference		reference	
fourth	+	+	+	+
fifth, highest	++	+	++	+
Parental class				
Classes 6 and 7	reference		reference	
Class 5	+	ns	ns	ns
Class 4	ns	ns	+	ns
Class 3	+	+	+	ns
Class 2	+	+	+	+
Class 1	+	+	+	+
Parental status	+	+	+	+
Parental education	++	+	+	+

Note (a) +: significant positive effect
++: significant and strong positive effect
−: significant negative effect
− −: significant and strong negative effect
ns: not significant

Source: Bukodi, Erikson and Goldthorpe (2014)

class or status positions, the more advantaged is taken. Parental education is treated on the basis of seven ordered categories that relate to both parents' qualifications in combination; and in view of the major changes in the distribution of parents' qualifications across the cohorts, a relativised measure is in this case adopted, following the same procedure as was described in regard to cohort members' own qualification in Chapter 5. Finally, cognitive ability is measured according to tests administered to cohort members at age 10–11 and is included in our analyses in the form of cohort-specific 'fifths' – or, in statistical terminology, quintiles.[5]

In the analyses underlying Table 6.1, our concern is not, we should stress, with determining the importance of cognitive ability in individuals' chances of attaining the two educational thresholds *as compared to that* of their parents' social class, status and education. Rather, we are concerned with the question of how far, once cognitive ability is included in our analyses, these parental attributes are still associated with children's educational success, *over and above any influence they may have had on the formation of children's cognitive ability*. Figure 6.1 shows statistically significant positive and negative effects and gives some indication of their relative strength.

It can be seen that, as would be expected in the light of previous research, cognitive ability has a quite consistently significant effect on the probability of cohort members reaching both of the two thresholds. Relative to being in the third – that is, the middle – quintile, taken as the reference category, being in the two lower ability quintiles is negatively associated with the chances of success, while being in the two higher quintiles is positively associated.

However, what Table 6.1 further reveals is that effects of parental class, status and education alike are *also* significant. Individuals with parents in Classes 1 and 2, the managerial and professional salariat, have consistently better chances of reaching the two thresholds, *independently of their cognitive ability*, than do those with parents in Classes 6 and 7, the broadly defined working class; and the same is true for those with parents in Class 3, that of ancillary professional and administrative employees, except in the case of women reaching the second threshold. The chances of cohort members of Class 4 and Class 5 origins are less consistently differentiated from those of Class 6 and 7 origins, although as regards the first threshold women with parents in Class 4, that of small employers and own-account workers, are

---

[5] For further details of the tests applied and score construction, see Schoon (2010). The use of cohort-specific quintiles serves to overcome the problem of 'Flynn effects' (Flynn, 1987): that is, the tendency for scores on cognitive ability tests to rise steadily and substantially over time – and at a far greater rate than could be accounted for by changes in gene pools, although possibly as a result of improved nutrition, better education and generally more stimulating environments. The statistical model applied – a binary logistic regression model – is fully described in Bukodi, Erikson and Goldthorpe (2014).

advantaged, and so too are men with parents in Class 5, that of lower supervisory and technical employees. The effects of parental status and education over and above those of cognitive ability are more straightforward than those of parental class. The higher parents' status and educational levels, the better their children's chances of attaining both educational thresholds.

From Table 6.1 we can then conclude that if the effects of individuals' social origins on their educational attainment are to be fully accounted for, parental class, status and education cannot be treated as interchangeable indicators. Rather, each, as we have suggested, relates to a different form of parental resources and has to be seen as having its own independent effects on children's chances of educational success.[6]

The further issue that has then to be addressed is that of whether the analyses underlying Table 6.1 reveal any changes across the cohorts. In fact, if we consider each cohort separately, the results we obtain show no changes of a consistent, directional kind. Parental class effects remain essentially constant, and while, between the 1958 and 1970 cohorts, parental status effects weaken somewhat, parental educational effects strengthen. Also between these two later cohorts there is some indication, in line with previous research findings, that the effects of cognitive ability weaken, although in our results this shows up in only a rather patchy way. For men, but not for women, being in the two lower ability quintiles becomes less damaging as regards the chances of reaching the higher-level secondary threshold but not the

---

[6] It would in principle be desirable to include parental income in our analyses as well as parental class, status and education. We do not do so because no data on parental income are available for members of the 1946 cohort and also because, as earlier noted, we have serious doubts about the quality of those available for the 1958 and 1970 cohorts. If, however, for these two cohorts, we do use these data, what we find (Bukodi, Erikson and Goldthorpe, 2014, Online Appendix 2) is that when parental income is considered alone, its effects on children's educational attainment appear quite sizable but that these effects are then much reduced once parental class, status and education are also brought into play. Thus, where in analysing educational inequalities, only parental income is considered, as is the usual practice among economists, origin effects are likely to be underestimated and effects attributed to income that are properly those of parental class, status or education. The use of children's eligibility for free school meals as a proxy for parental income is also very questionable, since, apart from being only a binary measure, it has been shown to have only a quite loose relation with parental income or family economic conditions more generally (Kounali et al. 2008; Hobbes and Vignoles, 2010).

degree-level threshold. Moreover, in further analyses, using data from a longitudinal study covering children born in the Avon region in 1991–2, ability effects are found to strengthen in comparison with the 1970 cohort – although without any overall weakening in social origin effects. It could be that these changes reflect, on the one hand, the move from selective to comprehensive secondary education during the 1960s and, on the other, the greater pressure on schools during the 1990s to replace mixed-ability teaching with forms of setting and streaming. But the extent of the changes is in any event not large.[7]

The general conclusion to which our findings point is therefore that over the historical period that our data cover, the independent effects of parental class, status and education on children's educational attainment persisted – *and persisted, too, in qualifying the effects of cognitive ability*. We can now move on to the second question that we raised, that of how far the eventual educational attainment of children who in early life were at the same level of cognitive ability differs according to their social origins when parental class, status and education are considered together.

To pursue this question, we allocate members of the 1946, 1958 and 1970 birth cohorts to three groups in relation to their social origins: the most advantaged, the least advantaged and an intermediate group. These groups are derived, in the way that is shown in Table 6.2, from a division of parental class, status and education each into three levels. In effect, the most advantaged group are predominantly the children of parents in the managerial and professional salariat or at least in white-collar occupations who have tertiary- or at least secondary-level qualifications, while the least advantaged group are predominantly the children of parents in wage-earning, mainly blue-collar occupations with no qualifications or at best only ones at a secondary level. Table 6.2 also shows the changing distribution of cohort members across the groups and, as would be expected in the light of the changing structure of employment and of educational expansion, the most advantaged group increases in size across the cohorts while the least advantaged decreases.

---

[7] The previous research indicating a weakening in the effects of cognitive ability between the 1958 and 1970 cohorts is Galindo-Rueda and Vignoles (2005). This research does, however, rely on less direct and more limited measures of social origins than does our own. For details of the analyses of the Avon Longitudinal Study data, see Bukodi, Bourne and Betthäuser (2018).

Table 6.2 *Composition of parental groups and distribution across cohorts*

Parental group	Level of parental characteristics			% by cohort		
	class	status	education	1946	1958	1970
Most advantaged	1	1	1	8	14	22
	1	2	1			
	1	1	2			
	2	1	1			
Intermediate	Other combinations of the three levels			40	55	51
Least advantaged	2	3	3	52	31	27
	3	2	3			
	3	3	2			
	3	3	3			
				100	100	100

Level 1: Classes 1 and 2; top third of status scale; degree-level qualification
Level 2: Classes 3, 4 and 5; middle third of status scale; qualification below degree-level qualifications
Level 3: Classes 6 and 7; bottom third of status scale; no qualifications

We can then examine the chances of men and women in the three groups attaining the two educational thresholds that we distinguish when we hold constant early life cognitive ability. In Figure 6.1 we show the results we achieve for the higher secondary threshold by graphing the probabilities of this threshold being reached by men and women in each group within each cognitive ability quintile and within each cohort.

It is evident, first of all, that, in line with the results we have already presented, the probability of reaching the threshold rises quite steeply, in each cohort and for both men and women alike, as one moves from the lowest ability quintile to the highest – although together with some tendency, especially among women, for success in this regard to increase across the cohorts for those at all ability levels alike. Second, though, it can also be seen that within each ability quintile the probability of reaching the threshold is higher in the group with the most advantaged social origins than it is in the intermediate group, and is

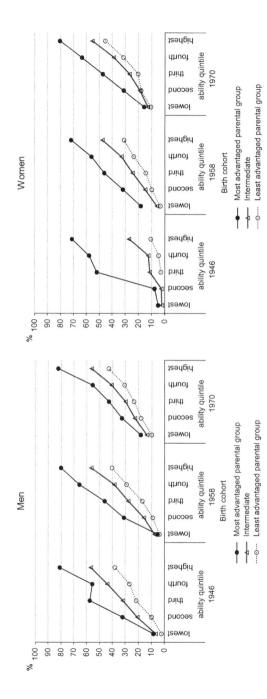

Source: Bukodi, Erikson and Goldthorpe (2014)

Figure 6.1 Estimated probabilities (%) of attaining upper secondary or higher level of qualification by parental group, cognitive ability quintile and cohort

higher in the intermediate group than it is in the group with the least advantaged social origins. And, third, it can be seen that as one moves from the lower- to the higher-ability quintiles, the disparities in the probabilities of success across the three parental groups clearly *widen*. There is, in other words, an 'interaction' between ability and social origins. Ability, one could say, counts for more, the more advantaged an individual's social origins or, alternatively, social origins count for more, the higher an individual's ability – a nice illustration of what has been called 'the Matthew effect'.[8]

Thus if, for purposes of illustration, we take men in the 1970 cohort, Figure 6.1 shows that for those in the bottom ability quintile the chances of attaining the higher secondary education threshold are in general quite low and that differences according to social origins range only from a 10 per cent probability for those in the least advantaged group to a 20 per cent probability for those in the most advantaged group. But for men in the top ability quintile, at the same time as the chances of success overall become much higher, the absolute differences between the groups in these chances considerably increase, ranging now from a little over a 40 per cent probability for those in the least advantaged group to as high as a 80 per cent probability for those in the most advantaged.[9]

Finally, Figure 6.1 also allows us to see the extent of changes across the cohorts. In the case of men, what is in fact most notable is the absence of any change of a significant kind: the graphs for the three cohorts are remarkably similar. In the case of women, the situation is somewhat different. Among women in the 1946 cohort, the disparities in the chances of attaining the higher secondary threshold, in relation to social origins, widen across the ability quintiles to a still greater extent than among men. For women in the top ability quintile, the probability of success is only 10 per cent for those in the least advantaged parental group, while being 70 per cent for those in the most advantaged. With the 1958 cohort, the disparities are a good deal reduced, as the chances of success of women in both the intermediate and the least advantaged parental groups markedly improve; and some

[8] After Matthew 25:29, the Parable of the Talents, 'For unto everyone that hath, shall be given.'
[9] In the binary logistic regression model underlying Figure 6.1 a term for the interaction between cognitive ability and the social origins variable was included and proved to be highly significant.

further reduction is apparent between the 1958 and 1970 cohorts. The result is that with the 1970 cohort the graphs for women come into a very close correspondence with those for men. What is therefore suggested by this pattern of change is that, although over the period covered some equalisation in educational attainment among women of differing social origins did indeed occur, this had less to do with changes in the educational system itself than with women's changing attitudes and ambitions in regard to education, with the result that in the latest of our cohorts women take up, to a similar extent as men, such opportunities as the system affords.

The results presented in Figure 6.1 do then indicate quite clearly that a wastage of talent occurs. Children with high levels of cognitive ability, as measured in early life, but who are disadvantaged in their social origins do not translate their ability into educational attainment to anything like the same extent as do their more advantaged counterparts. It is true that the overall amount of this wastage will be tending to decline insofar as fewer children are coming from social backgrounds of the kind that we have characterised as least advantaged. Nonetheless, we can – remarkably enough – still echo the conclusion reached by our sociological forebears researching inequalities in secondary educational attainment as far back as the 1930s: that a 'striking discrepancy exists' between 'the amount of good material in the community and the extent to which the existing machinery of social selection utilises it'.[10]

How far, then, do we find any different situation when we turn to the educational threshold set at degree level? Figure 6.2 has the same kind of derivation and format as Figure 6.1, with two exceptions. No graph is shown for women in the 1946 cohort since insufficient numbers attained degree level to permit any reliable analysis; and, again because of small numbers in the earlier cohorts, it is only with the 1970 cohort that we can make any estimate of the chances of cohort members in the bottom ability quintile reaching this threshold.

In the case of men, we see in fact much the same pattern of results as with the higher secondary threshold, although the disparities in chances of success between those in the least advantaged and most advantaged parental groups across the ability quintiles are somewhat

---

[10] The quotation comes from Gray and Moshinsky (1935: 115). Their outstanding work in quantitative sociology was carried out within the Department of Social Biology at LSE under the direction of Lancelot Hogben – a pioneer, incidentally, of research into gene–environment interaction.

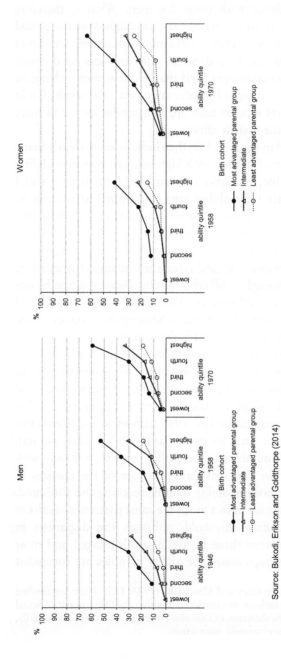

Source: Bukodi, Erikson and Goldthorpe (2014)

Figure 6.2 Estimated probabilities (%) of attaining degree-level qualification by parental group, cognitive ability quintile and cohort

smaller. There is also some indication of a slight narrowing of the disparities between the 1946 and 1958 cohorts but this tendency then disappears between the 1958 and 1970 cohorts.

In the case of women, however, the results do differ somewhat from those found with the higher secondary threshold. With the 1958 cohort, the disparities in women's chances of success across the parental groups are, at all ability levels, relatively small – generally smaller than those found for men; but with the 1970 cohort, the disparities quite clearly *increase* so as to become the same as or, if anything, wider than those for men. As can be seen, this comes about because, while women in the 1970 cohort of all social origins alike have a higher probability of attaining the degree-level threshold than women in the 1958 cohort, this greater rate of success is especially marked among more able women from the most advantaged parental group. Among these women in the highest ability quintile, over 60 per cent – a higher proportion than with their male counterparts – attained degree-level qualifications as compared with only around 25 per cent of those in this same ability quintile but coming from the least advantaged group.

Overall, then, a wastage of talent is just as evident at the second educational threshold that we have considered as it is at the first. Again, it is clear enough that educational potential is not being realised, and on a quite substantial scale.

Results of the kind we have presented do therefore go clearly against the position of those who, as we earlier noted, would claim 'the decline of the social' in regard to differences in educational attainment: that is, on the grounds that the educational systems of modern societies are already sufficiently developed to ensure that such differences as do now exist predominantly reflect variation in cognitive ability that is itself for the most part genetically determined. What our findings show is that even if one discounts the influence of early life family environment on the formation of cognitive ability – a very large discounting, it might be thought – children of similar ability *still* have very different chances of educational success depending on their parents' resources as these are represented by their class, status and education. There is no evidence at all of an emergent 'cognitive meritocracy'. Even if cognitive ability is taken as in itself meritorious, which may be thought a rather dubious supposition, its expression in educational attainment proves to be highly imperfect. And such a situation may be regarded not only as being, from a normative standpoint, unfair to those who lose out in not being able to fully realise their educational potential but also as damaging to society at large through the failure that is involved to make the best use of available human resources.[11]

Wasted talent? – 1

Dave

Dave grew up in a working-class family. His parents had only minimal education. At school he enjoyed sport but little else: 'I wasn't academic but I got by and got what I needed to get a job.' He left school at 16 – no one in his family or in his school suggested that he might stay on. He trained as a refrigeration technician and has spent almost all his life in this kind of work, making in the end 'good money' through overtime and shift working, although at some cost to his personal life. He has divorced twice.

However, apart from maintaining his sporting interests at a high level, winning trophies in football, table tennis, snooker and golf – 'I always have to win' – Dave has become an expert scuba diver and is taking courses on the theory – the physics and physiology – of diving. In addition, he has developed a strong interest in genealogy and is using internet sources to research his family history, which he has succeeded in tracing as far back as the early seventeenth century – 'rolls and rolls of paper'. He reads a lot, not fiction but mainly history; he wants to know 'what happened'.

---

[11] The phrase 'the decline of the social' is the subtitle of the book on educational inequalities by Marks (2014) already cited in note 3 above, and similar views are to be found in the work of Saunders, also there cited. The idea of a 'cognitive meritocracy' is problematic in that the possession of a high level of cognitive ability – whatever weight in its formation may be given to genetics or to early life environment – is essentially a matter of chance, outside of the individual's control. So merit, at least if understood with any connotation of moral worth, is scarcely involved. We would recognise that, in part, educational inequalities do arise from choice – children of less advantaged social origins tend to make less ambitious educational choices than do those from more advantaged backgrounds with the same level of previous performance (Jackson, Erikson and Goldthorpe, 2007). But, as is generally the case in social life, these are choices made under constraints.

Wasted talent? – 2

Harry

Harry's father was a self-employed carpenter. Harry's schooling was not successful, mainly, he believes, because he was made to write right-handed when he was really a 'lefty'. From that point 'I just disassociated from education.' He was told that he had an IQ of 147 but left school with only one O level: 'My sister was the prize pupil in the school and I was the prize prat.' In any case, his father thought that school work was less important than 'having a trade'. On his father's advice, Harry took up an apprenticeship in joinery.

After completing his apprenticeship, Harry was employed for twenty-five years in the same joinery shop but then suffered a serious industrial accident which meant he could no longer continue in manual work. While unemployed, he took a course in computing which he found 'quite easy'. Through a chance acquaintance, he was invited to go for an interview for a salesman's job in a firm manufacturing specialised industrial machinery. He got the job and has since remained with this firm, more recently being given some managerial responsibilities.

Harry played football and cricket at a high amateur level – 'I'm very competitive' – and has become a community coach. He is also a very active school governor, being first a parent and then a community representative. In this connection he has completed several training courses and is now passionately interested in education.

However, the further question that arises is that of the implications of our findings for the current political discussion of social mobility and related policy issues. Up to a point, what we have shown might be regarded as supportive of the importance that is attached to education as a driver of mobility. If it is the case that the educational system is failing children of less advantaged social origins in that many of them do not have the same educational success as do children from more advantaged origins of the same level of ability, then the need for further policy initiatives designed to ensure a greater equality in educational outcomes, and thus in opportunities in the labour market, would appear to be underlined. That is to say, there is no basis for supposing that existing disparities in educational attainment are predominantly the result of intergenerational genetic transmission – with the implication that further educational reform is likely to be subject to diminishing returns.[12]

Nonetheless, we would in fact wish to revert to the argument we have already advanced: that what can be achieved through educational policy alone in increasing equality of opportunity – and thus reducing the wastage of talent – in the face of inequality of condition has to be recognised as quite limited; and we would see the findings reported in the present chapter as providing further support for this argument. Too much is in this regard being asked of education, not on account of the resistance that comes from genetic determinism, but on account of that which comes from differences in a range of parental resources that can be deployed in furthering children's educational success.

Our previous finding that, at least with education being treated in absolute rather than relative terms, inequalities linked specifically to class origins have somewhat decreased now in fact requires significant qualification. When, while controlling for early life cognitive ability, we bring parental status and parental education into the analysis, in addition to parental class, we see that these also have independent effects on children's educational attainment, and, further, that when social origins are understood in this more comprehensive way, then over the period that our research covers, there is little indication that the influence they exert on children's absolute levels of educational attainment has been reduced – despite the almost continuous educational expansion and reform that has taken place. The liberal expectation that the exigencies of postindustrial society – its very 'logic' – would serve to bring into being an educational system in which inequality of opportunity was progressively reduced has not been borne out.

The disconnect between the findings of sociological research and the consideration of issues of educational inequality in political and policy

---

[12] Such an idea did apparently receive some attention during Michael Gove's time as Secretary of State for Education (2010–14), when one of his policy advisors, Dominic Cummings, produced a report in which it was claimed, on the basis of the work of the behavioural geneticist, Robert Plomin, that up to 70 per cent of population variance in cognitive ability was genetically determined; and, on this basis, the cost-effectiveness of preschool programmes for disadvantaged children was questioned. But although Gove apparently met Plomin to discuss the issues raised, the report appears to have been otherwise of no great consequence.

contexts could in fact be regarded as most apparent *in the inadequate attention that in the latter case is given to the importance of differences in parental resources*. In pursuit of policies capable of minimising 'social gaps' in educational attainment, especially at the primary and secondary levels, the importance of such differences has been largely disregarded, and the main concerns of policy have been directed elsewhere.

Perhaps the most obvious illustration of this is the emphasis that, since the years of New Labour, has been placed on 'school effectiveness': that is, on the part that it is believed can be played in reducing socially linked inequalities in educational attainment, as well as in raising general standards, by focusing on a number of so-called 'key factors' that include not only school organisation and resources and teaching styles but also 'leadership' and 'culture'. Research aimed at more precisely specifying these factors and at measuring their causal power has in the event proved highly controversial, and charges of both implicit ideological bias and methodological inadequacy have been raised. But what might more relevantly be noted is the body of available evidence that would indicate that insofar as 'school effects' can be established – and whatever the processes through which they operate – they still account for only a quite minor part of the total variance in pupils' educational performance as compared with that accounted for by pupils' own characteristics, and not least by those relating to their social origins. If ways of improving school effectiveness can be reliably identified, there would be obvious advantage in putting them into general practice. But what it might be possible thus to achieve in reducing inequalities in educational attainment would appear to have been seriously exaggerated in policy circles, and with, in turn, an inappropriate degree of responsibility being placed on schools in dealing with problems, the basic sources of which lie outside their walls.[13]

[13] On entering office in 1997, the New Labour government established a Standards and Effectiveness Unit within the Department for Education and Employment. For a review of the controversies arising over research promoted by this body and related studies of school effectiveness, see Goldstein and Woodhouse (2000). New Labour also initiated the academies policy, on which see Chapter 5, n. 12. In some policy quarters, much has been made of the supposed success of the London Challenge, a secondary school improvement programme, in raising levels of educational attainment and especially among pupils from disadvantaged local areas. However, subsequent research (Burgess, 2014)

Moreover, to the extent that any wider view has been taken, what is notable is that the concern has then been far less with differences in parental resources than with differences in parental *behaviour*: that is, with how far parents show an interest in their children's education, encourage them in their school work, engage with teachers, provide help with homework and study space, arrange educationally relevant out-of-school activities and so on. There can be no doubt that parental behaviour in these respects *is* a highly important factor in children's educational performance. But what appears to be seriously neglected in this regard – and with consequent policy failures – is the degree to which, and ways in which, differences in parental behaviour reflect the differing opportunities that are created and the differing constraints that are imposed by parents' resources, as these are conditioned by their class and status positions and their own educational level.[14]

What has been aptly called the 'concerted cultivation' model of parenting is far more easily engaged in by parents in salaried employment, with relatively secure, stable and potentially rising incomes, with social networks involving others in similarly advantaged positions, and with high levels of education than it is by parents in wage-work, with relatively insecure and fluctuating incomes, often dependent on overtime and shift working, with social networks of limited range, and whose own levels of education are low.[15] In the case of parents in situations approximating to the latter, simply pointing to shortcomings in the support they give to their children in their education and urging that they become more 'accountable' for their behaviour, without a full recognition of the disadvantaged conditions under which their

indicates that a very large part of the change that occurred can be attributed to the shifting ethnic composition of the London student body, with growing numbers of pupils coming from ethnic minority groups, often concentrated in disadvantaged areas but in which educational aspirations and levels of motivation are distinctively high. For research findings and more general discussion of the relative importance of school effects on children's educational performance, behaviour in school and psychological well-being, see Sellström and Bremberg (2008).

[14] The Department of Education's Parenting Early Intervention Programme (2008–11) and CANparent Programme (2012–14) were of very limited effectiveness and were discontinued. Subsequently, no comparable programmes have been centrally funded. See Social Mobility Commission (2017a: 26–7) and also the discussion of 'parenting policies' in Stewart and Waldfogel (2017).

[15] The concept of the 'concerted cultivation' of children is due to the American sociologist, Annette Lareau (2003).

parenting has to be undertaken, is a very questionable approach. Not only is it likely to have little success but comes dangerously close to 'blaming the victims'. The most detailed research carried out in the recent past into parental behaviour in ways relevant to children's education has found little evidence of any overall narrowing over time in differences in relation to parental class, status and education – and this could scarcely be regarded as surprising, given the general persistence, if not the widening, of social inequalities of condition. Yet adequate recognition of the problems that arise is still evidently lacking in official pronouncements and policy proposals.[16]

If education is to play a key role in promoting social mobility, the association between individuals' social origins and their educational attainment – as represented by the OE side of the OED triangle – should weaken. On the basis of more detailed analyses, we have now confirmed doubts we previously raised about whether in Britain any such weakening is in train – or could indeed be thought likely to occur in the present state of British society. In the next chapter, we move on to consider, also in greater detail than before, the further requirement of education being a key driver of mobility: that is, that the association between individuals' educational attainment and their eventual social destinations, as represented by the ED side of the OED triangle, should strengthen.

[16] The research referred to is that of Richards, Garratt and Heath (2016), a study of 'the childhood origins of social mobility' carried out for the Social Mobility Commission. Unfortunately, other studies in this area sponsored by the Commission are of lower quality, especially as regards the treatment of parental resources. For example, a study concerned in part with parenting in relation to the secondary school progress of 'low income pupils' (Shaw, Baars and Menzies, 2017) has in fact no data on parental income but uses the inadequate proxy of children's receipt of free school meals (see note 6 above), and gives no consideration at all to the effects of parental class, status or education. The proposals of Theresa May's administration for 'improving social mobility through education' that emanated from the Department of Education (2017), under Justine Greening, start out from an explicit recognition of the current wastage of talent but, yet again, the main policy emphases are on improving school effectiveness and parental behaviour. The proposals met with strong criticism from within the Conservative Party, and in the ministerial reshuffle shortly afterwards Justine Greening left the government.

7 | Education and the Labour Market: Is Education Now Class Destiny?

In Chapter 5 we noted that theorists of postindustrial society, writing in the later twentieth century from a broadly liberal position, claimed that a movement towards an education-based meritocracy was in progress. At the same time as inequalities in educational opportunity were being reduced, educational attainment was becoming increasingly important in determining individuals' economic futures – their life-chances in the labour market.

In this latter connection, the argument was developed along the following lines. In postindustrial society, characterised by rapid technological and economic advance, *theoretical* – as opposed to merely empirical – knowledge becomes of central importance. Thus, educational institutions, as the disseminators of theoretical knowledge and of associated expertise and skills, must take on a dominant role in the allocation of individuals to different positions within the division of labour. In particular, the university no longer serves, as in the past, chiefly to reproduce the status order of society but becomes, rather, 'the arbiter of class position' and in this way 'gains quasi-monopoly power over the fate of individuals'. Access to more advantaged class positions will lie beyond the reach of men and women, whatever their social origins and whatever their basic ability, if they lack appropriate qualifications; and a university degree serves as the essential 'passport of recognition'. This is the case, moreover, not only with professional and technical positions. With managerial and higher administrative positions also, the growing requirement for theoretical knowledge means that 'promotion from below' – as, say, on the basis of work experience and level of performance – which was once common, now becomes increasingly rare. In other words, it is achievement within the educational system, prior to entry into the labour market, that is, ever more, class destiny.[1]

The influence of such ideas remains pervasive. They are, implicitly if not explicitly, embedded in much present-day political discussion of education and social mobility. For example, references to the emerging 'knowledge economy' and its educational demands are frequent; formal qualifications are seen as ever more necessary for success in the labour market; and in turn educational policy, focused on expansion and the widening of opportunity, is regarded as vital in enhancing national economic performance and promoting social mobility alike. Nonetheless, the factual question remains of how far it is the case that in British society education is now class destiny or is, at all events, becoming more so. Remarkably little evidence of a directly relevant kind has thus far been produced.

In seeking to take matters further in this regard, we have to develop our approach from that of previous chapters. Hitherto, we have analysed data from the three successive birth cohort studies on which we concentrate in order, primarily, to gain an understanding of change – or constancy – *over historical time*. Now, in addition, we need to exploit more fully the possibility we noted in the Introduction of using the rich data provided by these studies in order to consider change or constancy *over individuals' life courses*. Insofar as education is becoming class destiny, we should find that there is a tendency across our cohorts for individuals' class positions to become more stable within their working lives: that is, a tendency for the class positions they obtain on first entering the labour market to become increasingly ones in which they subsequently remain. And, in particular, the probability of their achieving upward class mobility over the course of their working lives should fall away.

First of all, therefore, we aim to establish *typologies* of the 'class trajectories' that have in fact been followed by men and women in the 1946, 1958 and 1970 birth cohorts from the time of their labour market entry up to mid-life, so that, on the basis of these typologies, the extent of any changes in class trajectories occurring across the cohorts can be determined. Then, secondly, we move on to examine

---

[1] As we previously observed (Chapter 5, n. 2), the best-known theorist of postindustrial society is Daniel Bell, and the phrases quoted in the text are all taken from his work (Bell, 1972: 30–1; Bell, 1973: ch. 30).

how far and in what ways individuals' type of class trajectory is related to their level of education at labour market entry, and how far there are indications that an education-based meritocracy is emerging. In this regard, however, we need also to consider the further associations that independently exist between individuals' class trajectories and, on the one hand, their class of origin and, on the other hand, their cognitive ability. For if an education-based meritocracy is coming into being, these latter associations should be weakening. Class origins and cognitive ability should be of declining importance for individuals' class trajectories *except* insofar as their effects may be mediated through educational attainment.

For the majority of men and women in each birth cohort we have data that allow us to reconstruct, more or less completely, their employment and occupational histories from labour market entry up to age 38, an age by which, as we earlier noted, any occupational changes that an individual may make become increasingly less likely to entail a change in class position. Thus, for each of these cohort members there is the possibility of allocating them, year by year, for a period of twenty-two years – from age 16 to age 38 – to one or other of the classes of the seven-class version of NS-SEC (Table 1.1), refer-ring for this purpose to their 'modal' class in each year – that in which they had spent most time. In addition, though, we have to recognise two other possibilities for each year: first, that the cohort member had not yet entered the labour market; and, second, that for that year their class position is unknown – information is missing.[2] We have, there-fore, for each cohort member a total of nine different 'states' in which he or she may be found in each one of a sequence of twenty-two years. This is a unique body of data, and since for the three cohorts together

---

[2] In cases where for whatever reason – including, as often with women, their absence from the labour market – we have no information on a cohort member's class position for ten consecutive years, they are dropped from the analysis. We also, of necessity, exclude cohort members who have never been in employment, and further those whose first significant job – i.e. one lasting for six months or more – occurred only after age 30. The proportion of original cohort members excluded for one or other of these reasons is only around 6 per cent in the 1970 cohort but close to 20 per cent in the 1946 and 1958 cohorts. However, this would appear to be the result in these two earlier cohorts largely of operational shortcomings in data collection and coding procedures rather than of cohort members' non-response, and thus any associated biases should be minimised (Nathan, 1999).

we have such sequences for 12,886 men and 11,715 women, the data processing task that arises is a demanding one.

To enable us to move from the abundance of data we have available to the construction of typologies of class trajectories, we use a technique of sequence analysis known as 'optimal matching' – initially developed in molecular biology in order to study complex protein sequences. The basis of this technique is the pairwise matching of each individual sequence with each other individual sequence, in the sense of establishing the changes that would be necessary for the two sequences to be made identical. And it is then the degree of difficulty, or the 'cost', involved in this process of matching that is taken to determine the 'distance' between any two sequences. The costs reflect the nature of the substitutions, insertions or deletions of states that are required to make the matching in the most economical or 'optimal' way, and the costing system has to be theoretically derived. In our case, we do this by reference to the model of the pattern of social fluidity within the British class structure that we presented in Chapter 4. Most importantly, costs increase as the changes that are required to make two sequences identical involve class states that are further apart across the five hierarchical class divisions that we distinguished (see Table 4.1), with, however, modifications being made in two respects. First, the cost of all substitutions involving Class 4, that of small employers and self-employed workers, is increased on account of the high propensity for immobility in this class (see Table 4.2); and, second, a cost of substituting Class 3 for Class 5 or vice versa is introduced on account of the fact that these classes, while at the same hierarchical level, fall on different sides of the white-collar/blue-collar status divide (see Table 4.3). Figure 7.1 illustrates what is involved with some very straightforward cases.[3]

In this figure Sequence 1 captures the trajectory of an individual who remained outside the labour market up to age 22 – in full-time education, one might suppose – and then entered into a Class 1 position and remained in this, or in other Class 1 positions, continuously up to age 38. Sequence 2 captures the trajectory of another individual which is

---

[3] For full details of the costing and of the analyses undertaken, see Bukodi et al. (2016). For general discussion of the application of optimal matching and other forms of sequence analysis in sociology, see Abbott and Tsay (2000), Aisenbrey and Fasang (2010) and Halpin (2014).

Figure 7.1 Illustrative cases of costs of matching class sequences

The figure shows three class sequences across ages 16 to 38:

Age	16	17	18	19	20	21	22	23	24	25	26	27	28	29	30	31	32	33	34	35	36	37	38
Sequence 1	0	0	0	0	0	0	1	1	1	1	1	1	1	1	1	1	1	1	1	1	1	1	1
Sequence 2	0	0	0	0	0	1	1	2	1	1	1	1	1	1	1	1	1	1	1	1	1	1	1
Sequence 3	7	7	7	7	7	7	7	7	7	7	7	7	7	7	7	7	7	7	7	7	7	7	7

0 indicates pre-employment; otherwise numbers refer to NS-SEC classes

Costs of matching - i.e. distance between:

(1) Sequence 1 and 2 = 1; i.e. (cost of substitution of Class 2 for Class 1 = 1) x (number of occasions = 1) = 1

(2) Sequence 1 and 3 = 100; i.e. (((cost of substitution of any class for pre-employment = 2.5) x (number of occassions = 6) = 15) + ((substitution of Class 7 for Class 1 = 5) x (number of occassions = 17) = 85)) = 100

(3) Sequence 2 and 3 = 99; i.e. sequence (2) - (1) = 99

Source: Bukodi, Goldthorpe, Waller and Halpin (2016)

the same as Sequence 1 with the single exception that at around age 24 this individual – say, as a result of a career shift – spent a year in a Class 2 position before returning to Class 1 positions. In this case, matching the two sequences is very easy and 'low cost': for just one year one substitution is needed – Class 2 for Class 1 – and this involves only one level in the class hierarchy. Thus, following our costing system, the distance between Sequence 1 and Sequence 2 will be determined as very small, and is in fact, at 1, at the minimum possible level. In contrast, consider matching Sequence 1 – or Sequence 2 – with Sequence 3. In this latter case, an individual entered the labour market at age 16 in a Class 7 position and remained continuously in this or in other Class 7 positions through to age 38. That is to say, Sequence 3 differs from Sequences 1 in every one of the twenty-three years covered, and so far as class states are concerned the differences are as wide as could be within the class hierarchy. Thus, the distance between Sequence 3 and Sequence 1 will be determined as very large, and is, at 100, close to the maximum possible level under our costing system – while that between Sequence 3 and Sequence 2 is almost as large at 99.

We should, however, emphasise that the distances between the actual sequences followed by members of our three cohorts are very variable, lying on all intermediate points within the range indicated by the examples of Figure 7.1. Indeed, the really striking feature of the sequences is the enormous diversity that class histories display when considered at a detailed level.

On the basis of our costing system we can then apply an optimal matching algorithm in order to produce matrices – for men and women separately – that give, pairwise, the distances between the sequence followed by each man or woman in our cohorts and that followed by every other man or woman. As an analogy, think of the kind of chart found in a road atlas that shows the distance between each town or city and every other town or city. These distance matrices represent the initial step in the process of bringing the vast amount of data that we have on class histories into some manageable form. But – unlike road atlas charts – they are in themselves far too large to be readily inter-pretable. We are dealing with over 85 million pairs of distances for men and with over 68 million for women. Our next step, therefore, following the usual practice in optimal matching, is to move to a process of 'cluster analysis' – that is, one that involves searching the distance matrices for clusters of more or less similar sequences – and it is then the clusters thus found that serve as the basis for our typologies of class trajectories.[4]

In the light of our cluster analyses, we in fact opt for an eight-cluster typology of class trajectories for men and a nine-cluster typology for women. In Tables 7.1 and 7.2 we describe the types of class trajectory that emerge and for each type give an illustrative sequence in the same form as in Figure 7.1. But we would again stress that, because of the great diversity of the actual trajectories followed, very many variants on these illustrative sequences occur, even if ones that for the most part reflect short-distance shifts within the class hierarchy over short periods of time. We are dealing here with empirically derived, not pure or 'ideal', types.[5]

As can be seen from Tables 7.1 and 7.2, the typologies for men and women are broadly similar. In both cases there are types of class trajectory representing stability: that is, stability within Classes 1 and 2, the managerial and professional salariat (Types 1 and 2 for men and women alike); within Class 3, ancillary professional and administrative employees (Type 4 for men and Type 5 for women); within Class 4, small employers and self-employed workers (Type 5 for men and Type 6 for women); and within Class 6, the upper stratum of the wage-earning working class (Type 7 for men and Type 8 for women). The main differences that arise are three. First, for women there is no type representing stability in Class 5, lower supervisory and technical employees, corresponding to Type 6 for men. Second, while for men there is only one 'upward mobility' type (Type 3), for women there are two (Types 3 and 4) – a distinction being made between trajectories where mobility tends to occur relatively early in working life, before around age 30, or only later. And third, while for both men and

---

[4] We use what is known as 'Ward's method' of cluster analysis. This results in a treelike plot, or dendrogram, that moves from a large number of small, well-defined clusters (the leaves) through a smaller number of larger clusters (the branches) to a still smaller number of still larger but less well defined clusters (the trunks). The analyst has then to choose at what level the line is to be drawn through the dendrogram – usually somewhere among the branches – that will determine the number of clusters to be distinguished.

[5] We have checked the empirical quality of the clusters that we work with by using 'silhouette widths' which compare the distance of each individual sequence from its cluster centre with its distance from the centre of the next nearest cluster. In general, we achieve satisfactory results. The least well-defined clusters are those which become the Type 3 trajectory for men and the Types 4 and 9 trajectories for women.

women there are types representing mobility within the working class (Types 8 and 9 respectively), only for women is there a type for downward mobility to the working class (Type 7).

In carrying out our optimal matching exercise, in order to arrive at these typologies of class trajectories, we have worked with the class histories of men and women in all three of our cohorts taken together. Now, however, in order to address the question of whether there has been change in class trajectories over historical time – and in particular of whether an increasing stability in class positions from labour market entry onwards is apparent – we need to consider men and women in the three cohorts separately, and to ask how far types of class trajectory differ in their frequency from cohort to cohort.[6] The relevant distributions are shown in Figure 7.2 for men and in Figure 7.3 for women.

To begin with the distributions for men, it can be seen that there is a clear rise across the cohorts in the proportion following Type 1 class trajectories – those characterised by late entry into the labour market and then stability in the higher-level managerial and professional positions of Class 1. This finding is therefore consistent with the expectation that such positions should be increasingly ones that are directly entered into by individuals who have spent a lengthy prior period in full-time education – rather than being filled by promotion from below. However, it has also to be observed that there is no corresponding increase in the proportion of men following Type 2 trajectories – those characterised by late entry into and stability within the lower level managerial and professional positions of Class 2. Furthermore, while the proportion of men with Type 3 trajectories, involving upward worklife mobility, including into Classes 1 and 2, from labour market entry in less advantaged class positions does decline slightly between the 1946 and 1958 cohorts, this decline does not continue through to the 1970 cohort. And it is also of interest to find that there is no clear trend of change in the case of Type 5 trajectories that involve men being mobile from Classes 5, 6 and 7 positions to become small employers or self-employed workers in Class 4 – a form of possible worklife

---

[6] The question may be raised of how far, if we had treated our cohorts separately in constructing our typologies, we would have ended up with the same typology in each case. We investigated this possibility and found that, with both men and women, differences across the cohorts were very small, and insufficient to abandon the obvious advantages of using the same typology for all three cohorts.

Table 7.1 Typology of class trajectories, men

Types	Illustrative sequence[a]
	Age 16 → Age 38
(1) Majority: late entry and stability in Class 1	0 0 0 0 0 0 2 2 1 1 1 1 1 1 1 1 1 1 1 1 1
Minority: upward mobility to Class 1 from Classes 2 and 3, before age 30	
(2) Majority: late entry and stability in Class 2	0 0 0 0 0 3 3 2 2 2 2 2 2 2 2 2 2 2 2 2 2
Minority: upward mobility to Class 2 from Class 3, before age 30	
(3) Majority: upward mobility to Classes 1, 2 and 3 from Classes 4, 5, 6, 7, after age 30	0 0 6 6 5 5 5 5 5 5 5 5 3 3 3 2 2 2 2 2 2
Minority: downward mobility to Classes 4, 5, 6, 7 from Classes 1, 2, 3, after age 30	
(4) Majority: stability in Class 3	0 0 0 3 3 3 3 3 3 3 3 3 3 2 2 3 3 3 3 3 3
Minority: upward mobility to Class 2 from Class 3, after age 30	

136

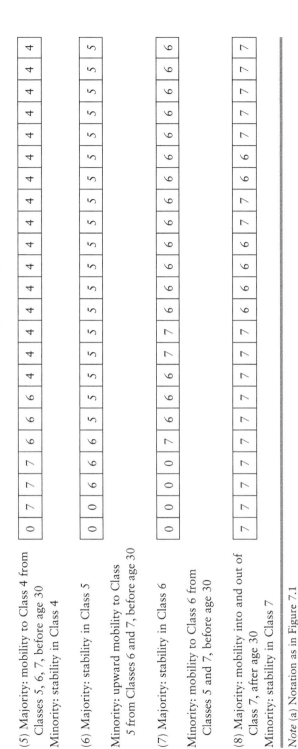

Note (a) Notation as in Figure 7.1

Source: Bukodi, Goldthorpe, Waller and Halpin (2016)

Table 7.2 *Typology of class trajectories, women*

Types	Illustrative sequence[a]
	Age 16 → Age 38
(1) Majority: late entry and stability in Class 1 Minority: upward mobility to Class 1 from Classes 2 and 3, before age 30	0 0 0 0 0 2 2 1 1 1 1 1 1 1 1 1 1 1
(2) Majority: late entry and stability in Class 2 Minority: late entry and stability in Class 3	0 0 0 0 0 0 3 3 2 2 2 2 2 2 2 2 2 2
(3) Majority: upward mobility to Class 2 from Classes 3 and 6, before age 30 Minority: stability in Class 2	0 0 6 3 3 3 2 2 2 2 2 2 2 2 2 2 2
(4) Majority: upward mobility to Classes 2, 3 and 5 from Classes 6 and 7, after age 30 Minority: mobility between Classes 4, 5, 6 and 7	0 7 7 6 6 6 6 6 6 6 5 5 5 3 3 5 2 2

(5) Majority: stability in Class 3

Minority: mobility to Class 3 from Class 6, before age 30

(6) Majority: mobility to Class 4 from Classes 3, 6, 7, before age 30

Minority: stability in Class 4

(7) Majority: downward mobility to Classes 6 and 7 from Class 3

(8) Majority: stability in Class 6

Minority: upward mobility to Class 6 from Class 7, before age 30

(9) Majority: mobility between Class 6 and 7

Minority: stability in Class 7

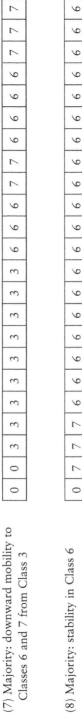

Note: (a) Notation as in Figure 7.1

Source: Bukodi, Goldthorpe, Waller and Halpin (2016)

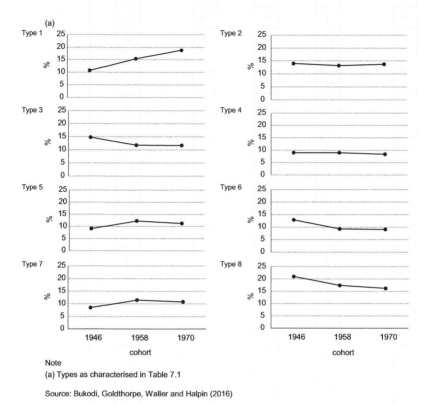

Source: Bukodi, Goldthorpe, Waller and Halpin (2016)

Figure 7.2 Distribution (%) of class trajectory types across cohorts, men

advancement that has also been seen as increasingly restricted in post-industrial society.[7] Overall, then, what is most notable about the results shown in Figure 7.2 is the rather modest degree of difference in the distributions that shows up across the cohorts, given the historical period that they span. In particular, no clear tendency is apparent for class trajectories that imply some degree of upward worklife mobility to become any less frequent.[8]

---

[7] See e.g. Bell (1972: 30) and for critical comment, Arum and Müller (2004). In recent years there has been a notable increase in essentially bogus self-employment where workers are constrained to take on self-employed status by those who are in effect their employers. However, this increase is unlikely to have had much effect on the results we report since these extend at the latest only to 2008: i.e. to men at age 38 in the 1970 cohort.

[8] Similar results have in fact been earlier reported by Mills and Payne (1989), using a different dataset, that of the ESRC Social Change and Economic Life Initiative, and a different analytical approach.

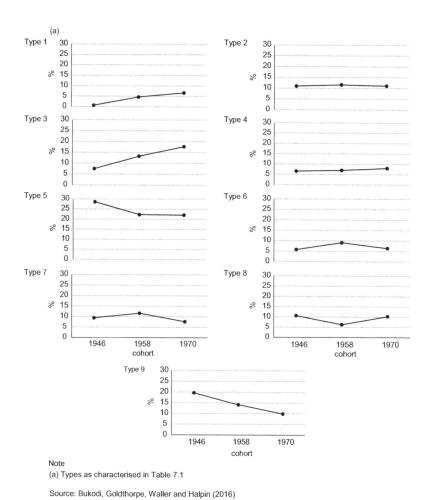

Note
(a) Types as characterised in Table 7.1

Source: Bukodi, Goldthorpe, Waller and Halpin (2016)

Figure 7.3 Distribution (%) of class trajectory types across cohorts, women

Turning to the corresponding distributions for women, as shown in Figure 7.3, we find in several respects a similar situation as with men. Most importantly, there is again an increase in Type 1 class trajectories characterised by late entry into the labour market and then stability in Class 1 positions, although, again too, this increase is not replicated with Type 2 trajectories characterised by late entry and stability in Class 2. However, a difference arises in that while with men Type 3, upward worklife mobility, trajectories could be said at all events not to be in steady decline, with women Type 3 trajectories, involving upward worklife mobility mainly from Class 6 and 7 to Class 2 positions and achieved before age 30 actually show an increase. And at the very least, no falling off is apparent in the case of Type 4 trajectories involving more limited upward mobility at a later stage in women's working lives. The growing importance of Type 1, 3 and 4 trajectories together is then chiefly offset by a quite substantial decline in the proportion following Type 9 trajectories, those characterised by mobility between Class 6 and 7 positions or, that is, within the wage-earning working class.

So far, therefore, the results of our analyses are somewhat equivocal as regards the question of whether in Britain an education-based meritocracy is emerging, so that the class positions in which individuals first enter the labour market on completion of their education become increasingly determinative of their class histories. We have shown that both men and women tend more frequently to take up Class 1 positions on labour market entry and to remain in such positions subsequently; but we have found no clear evidence, in the case of men, of a decline in class trajectories entailing upward worklife mobility while, in the case of women, such trajectories would appear to be rising in frequency. In order to gain a more decisive outcome, we now move on to results from analyses in which we directly examine the extent to which different types of class trajectory are associated with individuals' educational attainment at labour market entry – but also, for the reasons indicated at the start of the chapter, with their class origins and their cognitive ability. As we have seen in Chapter 6, individuals' class origins and cognitive ability are both strongly associated with their educational attainment. But what, for present purposes, we further wish to know is how far they have additional, independent effects on individuals' class trajectories – that is, effects *over and above those that operate via education.*

In Tables 7.3 and 7.4 we show, on the basis of the analyses we have undertaken, where these various possible effects on class trajectories of men and women are of positive or negative statistical significance, taking our three cohorts together, but with cohort being included in the analyses as a control variable. Since we are here primarily concerned with education as an investment good in relation to the labour market, we revert to treating educational attainment in terms of the four relative levels of qualification, the construction we explained in Chapter 5. To recall, the highest relative level includes all qualifications from A levels upwards for the 1946 cohort, but is restricted to tertiary-level qualifications for the 1958 cohort, and further to degree-level qualifications for the 1970 cohort, while the lowest level is no qualifications for the 1946 cohort but extended to no qualifications or any sub-secondary qualification for the 1958 and 1970 cohorts. We wish to determine individuals' qualifications at the start of their working lives. With men and women in the 1958 and 1970 cohorts we take their qualifications at the time of their first significant job (one lasting for at least six months) but, because of data limitations, with men and women in the 1946 cohort we have to take their qualifications at age 26.[9] To simplify the results somewhat, the NS-SEC classes are collapsed in the way indicated in the tables, and the two highest and two lowest cognitive ability quintiles are also collapsed. Since the results we obtain are on much the same pattern for men and women, we discuss Tables 7.3 and 7.4 together.

What may be observed, first of all, is that Type 1 and Type 2 class trajectories, characterised for men and women alike by stability within Class 1 and Class 2, are – as would be expected given the late entry into the labour market that is also involved – positively associated with the highest relative level of qualification. A clearly different situation is thus indicated from that in which, as revealed in the Nuffield mobility study of 1972, a large majority of those men born in the first half of the twentieth century who gained access to managerial and professional positions did so while having only very modest qualifications on leaving full-time education, if indeed, in the case of managers, any qualifications at all. And, conversely, it can be seen that those class trajectories that are largely restricted to positions within Classes 6 and 7 – that is, Types 7 and 8 for men and Types 8 and 9 for women – are positively associated with the two lowest qualification levels. In other words, for the period our data

---

[9] Some overestimation of level of qualification at labour market entry may in this case arise, on account of qualifications acquired between entry and age 26, but this is likely to be slight. We know that at age 26 still around three-fifths of the members of the 1946 cohort had no more than lower-level secondary qualifications. The statistical model from which the results reported in Tables 7.1 and 7.2 derive is a multinomial logistic regression model, full details of which are given in Bukodi et al. (2016).

Table 7.3 *Effects of relative level of qualification at labour market entry, class of origin and cognitive ability on probability of following different types of class trajectory, men[a]*

	Class trajectory type[b]							
	1	2	3	4	5	6	7	8
Relative level of qualification								
lowest	−	−	−	−	+	ns	+	++
next to lowest	−	−	ns	−	+	+	+	+
next to highest				reference				
highest	++	++	−	−	−	−	−	−
Class of origin								
Classes 6 and 7				reference				
Class 4	ns	ns	ns	ns	++	−	−	−
Classes 3 and 5	+	+	ns	ns	ns	ns	−	−
Classes 1 and 2	+	+	+	+	ns	−	−	−−
Cognitive ability quintile								
lowest two	−	−	ns	−	−	ns	+	+
middle				reference				
highest two	+	+	ns	ns	ns	−	−	ns

Notes (a) For symbols, see Table 6.1
     (b) As shown in Table 7.1
Source: Bukodi, Goldthorpe, Waller and Halpin (2016)

cover, educational attainment has evidently come to play an important part in determining whether individuals' class histories are largely spent within the managerial and professional salariat or within the wage-earning working class. To this extent, therefore, the idea of an emerging education-based meritocracy would appear to find support.

However, what has further to be observed is that Type 1 and Type 2 trajectories are *also* positively associated with Class 1 and 2 origins, while Type 7 and 8 trajectories for men and Type 8 and 9 for women are negatively associated with such origins, *even when qualifications are also included in the analysis.* That is to say, coming from advantaged class origins has a significant effect on individuals' class fates *quite independently* of the qualifications that they have, or have not, gained; and, likewise independently of qualifications, those trajectories that are

Table 7.4 *Effects of relative level of qualification at labour market entry, class of origin and cognitive ability on probability of following different types of class trajectory, women*[a]

	Class trajectory type[b]								
	1	2	3	4	5	6	7	8	9
Relative level of qualification									
lowest	ns	ns	− −	+	− −	ns	−	+	++
next to lowest	−	−	− −	−	ns	ns	+	+	+
next to highest				reference					
highest	+	++	−	−	− −	ns	−	−	−
Class of origin									
Classes 6 and 7				reference					
Class 4	−	ns	ns	ns	ns	+	ns	ns	ns
Classes 3 and 5	ns	ns	+	ns	+	ns	ns	−	−
Classes 1 and 2	+	+	+	−	ns	+	ns	−	−
Cognitive ability quintile									
lowest two	ns	ns	ns	+	−	ns	ns	+	+
middle				reference					
highest two	+	ns	+	ns	ns	ns	ns	−	−

Notes (a) For symbols, see Table 6.1
　　　(b) As shown in Table 7.1
Source: Bukodi, Goldthorpe, Waller and Halpin (2016)

largely confined to the working-class positions of Classes 6 and 7 tend to be positively associated with Class 6 and 7 origins (i.e. in Tables 7.3 and 7.4 almost all other classes of origin show significantly negative associations relative to Classes 6 and 7 as the reference category).

Further, cognitive ability also proves to be of importance over and above the effect it has on qualifications. For both men and women, class trajectories that are characterised by worklife stability within the managerial and professional salariat are, with one exception, positively associated with being in the two highest ability quintiles, while those characterised by stability within the working class are associated with being in the two lowest quintiles. In other words, the effect of individuals' ability in shaping their class histories would by no means appear to be fully expressed via their educational attainment at labour market entry. In the light of this evidence, extending

over the last half-century or more, one might then conclude that –
for better or worse – the realisation of an education-based meritocracy has still some way to go.

Such a conclusion is reinforced when we turn to those class trajectories that imply worklife mobility. For men and women alike Type
3 trajectories involve fairly early life upward mobility, including into
Classes 1 and 2. However, these trajectories tend, with both genders
alike, to be positively associated *not* with the highest, but with the
next-to-highest qualification level at labour market entry (i.e. in
Tables 7.3 and 7.4 to be negatively associated with all other levels as
compared with this reference category). And it can further be seen that
Type 3 trajectories are, again with both genders, positively associated
with Class 1 and 2 origins, and for women also with high cognitive
ability. What is thus suggested is the possibility that trajectories of this
kind may often reflect what has been referred to as 'counter mobility':
that is, upward worklife mobility that serves, in the case of individuals
from more advantaged class origins, to *offset* downward intergenerational mobility at labour market entry, as might be the result of only
modest educational performance. This possibility we explore further in
Chapter 9.[10]

Moreover, in two other mobility trajectories, educational attainment proves to have a yet more limited role. Type 5 trajectories for
men and Type 6 for women, which involve mainly upward mobility
from Class 6 and 7 positions into the small employer or self-
employed positions of Class 4, are shown to be positively associated
with both the next-to-lowest *and* the lowest qualification levels –
although also with Class 4 origins, and for women with Class 1 and
2 origins. The inheritance of capital or 'going concerns' may thus
often play a part in this kind of trajectory but it can also be followed
without this advantage as well as without that of a high level of
educational attainment.[11]

---

[10] The concept of counter mobility is due to the Swiss sociologist, Roger Girod
(1971).

[11] For cross-national evidence of the generally negligible importance of education
in regard to access to small employer of self-employed positions of the kind
covered by Class 4, see Ishida, Müller and Ridge (1995).

Upward mobility through self-employment

Colin

Colin grew up in a working-class family. His father always worked shifts at a factory and his mother was an office cleaner.

He enjoyed school, especially sports, but left at 16 with few qualifications – which now, looking back, he regrets – but at the time he 'wanted to earn money to buy things', especially a car. His father insisted that he should 'learn a trade' and so he became apprenticed to a roofer. He did not like his boss so left to take up a series of semi-skilled jobs in the construction industry. After some years working 'on the lump' – a form of casualisation of labour through subcontracting – he decided he might as well become independently self-employed. Following a difficult start, during which his marriage broke up under the pressure, he believes, of the financial problems involved when he was unable to obtain a steady stream of work, things steadily got better. He decided to advertise his services locally as a 'roofing contractor' and after that he began to prosper.

He now has a well-established business which demands 'continuous hard work' but which has made him 'comfortable' financially. He has a large house and garden and now that his children, who stayed with him after his wife left, have grown up, he lives there alone – 'very contentedly', he says.

Likewise, the Type 4 trajectory for women, which similarly involves upward worklife mobility from working-class positions, is positively associated with the two lowest qualification levels and – unlike the trajectories leading to Class 4 – is also associated with the two *lowest* cognitive ability quintiles. It may then be that in this case mobility is primarily promoted by non-cognitive attributes of some kind, such as personality characteristics. Support for this possibility is found in more detailed analyses we have undertaken which show that seven out of the ten occupations to which the trajectory most frequently leads are supervisory or managerial ones in the personal services or retail sectors.

Upward mobility with low qualifications

Angela

Angela enjoyed school, mainly because she excelled at sports: 'I always wanted to win.' She thought of training as a PE teacher but then decided to leave school at 16, with only one or two O levels, 'because I wanted to earn money'.

  She started work as a post-girl in an insurance company office but while still a teenager married, had a daughter and then divorced. After a period of single motherhood she returned to work in her late twenties in various part-time jobs in retail and services but then applied for, and got, a full-time job as a departmental manager in a furniture store where she had been previously employed and was well thought of. Over several years she 'worked her way up' to higher-level managerial positions in the firm: 'Again, I had to win, to be on top, there's no point, you know, in being down at the bottom.' She was eventually 'poached' by a rival firm for a top managerial position, and bargained a large salary increase: 'I'm good at my job.' She says that, although she still has problems with personal relationships, 'work-wise and money-wise' her life has become 'fantastic'.

The only worklife mobility trajectory in which the role of education appears to be quite dominant is in fact the downward mobility trajectory to working-class positions for women, Type 7. Being in the two lowest qualification levels is associated with this trajectory, but there is no association with class origins nor in any clear way with cognitive ability.

  Overall, then, the ways in which the class trajectories of the members of our three cohorts have been shaped would appear far more complex than envisaged in the liberal scenario of postindustrial society as outlined at the start of this chapter. The one question that remains, however, is that of whether, even if an education-based meritocracy does not as yet exist in Britain, there is evidence of some continuing movement towards it. To address this question, we have repeated the analyses that underlie Tables 7.3 and 7.4 for each cohort separately. What we find may be best described as merely minor variations on the pattern of results we have presented for the cohorts taken together. There is no indication of any directional change across the cohorts, and certainly not of a kind that could be interpreted as showing an increasing importance of individuals' qualifications at labour market entry for the class trajectories that they subsequently follow.[12]

In sum, the results we have reported would indicate that, if the comparison is between cohorts born before and after the Second World War, then entry into higher-level managerial and professional positions has become more strongly associated with the possession of higher-level educational qualifications; but that over the postwar decades further change of this kind, in the direction of an education-based meritocracy, has not been sustained. Or, in other words, there is little reason to believe that education *per se* – that is, *considered independently of class origins and cognitive ability* – is any more class destiny today than it was fifty or sixty years ago.

In conclusion, it is then relevant to ask why liberal expectations in this regard have not been met, and further what are the implications for current discussion of social mobility in political and policy contexts, which, as we have noted, has been much influenced, even if only implicitly, by theories of postindustrial society that underlie these expectations. To begin with, two misjudgments can be identified.

First, the extent and the durability of the effects of individuals' social origins on their class histories have been inadequately appreciated. As we have previously shown, inequalities in individuals' educational attainment in relation to their social origins – that is, in relation to the level and range of their parents' resources – have remained more or less unchanged across our birth cohorts. Now, we have further shown that individuals' social origins have a similarly persisting effect on their chances in the labour market *over and above* that which is mediated through the educational qualifications they obtain prior to entry. In this way, therefore, the issue of the degree of compatibility between equality of opportunity and inequality of condition again arises.

Second, the importance of theoretical knowledge within the postindustrial economy has been exaggerated. Advancing technology and more complex organisational and economic contexts undoubtedly increase the demand for such knowledge in some sectors. But this is far less the case in others – and including in ones in which employment growth has tended to be strong. For example, in Britain since the 1970s employment growth has been most marked not in those sectors that

---

[12] Further details of the analyses undertaken can be found in Bukodi et al. (2016).

might be regarded as constituting the 'knowledge economy' but rather in a range of personal services – including various forms of care, hospitality, leisure and travel services – and in retail.[13] In these latter sectors many jobs do of course involve only quite routine wage work, but there are also higher-level supervisory and managerial positions, and these are not for the most part ones that call for any great theoretical knowledge as opposed to the kind of practical knowledge that can be readily gained through work experience. Thus, opportunities can still exist for promotion from below for men and women with perhaps few formal qualifications but who can, through their work performance, directly demonstrate their suitability for it.

Finally, the yet more basic question can be raised, although it is one that seems little considered in political circles, of the unintended and perhaps unwanted consequences of taking an education-based meritocracy as in effect an ultimate policy objective. It could obviously be thought desirable, on efficiency as well as normative grounds, that selection for more demanding, and better-rewarded, social positions should be based on evidence of relevant competencies. But how far formal educational qualifications are to be seen as providing the only, or in all cases the most reliable, such evidence is open to some doubt. The danger always attending the idea of an education-based meritocracy is that of 'credentialism': that is, the danger that certain formal qualifications become a strict requirement for gaining entry to certain occupations, whether or not such knowledge, expertise and skills as they serve to certify are actually required in carrying out the work involved. And what has then to be recognised is that credentialism can in this way constitute a serious and unnecessary *barrier to* social mobility – reinforcing in the labour market the inequalities of opportunity initially arising within the educational system.[14]

With this danger in mind, the findings that we have reported of the persistence of trajectories of upward worklife class mobility, with no strong association with level of qualification at labour market entry,

---

[13] The particular occupations in which numbers increased most in the last quarter of the twentieth century include care assistants and attendants, educational assistants and hospital ward assistants – all in the top ten – with travel and flight attendants, hotel porters, merchandisers and window dressers not far behind (Goos and Manning, 2007).

[14] Concerns over credentialism have been far more marked in the US than in Britain, stemming from the influential work of Collins (1979).

could be viewed quite positively – and could, moreover, point to the potential value of some reorientation of attempts aimed at increasing mobility via the practices of employers. So far, the main focus of such attempts has been on employers' *recruitment* practices, mainly as a result of concerns that the use of a range of job applicants' personal characteristics, as well as their qualifications, as signals of their suitability, is likely to lead to social biases that impede mobility. But a focus on employers' *promotion* practices might prove to be at least as, if not more, rewarding: that is, with the aim of discouraging credentialism that effectively blocks promotion from below for those without some, perhaps quite arbitrarily determined, level of qualification, and of encouraging the wider development of internal promotion programmes and associated training provision.[15] In this way, greater opportunity could be created for upward mobility over the course of working life on the part of men and women who have actually shown themselves to be capable of moving on to a higher grade of work, and regardless of their possession or otherwise of 'passports of recognition' in paper form.

[15] The Social Mobility Employer Index, sponsored jointly by the Social Mobility Commission and the Social Mobility Foundation, aims to rate employers – but only those who volunteer to be evaluated – according to their procedures in regard to both recruitment and 'progression'. The emphasis so far has been heavily on recruitment, although the Commission has recently shown some greater concern over the improvement of 'internal pathways to promotion' and especially for men and women with low level qualifications (Social Mobility Commission 2016: 147–54).

8 | *Origins versus Education: Are there 'Glass Floors' and 'Glass Ceilings'?*

In the two preceding chapters we have examined in some detail the associations that exist between individuals' social origins and their educational attainment and between their educational attainment and their class histories and eventual class destinations – that is, the associations on the OE and the ED sides of the OED triangle. The results we have presented show that the OE association has not weakened nor the ED association strengthened in the ways that would be expected if the expansion and reform of the British educational system over the last half-century or more had resulted in movement towards an education-based meritocracy.

In the present chapter we turn to the third side of the triangle, the OD side. This relates to the 'direct' effect of origins on destinations or, that is, to that part of the association between origins and destinations that is *not* mediated via education. If an education-based meritocracy were emerging, then, with the weakening of the OE association and the strengthening of the ED association, the direct OD association should also weaken (see Figure 5.1). In other words, the overall association between origins and destinations should become *increasingly mediated through education*, while the direct effect falls away. Conversely, the persistence of a direct effect must imply that individuals' origins continue to qualify the effects of their education on their destinations; and, insofar as this is so, the degree to which any reduction in social inequalities in educational attainment is translated into a weaker overall OD association – that is, into greater social fluidity – will be restricted. 'Glass floors' will prevent children of more advantaged origins but with relatively poor educational attainment from being downwardly mobile, while 'glass ceilings' will limit the upward mobility of children from less advantaged origins who have performed well educationally.

In Chapter 5 we noted previous research that has indicated that in Britain the direct effect of social origins – or DESO in the usual sociological abbreviation – has remained remarkably stable over time, and we reported results consistent with this conclusion from our own analyses of data from the 1946, 1958 and 1970 birth cohorts.[1] Then in Chapter 7 we have also shown how, across these cohorts, individuals' social origins have a persisting effect on the class trajectories that they follow, independently of the level of their educational qualifications at labour market entry. However, we now wish to take the question of DESO further in three different respects.

First, we examine how DESO is affected if we consider social origins not simply in terms of class but in the more comprehensive way that we introduced in Chapter 6 in regard to social inequalities in educational attainment: that is, if we take into account, in the way there described, parental status and education in addition to parental class. If this is not done, it could be that DESO will be *under*estimated. Second, though, we also move to a larger view of educational attainment and take into account the further qualifications that individuals may obtain *after* labour market entry – that is, in the course of their working lives. If this is not done, it could be that DESO will be *over*estimated. And third, having arrived at our best estimates of DESO, we seek to gain some better idea of how DESO comes about. To refer to the direct effect of social origins on destinations, in the sense of the effect that is not mediated via education, is in fact to refer to an *unexplained* effect

---

[1] One of the papers previously cited, Vandecasteele (2016), appears in a collection (Bernardi and Ballerino, 2016) in which the extent of, and changes in, the direct OD association are examined in fourteen modern societies. It is found that whether origins and destinations are considered in terms of income, socioeconomic status or class, a significant direct association is in all cases present. This association is weakening in only two cases, is strengthening in two, and stable over time in the rest. A recent British study (Sullivan et al., 2017), drawing on the 1970 birth cohort dataset, claims to show that there is *no* residual effect of social origins on destinations once education is taken into account. However, several limitations of this study have to be noted. First, it is concerned only with access to NS-SEC Class 1 and not with the association between class origins and destinations more generally; second, class origins are not likewise treated on the basis of NS-SEC but on that of the now outmoded Registrar General's Social Classes, which very likely underestimates their effect; and, third, the definition of 'education' is extended to include not only qualifications obtained but also type of school and university attended. But the effect on class destination of attending a 'Tatler public school' or a Russell Group university *over and above the level of qualification obtained* could as well be seen as an effect of social origins as of educational attainment per se.

of social origins. If education is not the mediating factor, then what other factors are involved?

These more detailed concerns do, however, mean that, because of data considerations, we have to limit our analyses to the 1970 birth cohort. It is for this cohort that we have the fullest information on the nature and timing of qualifications gained after labour market entry; and it is only for members of this cohort that we have information about whether they have ever received any kind of direct help from their parents in searching for and obtaining jobs – which is of course one possible way through which DESO could operate. In turn, because the numbers in our analyses are thus reduced, we work with only a threefold version of NS-SEC, in which Classes 1 and 2 and Classes 6 and 7 are collapsed, as well as Classes 3, 4 and 5, and we focus on the chances of individuals being found, at age 38, either in Classes 1 and 2, the managerial and professional salariat, or in Classes 6 and 7, the wage-earning working class. Further, as regards educational attainment at labour market entry and again at age 38, we form, on the basis of a detailed classification of cohort members' academic and vocational qualifications, three relative qualification levels, rather than the four we have previously used, with qualifications being relativised according to age at labour market entry.[2] We label these levels, which cover roughly equal numbers of individuals, as low (comprising no, or only sub-secondary, qualifications) intermediate and high (comprising higher secondary and tertiary qualifications). And finally, since preliminary analyses revealed no significant gender effects, we treat men and women together, although in the analyses on which we report gender and also part-time working are always included as control variables.

Table 8.1 derives from analyses in which we fit three successively more inclusive statistical models to data for the 1970 cohort, and shows significant positive and negative effects on the chances of being found at age 38 either in the salariat or in the working class for

---

[2] The logic of this relativising of qualification level by age at labour market entry is the same as that of relativising across birth cohorts, i.e. that what matters as regards labour market returns is not just how much education individuals have but how much relative to those with whom they are in most direct competition. Five age groups are used covering the entire age range from 16 to 38. Further details can be found in Gugushvili, Bukodi and Goldthorpe (2017: Online Appendix A).

Table 8.1 *Effects of social origins and of change in relative level of qualification on class position at age 38, by relative level of qualification at labour market entry*[a]

	Relative level of qualification at labour market entry					
	Low		Intermediate		High	
	Class at age 38		Class at age 38		Class at age 38	
	1 and 2	6 and 7	1 and 2	6 and 7	1 and 2	6 and 7
Model 1						
Class of origin						
Classes 6 and 7	−	++	ns	+	ns	+
Classes 3, 4 and 5	reference		reference		reference	
Classes 1 and 2	++	− −	+	−	+	ns
Model 2						
Class of origin						
Classes 6 and 7	ns	+	ns	+	ns	+
Classes 3, 4 and 5	reference		reference		reference	
Classes 1 and 2	+	ns	ns	ns	+	ns
Parental status	ns	− −	+	ns	ns	ns
Parental education	++	− −	++	− −	++	ns
Model 3						
Class of origin						
Classes 6 and 7	ns	+	ns	+	ns	+
Classes 3, 4 and 5	reference		reference		reference	
Classes 1 and 2	+	ns	ns	ns	+	ns
Parental status	ns	− −	+	ns	ns	ns
Parental education	++	− −	++	− −	++	ns
Change in relative level of qualification						
Worsened			−	+	− −	+
Did not change	reference		reference		reference	
Improved	++	− −	++	− −		

Note (a) For symbols, see Table 6.1
Source: Gugushvili, Bukodi and Goldthorpe (2017)

individuals who entered the labour market at the three relative qualification levels that we distinguish.[3]

With Model 1 the only explanatory variable included is that of parental class. It can be seen that this has rather systematically significant effects. Compared with individuals of intermediate class origin (the reference group), individuals of salariat origin have a higher probability of being themselves found in the salariat, and individuals of working-class origin a higher probability of being themselves found in the working class *regardless of their level of qualification at labour market entry*. And for individuals with low- or intermediate-level qualifications, being of salariat origin also has a negative effect on their risk of ending up in the working class. In other words, there is here clear evidence of DESO being in general operation and in creating glass ceilings and, especially, glass floors.

With Model 2 we introduce parental status and education in addition to parental class. It can be seen that the effects of parental class now in some instances weaken or indeed become non-significant, although they still play a part in maintaining intergenerational immobility. Parental status is of rather limited importance – perhaps the main point of interest to emerge is that it is now higher parental status, rather than more advantaged parental class, that appears to create a glass floor protecting individuals with low entry qualifications from ending up in the working class. But parental education proves to have rather consistent effects. Higher parental education has a positive effect on the chances of individuals at all qualification levels accessing the salariat, and a negative effect on the risks of those with low and intermediate levels of qualification being found in the working class.

These results do then indicate that DESO will tend to be underestimated if only parental class is considered. As we argued in Chapter 6, although parental class, status and education are correlated, the correlations are not perfect, and *cumulative* effects may therefore be expected in some degree to arise. We take this matter further in Figure 8.1. In the left-hand panel of the figure we show the probabilities, under Model 1 of Table 8.1, of men of salariat, intermediate and working-class origins being found in the salariat and in the working

---

[3] Full details of the models – known as linear probability models – and of the construction of the variables included are given in Gugushvili, Bukodi and Goldthorpe (2017).

class in relation to each of the three qualification levels that we distinguish at labour market entry. Then in the right-hand panel we show, under an analogous model, the corresponding probabilities for men allocated to the three parental groups defined by *combinations* of class, status and education that we introduced in Chapter 6. It is evident that the effects of social origins are greater in the latter case than in the former – and results for women are on much the same pattern.[4] In other words, as regards the first issue that we raised, we can directly confirm that DESO will be underestimated insofar as social origins are not treated in a sufficiently comprehensive way.

At the same time, though, what also emerges from Figure 8.1 is that the differences resulting from DESO are more marked, *the lower the level of qualification* – and this shows up especially strongly in the right-hand panel. Thus, it can be seen that for individuals with low-level qualifications the difference between those with parents in the least and most advantaged groups is up to almost 30 percentage points in their chances of being found in the salariat and to over 30 percentage points in their risks of being found in the working class. These are disparities of a rather remarkable order, testifying to the actual extent to which the experience of men and women in the 1970 birth cohort diverges from what would be expected if an education-based meritocracy had been brought into being. They also reinforce previous indications that DESO contributes more to the creation of glass floors than glass ceilings. This is an outcome much in line with the importance that we have attached to the particular concern of parents and their children – stemming, we suggest, from the psychology of loss aversion – to avoid intergenerational *downward* mobility. Where the children of more advantaged parents do not perform well educationally before entering the labour market, other factors would appear to operate that still give them a good chance of maintaining their parents' position or, at all events, of not falling too far below it.

Moving on now to the second issue we wish to address – that of the effect on DESO of taking account of qualifications gained after labour market entry – we introduce in Model 3 in Table 8.1 a further variable that we have constructed specifically to allow for change in individuals' relative qualification level in the course of their working lives. We compare each cohort member's relative qualification level at labour

---

[4] See further Gugushvili, Bukodi and Goldthorpe (2017: Online Appendix B).

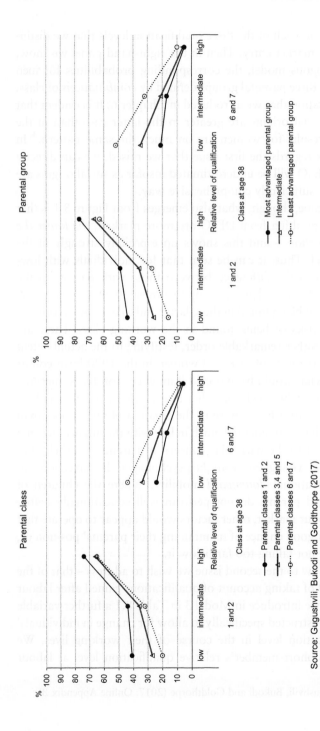

Source: Gugushvili, Bukodi and Goldthorpe (2017)

Figure 8.1 Estimated probabilities of men working full-time being found in different class positions at age 38 by parental class (left panel) and parental groups defined by class, status and education (right panel), by level of qualification at labour market entry (%)

market entry and at age 38, and then categorise them according to whether, over the intervening period, their level improved, stayed the same or worsened. The positions of almost a third of cohort members did in fact change, with the level of 11 per cent improving and that of 22 per cent worsening. Because we are here treating qualifications relatively, it is of course possible for individuals' positions to worsen simply because, while others raised their qualification level, they did not do so or at least not to the same extent. There are no significant differences in relation to class origins in the proportions of men and women changing their levels or in the direction of any change.

As can be seen from Table 8.1, when this new variable is brought into the analysis, its effects prove to be of a very clear kind. An improvement in relative qualification level significantly increases an individual's chances of being found in the salariat at age 38 and reduces his or her risk of being found in the working class, while a worsening in level has the opposite effect. It has therefore to be recognised that the importance of education for the class positions that individuals eventually achieve does not end at labour market entry but can be continued over a lengthy period afterwards. And we can now in fact say that DESO will be overestimated – at all events in the sense that the effects of educational attainment on class destinations will not be fully recognised – if qualifications gained during working life are disregarded.

At the same time, though, it can also to be seen from Table 8.1 that when with Model 3 we do take account of such qualifications, *the pattern of the significant effects of the social origin variables remains exactly the same as under Model 2.* In other words, while we gain a fuller understanding of the way in which class destinations are determined, DESO is not eliminated. This means, therefore, that the third question we posed retains its relevance: if DESO is the effect of social origins on destinations that is not mediated through education, how is it mediated?

To address this question, we move on to a yet further model in which all of the variables included in Model 3 are retained but in which three additional variables are included. In the case of each of these variables there are grounds for supposing that it could capture a mediating factor in DESO.

Two of the variables relate to individual characteristics, the first of these being cognitive ability. As we have already shown in Chapter 7, cognitive ability can in itself play a significant part in individuals' class trajectories – independently, that is, of the influence that it also has via their educational attainment. We allocate cohort members to cognitive ability quintiles in the same way as previously. The second individual characteristic that we consider relates to what psychologists call 'locus of control': that is, to the extent that individuals feel they have control over their lives and can influence their own futures rather than being 'fatalistic' and seeing their lives as being primarily shaped by circumstance and chance. Previous studies have in fact shown that a high sense of 'internal' as opposed to 'external' control is associated with more ambitious educational choices and more extensive job searches, and in turn operates as a mediating factor in both intergenerational income and class mobility.[5] In the 1970 cohort locus of control was measured at age 10 on a multi-item scale, and we allocate cohort members to quintiles according to whether they revealed a lower or higher sense of internal control. It should be noted that men and women of more advantaged class origins prove, on average, to rank higher on *both* cognitive ability and a sense of internal control than do those of less advantaged origins.

Our third additional variable concerns help in their working lives that individuals may have received from their parents. It is widely believed that family social networks and influence are not only often used in assisting individuals to obtain employment but, further, in actually advancing their careers.[6] Cohort members were asked: 'Have your parents ever done any of the things on this card to help you get any job you have ever had? Please include internships and placements, even if unpaid.' Of the various forms of possible parental help that were listed, we selected the following as those most relevant to our concerns: parents giving advice, providing recommendations to an employer, directly employing the cohort member, and using their

---

[5] See, for example, Osborne Groves (2005), Blanden, Gregg and Macmillan (2007), McGee (2015), Caliendo, Cobb-Clark and Uhlendorff (2015) and Betthäuser and Bourne (2017). Of late, a good deal of interest has arisen in the role of 'non-cognitive' attributes in individuals' educational and occupational success, but research findings have so far been somewhat inconsistent. Locus of control is one of the attributes that most regularly emerges as significant.

[6] See for some (limited) supporting evidence Ioannides and Loury (2004) and Loury (2006).

contacts to help find the cohort member a job.[7] Parental advice was the most frequently reported kind of help – by 36 per cent of respondents – while the other forms of help were each reported by around 10 per cent. Advice was more likely to be reported by men and women of more advantaged class origins, but reports of the other forms of help were not associated with class origins.

Table 8.2 has the same format as Table 8.1 but with the three variables representing potentially mediating factors of DESO being now included in the analysis. It may be noted, first of all, that the two individual characteristics of cognitive ability and locus of control both have certain significant effects.

As regards cognitive ability, it can be seen that (with the intermediate quintile being taken as the reference category) being in the lowest quintile further increases the likelihood of being found in the working class for individuals with low or intermediate qualification levels at labour market entry. But of greater interest so far as DESO is concerned are the effects of being in the highest or next-to-highest quintile. This adds to the effect of a high relative qualification level at labour market entry, and of any subsequent improvement in this level, in raising the chances of being found in the salariat, and being in the highest quintile also offsets the negative effects on these chances of starting working life at a low qualification level and of failing to improve on this. Furthermore, for those who thus remain at a low qualification level, being in the two higher ability quintiles reduces the risk of ending up in the working class. In other words, while high cognitive ability can reinforce the effects of educational attainment, it can also compensate for educational shortcomings. And insofar as high cognitive ability is associated with more advantaged class origins, it could then be regarded, from the standpoint of a meritocracy based on educational attainment rather than simply on ability, as a factor

---

[7] The other forms of parental help that were listed were help with job application forms and writing references. It should be added that the item on parental help was included in interviews with members of the 1970 cohort carried out in the 2012 'sweep' when they were aged 42, while we focus on their class destinations at age 38. It is therefore possible that some few instances of help that were reported occurred between these two ages, and should have been excluded from our analyses.

Table 8.2 *Effects of cognitive ability, locus of control, parental help, change in relative level of qualification and social origins on class position at age 38, by relative level of qualification at labour market entry*[a]

	Relative level of qualification at labour market entry					
	Low		Intermediate		High	
	Class at age 38		Class at age 38		Class at age 38	
	1 and 2	6 and 7	1 and 2	6 and 7	1 and 2	6 and 7
Cognitive ability						
first, lowest	−	+	ns	+	ns	ns
second	ns	ns	ns	ns	ns	+
third	reference		reference		reference	
fourth	ns	−	ns	ns	+	ns
fifth, highest	++	− −	ns	ns	+	ns
Locus of control						
first, lowest	−	+	ns	+	ns	+
second	−	+	ns	+	ns	+
third	reference		reference		reference	
fourth	ns	ns	ns	ns	ns	ns
fifth, highest	ns	ns	+	ns	ns	ns
Parental help						
advice	ns	ns	ns	ns	ns	ns
recommendation	ns	ns	ns	+	ns	ns
direct employment	ns	−	ns	ns	ns	ns
help finding job	ns	ns	ns	ns	ns	ns
Change in relative level of qualification						
Worsened			−	+	− −	+
Did not change	reference		reference		reference	
Improved	++	− −	++	− −		
Class of origin						
Classes 6 and 7	ns	ns	ns	+	ns	+
Classes 3, 4 and 5	reference		reference		reference	
Classes 1 and 2	+	ns	ns	ns	+	ns
Parental status	ns	− −	ns	ns	ns	ns
Parental education	+	−	++	− −	++	ns

Note (a) For symbols, see Table 6.1
Source: Gugushvili, Bukodi and Goldthorpe (2017)

that mediates DESO, though, again, more through the creation of a glass floor than a glass ceiling.[8]

As regards locus of control, it is, in some contrast, the effects of being in the lowest and the next-to-lowest quintiles, as regards a sense of internal control, that are most notable. These effects further reduce the chances of individuals with low levels of qualification at labour market entry being found in the salariat, and they also increase the risks of being found in the working class for individuals *at all levels of qualification, including the highest,* and independently of whether or not they have improved their qualification level since labour market entry. Thus, insofar as children of less advantaged class origins are more likely to have a low sense of internal control, this could be taken as a further mediator of DESO and as one that in this case tends to create a glass ceiling.

Turning now to our third potential mediating variable, that of parental help, we have what might appear to be the most surprising finding. As Table 8.2 reveals, the various forms of parental help that we consider appear to be of no great importance for individuals' chances of accessing the salariat or being confined to the working class. Only two significant effects show up – one of which is in fact rather readily interpretable: direct employment by a parent reduces the risk of being found in a working-class position for those who at labour market entry were at a low qualification level. This is much in line with what we have earlier shown in Chapters 4 and 7 that in the case of Class 4, in which small employers are included, there is a relatively high propensity for intergenerational succession – with,

---

[8] In research undertaken by economists – as, for example, by McKnight (2015) for the Social Mobility Commission and in the US by Reeves and Howard (2013) – and focused on the presence of glass floors, DESO is in effect defined not in contradistinction to the part played by education in the OD association but to the part played by cognitive ability, with education then being brought into the analysis as a factor through which DESO may be mediated. We see advantage in the opposite approach that we, along with most other sociologists, have adopted, at all events if it is meritocratic selection that is at issue. In this case, departures from selection by educational attainment must be of greater concern than departures from selection by cognitive ability. For, as we have earlier remarked (Chapter 6, n. 11), the possession of a high level of cognitive ability is essentially a matter of chance, whereas educational attainment could be better regarded as meritorious in that it does in some degree involve effort and choice for which individuals could be held responsible.

say, children taking over family concerns – in which educational attainment plays little part.[9]

DESO through intergenerational succession

Barry

Barry grew up as the eldest son of a sheep farmer, and knew from an early age 'that I was always meant to be a farmer myself'. His upbringing was 'homely'; having to go to school 'meant tears'. He learnt the business of farming – 'fencing, hedging, ditching, caring for stock' – from his father and from the farmhands. He left school at the minimum age, without any qualifications, to work for his father on the farm. He has generally negative views about modern education and its value.

When he was 21 his father died suddenly, so Barry, together with his mother, took over the running of the farm – 'I felt a responsibility to keep it all going.' Subsequently he took sole charge himself and then acquired a second farm. Around the same time he and his wife divorced. His social life is limited as he lives in a remote valley. Farming, he says, is 'as much a lifestyle as a career'. Questions of 'getting on' and social mobility mean little to him: 'I just think of myself as running my own business and being comfortable – modestly comfortable – out of the income.'

We do of course recognise the possibility that cohort members may have failed to report the parental help that they received, whether because they had forgotten about it or because they did not wish to admit to it. But the important point that emerges is that *in those cases where help was reported*, there is little indication that it was of any consequence for the class destinations eventually reached by the men and women concerned. Moreover, our finding in this regard is actually not as surprising as it might at first seem, in that it has been essentially foreshadowed in a number of earlier studies. Whatever may be the case with access to certain elite positions, very little evidence has in fact been

---

[9] One might speculate that the other significant effect – a parental recommendation increasing the probability of individuals with intermediate levels of qualification being found in the working class – reflects what would appear still to be the fairly common practice within the skilled trades of fathers 'speaking for' their sons to their own employers.

produced to indicate that parental or wider family social networks are of more general importance in improving individuals' labour market chances or, at all events, in increasing their chances of obtaining jobs that enable them to achieve upward mobility intergenerationally or to avoid downward mobility.[10]

Individuals' cognitive ability and sense of internal control, if not, for the most part, parental help, can then be shown to play some significant role in mediating DESO and in thus creating glass floors and glass ceilings that limit the amount of mobility that would be expected if the association between class origins and destinations did in fact derive from educational attainment alone. However, we cannot claim to have provided a complete account of how DESO is brought about. If we had done so, we would have found that in Table 8.2 under Model 4 all social origin effects became insignificant. But, as can be seen, the pattern of these effects is only rather slightly modified from what it was under Model 3 in Table 8.1. We have therefore to recognise that DESO is likely to result from a wide variety of social processes and to involve a range of other factors than those that we have been able to identify and to include in our present analyses. For example, the persisting effect of parental class may be in part mediated through family *wealth* (recall Figure 1.7) which, even if not directly drawn upon, can serve as what has been called 'a general insurance factor', facilitating more ambitious, and thus perhaps more risky, educational and occupational choices on the part of children. And the persisting effect of parental education may reflect family environments in which education is highly valued and children are expected to continue to

---

[10] A further study based on the 1970 birth cohort (Gutierrez, Micklewright and Vignoles, 2015) takes a somewhat different approach to ours in covering all forms of help reported and also help from friends, but still finds no evidence that men and women who said that they had received help had derived any benefit from it as regards either higher average earnings or higher socioeconomic status. These authors also note that less than a third of cohort members who reported help believed that it had contributed 'a lot' to their occupational careers, with the remainder believing that it had contributed 'a little' or 'nothing at all'.
A study using a different dataset, obtained from the Higher Education Statistics Agency (Macmillan, Tyler and Vignoles, 2014), and focused on access to NS-SEC Class 1 positions finds that for men and women graduating in 2006–7 social networks appeared to have 'very little impact on the residual relationship between family background and entering a top occupation' – i.e. on DESO as we would term it.

'improve themselves' in adult life, even if in ways not necessarily reflected in further formal qualifications.[11]

What, then, are the wider implications of our investigation of DESO? To begin with, we have established that still with the latest cohort we can consider, that of men and women born in 1970, DESO is readily apparent, and especially so if we treat social origins as comprising parental status and education as well as parental class. Social origins still significantly qualify the effects of educational attainment so far as individuals' chances in the labour market are concerned. The doubts we have expressed concerning the capacity of educational policy alone to bring about a greater equality of opportunity within the class structure are thus again underlined.

Further, DESO is most marked in relation to educational attainment at labour market entry. The degree to which social origins can influence class destinations independently of individuals' relative level of qualification at this point is strikingly brought out in the graphs of Figure 8.1, and especially in the case of those with low levels of qualification. At the same time, though, we have found that the effects of education on class destinations can extend well beyond labour market entry. Qualifications obtained in the course of a working life that raise an individual's relative level increase their chance of accessing the salariat, while if their level falls, their risk of ending up in the working class increases. In these ways, therefore, evidence is again provided, complementary to that of Chapter 7, to show that the idea of educational attainment at labour market entry becoming class destiny is far from realisation. And in this regard we can now add that a high level of cognitive ability, as a mediating factor in DESO, can compensate for a low level of qualification at labour market entry, and even where no improvement in qualifications is later made.

Furthermore, the results of our attempt to find mediating factors in DESO are of some consequence in regard to policy in two other respects. First, a good deal of attention has of late centred on identifying – in the hope of then reducing – influences on occupational achievement deriving from what has been labelled as 'opportunity hoarding' on the part of more advantaged classes.[12] For example, there

---

[11] The idea of wealth as a general insurance factor comes from Pfeffer and Hällsten (2012). On parental education as an influence on lifelong learning, see Tuckett and Field (2016).

[12] The term comes from the American sociologist, Charles Tilly.

has been much discussion of the use of family resources in advancing young peoples' career prospects through internships or placements, often unpaid, that are in effect restricted to those with the social contacts needed to obtain them and the financial support to make them viable. However, while opportunity hoarding of this kind may well be of importance in regard to career progression to higher-level positions in some particular cases – such as, say, finance, the law or the media – our findings would suggest that the degree of concern shown in this regard has become somewhat exaggerated, at all events if the focus is on mass rather than certain kinds of elite mobility.[13] We confirm the conclusion reached in a number of other studies that direct parental help is not a 'non-meritocratic' factor of any great importance in determining the degree of individuals' success in working life within the population at large.

Second, and in some contrast, our finding that low levels of internal locus of control are likely to restrict the chances of upward mobility even of men and women with relatively high levels of qualification could be taken to point to what might be a far more extensive, if largely overlooked, problem, and especially insofar as a low sense of internal control tends to be associated with disadvantaged social origins. The Social Mobility Commission has sought to identify geographical localities in which the chances of upward mobility appear to be particularly poor – so-called social mobility 'cold spots' – and many of these turn out to be deindustrialised areas in the north and Midlands, areas around decayed coastal towns or more remote rural areas. If these areas are indeed ones characterised by low rates of upward mobility, problems in local schools and the state of local labour markets, on which the Commission's analyses have so far concentrated, no doubt play a part. But more consideration could certainly be given to the possibility that in such areas working-class children, especially, may very well grow up with a fatalistic sense that people, or at least people of their kind, do in fact have little control over what happens to them in their lives, which then limits the extent to which they actively seek to

---

[13] It may further be noted that the economic advantages of unpaid internships are in any event questionable. Holford (2017) shows that graduates who take up such internships rather than moving directly into paid employment incur a substantial earnings penalty for up to three years afterwards, although this penalty is mitigated somewhat in the case of those from more advantaged social origins.

translate such educational success as they may achieve into such labour market opportunities as may exist.[14]

Finally, though, perhaps the most significant question that arises from the analyses we have presented in this chapter is the following. Given that DESO is overestimated if attention is limited to educational attainment at labour market entry, and that whether or not individuals later make improvements in their relative qualification level has a significant effect on their eventual class destinations, does this continuing role of education make in the end for greater mobility – or greater immobility? This question becomes of heightened interest in view of a growing importance that has been attached in government circles over recent years to 'lifelong learning'. Insofar as the implications for social mobility of policy initiatives in this regard have been considered, it would appear to have been supposed that they will be positive – if only perhaps on the basis of the rather simplistic assumption that more education, of whatever kind, must mean more mobility. But relevant evidence is in fact very limited. In the next chapter we take further our analyses of the experience of men and women in the 1970 birth cohort to try to throw a clearer light on the matter.

---

[14] On social mobility cold spots, see further Social Mobility Commission (2016: chs. 3 and 4; 2017b) and the discussion in our concluding chapter. One may, incidentally, doubt if in places like Stoke, Blackpool and west Somerset worries over the availability of internships, paid or otherwise, are all that widespread.

9 | *Lifelong Learning: Compensation or Cumulative Advantage?*

Provision for lifelong learning has been widely regarded as a way in which men and women who have not performed well within the normal course of full-time education can later upgrade their levels of qualification. In the case of those of more disadvantaged social origins, who are likely to have below average levels of educational attainment on entering the labour market, lifelong learning has then been taken to have a particular value. For such men and women it can offer a 'second chance' through which they can compensate for their earlier lack of educational success and, in turn, improve their prospects of upward social mobility during worklife and thus intergenerationally. An influential report published by the Ministry of Education in 1959 made explicit the idea of an 'alternative route', via mainly part-time further education, which would enable those children, predominantly of working-class origin, who had failed to reach grammar schools or who had been 'early leavers' still to gain higher-level qualifications while in employment and in turn access managerial and professional occupations.[1]

However, another possibility has to be recognised – as sociologists were in fact rather quick to point out. It may be that lifelong learning is not only, or not even primarily, pursued by men and women from less advantaged social origins but rather by those from more advantaged origins, and especially in cases where the latter had levels of educational attainment which, if not especially poor, were still insufficient to give them a strong assurance of maintaining their parents' social position. Through further education, these individuals could take the opportunity of building on their previous qualifications, and in this case lifelong learning would serve less to give a second chance in a

---

[1] See Ministry of Education (1959). The report became widely known as the Crowther Report, after Sir Geoffrey Crowther, chairman of the Central Advisory Council for Education (England), which was responsible for its production.

compensatory sense and more to give a second chance of realising cumulative advantage; the 'Matthew effect' would again be apparent. And, to the extent that this was so, lifelong learning would be likely to contribute less to social mobility than to social immobility.[2]

In the previous chapter we have seen that if individuals do improve their relative qualification level in the course of their working lives, this increases their chances of being found in the managerial and professional salariat, while if their relative level worsens their chances of being found in the wage-earning working class increase. We now wish to go into more detail in this connection by focusing on the two following questions. First, what is the association between individuals' class origins and the likelihood of their participation in lifelong learning that leads to further qualifications? And, second, what is the association between obtaining such qualifications and changes in individuals' class positions in working life and also in relation to their class origins?

We again confine our attention to the 1970 birth cohort. We draw on the data we have on cohort members' class origins and their complete employment and class histories up to age 38 as described in Chapter 7, and, in addition, we are also able to construct their complete educational and qualifications histories. In this latter case, we take into account all formal qualifications, whether academic or vocational, that cohort members had obtained, again up to age 38, and categorise these on the same lines as shown in Table 5.1 – although now with academic and vocational qualifications being treated separately. We then define qualifications resulting from some form of lifelong learning provision – or, for short, 'further qualifications' – as those that were gained following an individuals' first period of full-time education and entry into their first significant job, that is, one lasting for at least six months. We do not distinguish between qualifications gained from full-time and part-time further education since it is in fact the latter that very largely predominate.[3]

To begin with, it may be noted that among members of the 1970 birth cohort participation in lifelong learning was at quite a high

---

[2] For an early paper raising this possibility and discussing results obtained on the basis of data from the Nuffield mobility study, see Raffe (1979).

[3] Data from the British Household Panel Study and its successor, the Understanding Society survey, show that over the period 1998–2012 less than 5 per cent of recorded 'adult learning episodes' were ones of full-time education.

level. Over half, 57 per cent of men and 54 per cent of women, had obtained further qualifications, mainly in early working life – that is, by their late twenties. Vocational qualifications were far more frequently acquired than academic qualifications – twice as often in the case of women and somewhat more than twice as often in the case of men.[4]

To establish the association between participation in lifelong learning and class origins, we start with a statistical model designed to show the effect of an individual's class origins on the probability that he or she obtained a further academic or a vocational qualification in any year of his or her working life up to age 38. The model includes a number of other variables apart from class origins that are known also to influence participation, such as previous qualifications and employment status (employee, self-employed, unemployed, inactive, etc.).[5] Although these other variables are intended, given our focus on class origins, primarily to serve as controls, one outcome of particular relevance is the following. Consistently with most previous research, we find that an individual's previous level of *academic* qualification is an important factor in participation: the higher this level, the greater the probability that he or she will obtain a further qualification, whether of an academic *or* a vocational kind.[6]

Turning then to the effects of class origins, we show in Table 9.1 results from our initial model, labelled Model 1, for men and women separately. It can be seen that significant class origin effects occur mainly at the extremes of the class hierarchy and in relation to academic qualifications. Men and women originating in Class 1, the higher level of the managerial and professional salariat, are more likely

---

[4] The extent of participation in lifelong learning in Britain seems to be often underappreciated. The Social Mobility Commission has claimed (Social Mobility Commission 2016: 148) – though without citing supporting evidence – that Britain has 'fallen behind other countries in its adult skills agenda'. But in a study based on data for 2007, Dämmerich et al. (2014) found that Britain in fact ranked top among European countries in terms of the proportion of its working-age population who were engaged in further education or training of some formal kind.

[5] For a useful review of previous work on factors affecting participation in lifelong learning, see Tuckett and Field (2016).

[6] The model is a binomial logistic regression model in which time dependency is taken into account via age year dummy variables and in which a person-specific random error term is included. For further details of the model and of all the analyses referred to in this chapter, see Bukodi (2017).

Table 9.1 *Effect of class of origin on the probability of obtaining further qualifications*[a]

	Men		Women	
	Further qualification		Further qualification	
	Academic	Vocational	Academic	Vocational
Model 1				
Class of origin				
Class 7	—	ns	— —	ns
Class 6	ns	ns	— —	+
Class 5	ns	ns	ns	++
Class 4	reference		reference	
Class 3	ns	ns	ns	ns
Class 2	ns	ns	ns	ns
Class 1	+	—	++	ns
Model 2				
Class of origin is higher than own class in year before qualification obtained	++	ns	++	ns

Note (a) For symbols, see Table 6.1
Source: Bukodi (2017)

than those originating in other classes to obtain further academic qualifications, while men and women originating in Class 7, the lower level of the wage-earning working class, are less likely to do so – as also are women originating in Class 6. In contrast, the acquisition of further vocational qualifications shows no very systematic association with class origins. Men of Class 1 origin are less likely to obtain vocational qualifications than others, while women of Class 5 and Class 6 origins appear more likely.

　　Class origin effects can, however, be treated in a different way, which adds to – and also suggests some explanation of – our results under Model 1. From our class and qualifications histories of members of the 1970 cohort, we can create a further variable that refers to whether or not at any point in their working lives individuals were in a less advantaged class position than that in which they originated, according to fivefold hierarchical division of NS-SEC (Table 1.1).

In Model 2 in Table 9.1, this variable replaces the class of origin variable of Model 1 – and with rather striking results. As can be seen, *being in a less advantaged class than that of their parents* strongly increases the probability that individuals will subsequently gain a further academic, though not a vocational, qualification. In other words, here we do find a rather clear indication that participation in lifelong learning provides a second chance of realising the advantages of social origins rather than a second chance of overcoming the disadvantages; at the same time, there is a still further indication that 'class maintenance' – the avoidance of downward class mobility – is a powerful motivational force.

The findings presented in Table 9.1 do not, however, take any account of the age at which further qualifications are obtained. Could it be the case that, insofar as a gap exists between the qualification levels of men and women of differing class origins at labour market entry, participation in lifelong learning does at all events bring about some narrowing in this gap over the course of working life? Does it, in other words, allow for some degree of 'catch-up' on the part of those who start out from disadvantaged origins?

In Figures 9.1 and 9.2 we show probabilities estimated under a version of Model 1 of Table 9.1 of a man or women of Class 1 and 2 or of Class 6 and 7 origins obtaining further academic and vocational qualifications at all ages from 18 to 38. To simplify, we focus on the case of a hypothetical man or woman who is currently in full-time employment in a Class 3 position, who has higher secondary qualifications (category 5 in Table 5.1) and who has not experienced worklife mobility in the last five years. With different hypothetical persons we would of course have different results; but, unless rather extreme cases were to be taken, the probabilities produced could be expected to be on the same pattern so far as comparisons between individuals of Class 1 and 2 and Class 6 and 7 origins are concerned.

As regards gaining further academic qualifications, it can be seen that there is in fact no very great change in the difference in the probabilities of doing so for individuals of salariat and working-class origins over the age range covered. The probabilities for the former remain always above those for the latter; and, while the difference does reduce slightly from the early to the late twenties, it then with men falls very little further and with women stays essentially unaltered. There is, in other words, no evidence that catch-up occurs to any substantial extent.

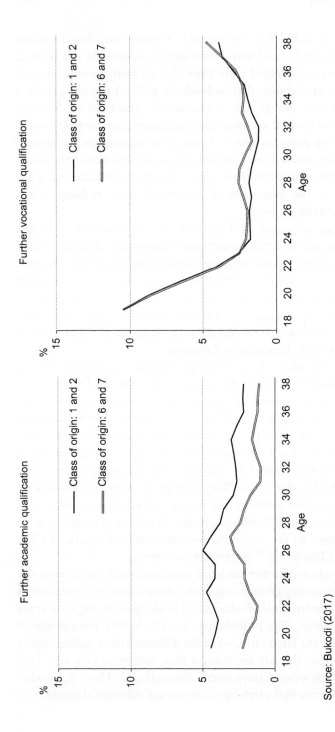

Source: Bukodi (2017)

Figure 9.1 Estimated probability of attaining further qualifications by class of origin and age, men

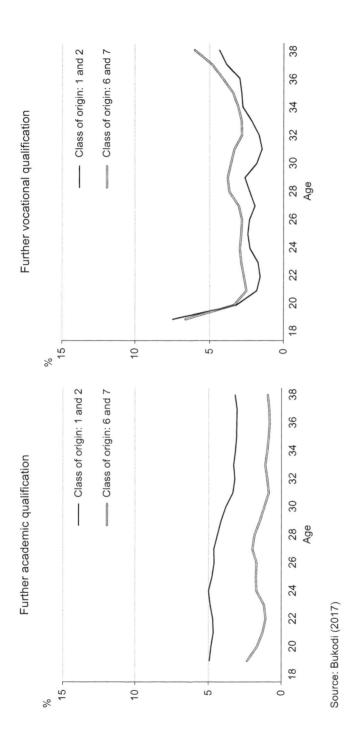

Source: Bukodi (2017)

Figure 9.2 Estimated probability of attaining further qualifications by class of origin and age, women

As regards vocational qualifications, the situation is, again, a contrasting one, and so much so that the question of catch-up does not in fact arise. With men, there is very little difference at any age between those of salariat and of working-class origins in the probability of their gaining a vocational qualification, and with women it is those of working-class origin who, at all ages from the early twenties onwards, have somewhat the higher probability.

The results we have so far presented do then clearly show that in answering the first question we raised, that of the association between individuals' class origins and their acquisition of further qualifications through lifelong learning, the distinction between academic and vocational qualifications is crucial. In the case of academic qualifications, an association clearly exists. In the course of their working lives, men and women of the most advantaged class origins are more likely than those of the least advantaged to gain further academic qualifications; and, further, being in any class position that implies downward intergenerational mobility increases the probability that an individual will go on to acquire a further academic qualification. But in the case of vocational qualifications, no comparable associations with class origins exist; and, with women, it is, if anything, those of working-class origin who appear the most likely to obtain such qualifications. An evident consideration in explaining these findings is that courses leading to academic qualifications are likely to be more costly to pursue than those leading to vocational qualifications. However, the whole question of cost to the individual of further education, including opportunity costs as well as direct ones, would not appear to have been the subject of any detailed research.

At all events, what is important is that we should maintain the academic–vocational distinction in moving on now to our second question, that of the association between individuals' acquisition of further qualifications and their class mobility viewed in both worklife and intergenerational perspective – or, in other words, the question of the 'class returns' that further qualifications bring.

In seeking to answer this question, we have undertaken preliminary analyses of the time relationship between an individual gaining a further qualification and any subsequent change in his or her class position. We find that, if any change in class position does occur, this happens fairly quickly after the new qualification – most often within a year and almost always within two or three years.

We then develop our modelling strategy on the following lines. Using the same form of model as Model 1 of Table 9.1 and keeping the same set of control variables, we focus, to begin with, on the association that exists between individuals obtaining further academic or vocational qualifications and their experiencing, within the next three years, upward or downward class mobility in the course of their working lives. As well as distinguishing between academic and vocational qualifications, we also distinguish between qualifications that do and do not raise individuals' levels of such qualification. And we also consider upward and downward mobility in three different ways: first, upward or downward mobility of any kind, in terms of the fivefold hierarchical divisions of NS-SEC; second, upward mobility to and downward mobility from Classes 1 and 2, the managerial and professional salariat; and, third, upward mobility to and downward mobility from Class 1 alone, the higher level of the salariat. Tables 9.2 and 9.3 are based on our results for men and for women treated separately.

For men, a fairly clear pattern of results emerges. As regards upward mobility, it can be seen from Table 9.2 that if a man obtains a new academic qualification that raises his level of such qualification, this significantly and quite strongly improves his chances of experiencing upward class mobility over the next three years, both of any kind and more specifically into Classes 1 and 2 or into Class 1 alone. And also a new academic qualification that does not upgrade his level of qualification still improves his chances of mobility into Class 1 – as a result, one might suppose, of widening his *range* of qualification. In contrast, a new vocational qualification has no effect on a man's chances of upward class mobility, whether it is one that raises his level of vocational qualification or not.[7] As regards downward mobility, our findings are yet more straightforward. New qualifications, whether academic or vocational and whether marking an upgrading in qualification or not, appear to have no effect on reducing a man's risk of downward worklife mobility in any of the ways considered: that is, in no cell of the right-hand panel of Table 9.2 is there a negative sign. In short, we may say that, so far as men are concerned, further qualifications gained through lifelong learning are associated with their experience of class mobility in the course of working life in just one way: obtaining further *academic* qualifications increases their chances of *upward* mobility.

[7] It is of course possible that further vocational qualifications bring earnings returns if not class returns, although the extensive research on this issue by economists would suggest that, at least in the case of men, earnings returns tend to be limited, if evident at all. See e.g. Jenkins et al. (2003), Wolf, Jenkins and Vignoles (2006) and Blanden et al. (2012).

Table 9.2 *Effect of further qualifications on the probability of upward and downward worklife mobility, men*[a]

	Upward worklife mobility to			Downward worklife mobility from		
		Class			Class	
	any class	1 and 2	Class 1	any class	1 and 2	Class 1
New academic qualifications attained in past three years that						
raise level of qualification	++	++	++	ns	ns	ns
do not raise level of qualification	ns	ns	++	ns	ns	ns
New vocational qualifications attained in past three years that						
raise level of qualification	ns	ns	ns	ns	ns	ns
do not raise level of qualification	ns	ns	ns	ns	ns	ns

Note (a) For symbols, see Table 6.1
Source: Bukodi (2017)

For women, the results presented in Table 9.3 turn out, in the case of further academic qualifications, to be on much the same lines as those for men. Where a woman raises her level of academic qualification, this increases her chances of upward worklife mobility in all three ways considered, and a new academic qualification that does not raise her academic level still improves her chances of upward mobility into the salariat. At the same time, further academic qualifications do no more for women than for men in reducing their risks of downward mobility.[8] However, in the case of further vocational qualifications, a contrast shows up. While for men, these qualifications prove to be unassociated with their worklife class mobility, for women they are, in certain respects, associated with their chances of upward mobility and – what may appear a quite counterintuitive finding – also with their chances of downward mobility.

[8] It should, though, be added that such further qualifications could have an indirect effect in this regard, in the case of men and women alike, insofar as they prevent an individual's *relative* qualification level from worsening, which, as was shown in Chapter 8, does increase the risk of downward mobility.

Table 9.3 *Effect of further qualifications on the probability of upward and downward worklife mobility, women*[a]

	Upward worklife mobility to			Downward worklife mobility from		
	Class			Class		
	any class	1 and 2	Class 1	any class	1 and 2	Class 1
New academic qualifications attained in past three years that						
raise level of qualification	++	++	++	ns	ns	ns
do not raise level of qualification	ns	++	++	ns	ns	ns
New vocational qualifications attained in past three years that						
raise level of qualification	++	++	ns	+	++	++
do not raise level of qualification	++	++	ns	++	++	ns

Note (a) For symbols, see Table 6.1
Source: Bukodi (2017)

As regards upward mobility, further vocational qualifications do appear to help women to increase their chances of relatively short-range movement – from, say, working-class to intermediate class positions or into the lower-level managerial and professional positions of Class 2 – although not into the higher-level positions of Class 1 – following, say, the Type 3 class trajectory for women that was identified in Chapter 7. As regards the association between further vocational qualifications and downward mobility, more detailed analyses reveal that this very largely comes about in rather specific circumstances involving women's balancing of work and family life. That is, as a result of women who were previously in salariat or intermediate class positions obtaining relatively low level vocational qualifications during or after some time out of the labour market, usually on account of priority being given to family commitments, and in preparation for re-entry although often only part-time and in some less advantaged class position.[9]

---

[9] See further Bukodi (2017). It should be noted that with many of these women, even a low-level vocational qualification will count as one raising their level of such qualification simply because they had no previous vocational qualifications at all. In the context of the discussion of women's mobility in Chapter 3, the

Vocational qualifications do then play a greater part in influencing women's worklife class mobility than men's. But it would still seem apparent that, in this regard, it is academic qualifications that are in general of main importance. And since we have previously shown that acquiring further academic qualifications is associated with more advantaged class origins, and especially with initial downward mobility from such origins, the evidence so far produced would suggest that, in intergenerational perspective, participation in lifelong learning may indeed contribute at least as much to class immobility as to class mobility. However, to complete our analyses, we need to go into somewhat more detail about how class origins and further academic qualifications come together in determining intergenerational mobility chances.

To do this, we work with a variant of our basic model, Model 1, under which we can estimate the probabilities of men and women experiencing upward mobility over the course of their working lives – that is, at all ages from 18 to 38 – according to whether or not they had obtained further academic qualifications within the past three years.[10] And we then compare these probabilities for individuals of Class 1 and 2 origins and Class 6 and 7 origins, again focusing on the same hypothetical persons as in Figures 9.1 and 9.2: that is, men and women in Class 3 positions with higher secondary qualifications. In the case of men, we consider upward mobility to Class 1 but in the case of women, because of the relatively small numbers accessing Class 1, we consider upward mobility to Classes 1 and 2 together. Results for men are graphed in Figure 9.3 and for women in Figure 9.4.

What may first be observed is that in all graphs the chances of our hypothetical persons being upwardly mobile from their initial Class 3 positions to a Class 1 position, or with women to a Class 1 or 2 position, are always greater for those of Class 1 and 2, or salariat, origins than for those of Class 6 and 7, or working-class, origins – regardless of whether or not they have obtained a new academic qualification in addition to their higher secondary qualification. In

women in question here would number among the part-timers who did *not* move into relatively low-level employment from the first. On women's downward worklife mobility linked with a move to part-time working, see Dex and Bukodi (2012).

[10] The same set of control variables are included as previously and also allowance is made for any interactions between obtaining further qualifications and age.

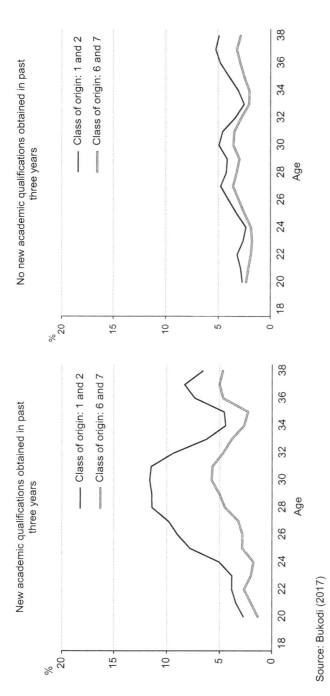

Source: Bukodi (2017)

Figure 9.3 Estimated probability of men moving up to Class 1 in the course of their working lives by class of origin and age, for men obtaining or not obtaining new academic qualifications in past three years

182

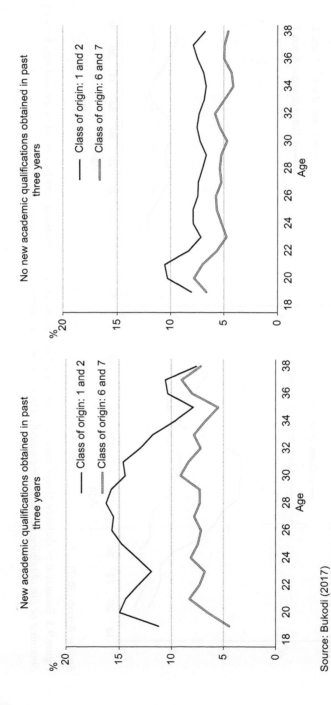

Source: Bukodi (2017)

Figure 9.4 Estimated probability of women moving up to Classes 1 and 2 in the course of their working lives by class of origin and age, for women obtaining or not obtaining new academic qualifications in past three years

other words – and as would be expected from the results reported in Chapter 8 – DESO is clearly present.

However, what can also be observed, in comparing the graphs in the left-hand and right-hand panels of the two figures, is that gaining a further academic qualification does increases the chances of upward mobility – *and more so, in absolute terms, for our hypothetical persons who are of salariat origins than for those who are of working-class origins*. Thus, for men who have gained no further academic qualification the chances of moving up to Class 1 remain generally low across the age range covered – never more than 5 per cent at any age even for those of salariat origin; for women, the chances of moving up to Classes 1 or 2 reach at most to around 10 per cent. But in the case of men and women who do obtain a further academic qualification, while the chances of upward mobility of those of working-class origins improve to some extent, the chances of those of salariat origins improve clearly more, and especially from the mid twenties to the early thirties: that is, the gaps that show up in the graphs are in general wider in the left-hand panels of the two figures than in the right-hand panels.

In answering the two questions from which we set out in this chapter, we have then produced fairly consistent evidence that further qualifications gained through lifelong learning do rather little to compensate for relatively low levels of educational attainment at labour market entry on the part of individuals of disadvantaged class origins, but that they do help individuals of more advantaged origins to add to the qualifications they have already acquired. On the one hand, vocational qualifications are those most frequently obtained, and while obtaining them is not associated with class origins in any systematic way, such qualifications have only limited effects in improving individuals' chances of upward worklife mobility. They do so for those women who acquire them, although not as regards accessing the higher-level managerial and professional positions of Class 1, but for men they would appear to have little effect at all. On the other hand, further academic qualifications are less often gained and it is individuals of advantaged class origins who are most likely to gain them. And while qualifications of this kind are in turn associated with generally improved chances of upward class mobility in the course of working life, it is individuals of advantaged origins who would appear to benefit most in this way. Taken overall, our results would therefore rather clearly indicate that while further qualifications obtained through lifelong learning may play some, rather modest, part in promoting class mobility, they are of greater importance as a driver of what we have earlier referred to as 'counter mobility': that is, upward mobility achieved by individuals in the course of their working lives that *offsets* their earlier downward mobility by reference to the position of their parents and thus leads to intergenerational *im*mobility.[11]

Counter mobility through further education – 1

Adam

Adam's father was a ship's captain in the Merchant Navy. Adam passed the 11-plus – 'you would have to be thick not to pass it' – and was in the top stream at grammar school. He did well in O levels and took maths, physics and chemistry at A level. He got an A in maths but failed physics and chemistry. His parents were divorcing at the time but he does not believe this is why he failed: 'We were 17, 18 and we were going out clubbing it ... every night. That was the only reason why.' He could not take up the university place he had been offered in civil engineering, and after various short-term jobs ended up working as a hospital laboratory technician.

However, after several years he found this work boring and decided he wanted to move on. In his mid twenties, he took ONCs and HNCs on day release courses and on this basis was able to enter university as a mature student. He obtained degree-level qualifications in psychology and biology, and has since followed a career as a biological scientist in industry and government. While at university, he married a fellow student: 'It worked out quite well, you know.'

---

[11] If – as we would think quite possible – counter mobility is more frequent in Britain than in many other countries, in part at least because of the high level of participation in further education, this could account for the fact, referred to in Chapter 5 (n. 3), that in the 1970 cohort the interaction effect within the OED triangle favouring greater fluidity among those with higher education disappears by the time individuals have reached their late thirties. It could be that the previously weak OD association existing for those with higher levels of E is subsequently strengthened as a result of more individuals from more advantaged origins improving their level of qualification and achieving upward mobility during the course of their working lives.

Counter mobility through further education – 2

Graham

Graham grew up in what he describes as a 'definitely middle-class' family. He was expected to do well at school and reached the sixth form without difficulty – but then failed all his A levels: 'I didn't want to be at school in the sixth form.' What he wanted was to get away from home and 'to see the world', so he entered the Merchant Navy College to train as a ship's radio operator. But, having qualified, he was unable to find a job of this kind and, rather than 'going on the dole', went to work as a technician at an engineering firm. A few years later he was made redundant but then, after various routine jobs, was taken on as a radio technician at a military airbase.

At this point he decided to resume his education, while continuing in his job, and enrolled on an Open University course in mathematics and computing. He completed this over a five-year period, obtaining a B.Sc. degree. He now works for an aeronautical engineering company. His salary is such that he has been able to pay off the mortgage on the house that he and his wife have bought in an attractive coastal area, and he looks forward to retiring 'on a good company pension'.

His relations with his family, especially with his father, were never close after he left school and home, but now, after his father's death, he is re-establishing closer ties with his mother and brothers.

Lifelong learning does, then, represent a particularly significant case as regards the relation between educational policy and social mobility. As noted at the end of the last chapter, there has of late been growing governmental interest in increasing participation in lifelong learning. This is seen as an important means of ensuring adequate levels of skill and expertise within the workforce in the context of continuing rapid technological and organisational change and of an aging population. And, as also noted, it has at the same time been supposed that greater participation in lifelong learning will serve to increase social mobility. However, research that has been officially commissioned with the apparent expectation of producing supportive evidence in this latter respect has in fact produced results that could, at best, be described as ambivalent.

Most notably, a Department of Business, Innovation and Skills Research Paper, specifically concerned with the contribution of further education to social mobility, turned out to show that this contribution was quite problematic. Unsurprisingly, the paper confirmed the findings of previous research that, far from further education fulfilling a compensatory role, it was individuals with already relatively high levels of qualification who were most likely to participate; and, on the basis of further analyses – which would in fact appear likely to underestimate the association between social origins and destinations – still only very patchy evidence could be produced of qualifications obtained through lifelong learning raising individuals' chances of upward mobility intergenerationally.[12]

Our own results point to some clearer, if perhaps still less congenial, conclusions. We have already observed at a number of points that, if a long view is taken, little evidence is apparent that educational policies of expansion and reform can, on their own, do much to increase levels of social mobility, whether considered in absolute or relative terms. But with lifelong learning a different, and yet more challenging, situation is indicated. An educational policy of more extensive and higher-quality provision for the upgrading of qualifications in the course of working life, with its own well-defined rationale in terms of benefits for the national economy as well as for the individuals involved, would at the same time appear likely to have actually *adverse* effects so far as social mobility is concerned. That is, because opportunities for lifelong

---

[12] The research was the work of economists (Gloster et al., 2015), based on the datasets of the British Household Panel Study and the Understanding Society survey. The main shortcoming of the research is the same as that which we have noted in other work by economists on social mobility: i.e. the remarkably casual way in which both social origins and destinations are understood and measured. Social origins are treated only on the basis of parents' education, and social destinations on the basis of a 'compressed' version of the old Registrar General's Social Classes, although, and contrary to what is suggested in the research report, it is entirely possible with the datasets in question to use NS-SEC as regards both origins and destinations. A further relevant official inquiry is the Government Office for Science project on the Future of Skills and Lifelong Learning. A commissioned literature review on factors influencing participation in lifelong learning (Tuckett and Field, 2016) has already been referred to (n. 5 above) – the findings of which have been nicely summed up by its lead author as 'If you don't at first succeed – you don't succeed.' We were ourselves involved in the early stages of this project and presented some of our results relating to further education and social mobility; but this topic would seem subsequently to have dropped off the agenda.

learning turn out to provide 'second chances' not so much for men and women whose disadvantaged social origins have had limiting effects on their educational attainment prior to labour market entry, but more for those of more advantaged origins who while in full-time education have not realised their advantages to the full extent that they might.

What emerges from this situation that is of wider societal significance is in fact reinforcement for an argument we put forward earlier in Chapters 5 and 6. The consequences of educational policies will only be adequately assessed if the individuals they affect are not regarded as being uniform and passive, and if their probable reactions to particular policies are taken into account on the basis of an understanding of their differing motivations and resources. Thus, opportunities that allow for the avoidance of downward mobility on the part of individuals with resources adequate to pursue them could be expected to be more often exploited than opportunities for upward mobility for individuals whose more limited resources must mean that in deciding whether or not to take up these opportunities far more difficult cost–benefit considerations are likely to arise. Or, more generally, one could say, the impact of educational policy on the existing social order will always be strongly conditioned by the nature of the reception that policy initiatives receive from individuals holding more or less advantaged positions within this order.

10 Social Mobility in Britain in Comparative Perspective: Is Britain a Low Mobility Society?

As we noted in the Introduction, although the main concern of our work is with the detailed analysis of social mobility in Britain, it is often revealing to take a cross-national comparative view; and the question that in this case most obviously arises is that of how levels of mobility in Britain match up with those found in other modern societies.

In official circles, it has become widely believed, and asserted, that Britain is a low mobility society. Most notably, claims to this effect have been repeatedly made in the annual reports of the Social Mobility Commission. For example, the 2013 report states that Britain 'is a low mobility society compared to other developed countries'; the 2015 report starts out from the proposition that 'Britain has lower levels of social mobility than most other comparable countries'; and the 2016 report reaffirms that Britain has a 'deep social mobility problem'.[1] Such contentions then serve, in the same way as those of declining mobility, to justify the importance that is given across the political spectrum to increasing mobility. However, in Chapters 2 and 3 we have shown that the evidence of mobility in decline is open to serious question, and we can now ask whether the same might not be true of the evidence that underlies the view that in British society mobility is unusually restricted.

To begin with, it may be observed that in this latter case just as in the former, it turns out that such supporting evidence as exists relates only to income – or in fact for the most part only to earnings – mobility, which could in itself be thought a significant limitation. And what can then be further said is that the evidence in question derives from analyses that are based on data of often doubtful reliability, that involve uncertainty as to whether it is absolute or relative mobility

---

[1] See Social Mobility and Child Poverty Commission (2013: 126); Social Mobility Commission (2015: 1, 2016: 1–3).

that is at issue, and that are not confirmed in their conclusions by other analyses of generally superior quality.

The sources most often invoked when the claim is made that Britain is a low mobility society are two: a report sponsored by the Sutton Trust and a report of the Organisation for Economic Co-operation and Development. These reports relate to different sets of countries and apply different measures of mobility but both purport to show that, at least so far as men are concerned, Britain (or, in the case of the OECD report, the UK) has clearly lower levels of income mobility than do the other countries that are covered – apart from the US – and, in particular, lower levels than the Nordic countries, which appear the most mobile.[2]

However, the data problems generally associated with studies of income mobility that we referred to in Chapter 1 are clearly present. Thus, for some of the countries in the OECD report, fathers' earnings are not observed but are imputed from other data, usually on fathers' education or occupation, with a consequent large increase in the margin of error involved. And in the Sutton Trust report, cross-national comparability is impaired in that for some countries, including Britain, it is parental income from all sources rather than father's earnings that serves as the 'origin' variable – and it is notable that in all such cases *lower* mobility is indicated than in the others. Further, the OECD report relies largely on a measure of income mobility, known as 'the intergenerational earnings elasticity', that reflects not only the strength of the net association between the earnings of fathers and sons but also changes in the degree of earnings inequality between the fathers' and sons' generations. Absolute and relative mobility are thus confounded. Intergenerational changes in earnings inequality should not enter into the comparative assessment of relative earnings mobility, which – it would appear – is the main concern of the report.[3]

---

[2] The report sponsored by the Sutton Trust is Blanden, Gregg and Machin (2005b), who for Britain draw on the analyses of data from the 1970 cohort study by Blanden et al. (2004) referred to in Chapters 2 and 3. The OECD report is d'Addio (2007). Further OECD reports that seek to underwrite d'Addio's conclusions, though without adding any results of direct relevance, are Causa, Danton and Johansson (2009) and OECD (2010).

[3] The intergenerational earnings elasticity indicates the proportion of the difference in parents' earnings that is transmitted, on average, to children. It may thus serve some descriptive purposes but it is of very doubtful value for comparative analyses, since the confounding of factors involved means that countries can have

Not surprisingly, then, other researchers in the field have shown some scepticism over these findings, and from analyses in which problems of data and measurement have been more seriously treated results have been obtained that differ in two main respects. First, once due account is taken of the likely error in estimates, the range of cross-national variation in income mobility appears a good deal less than might otherwise be supposed; and second, within this more limited range of variation, Britain would seem most reliably placed in a middling rather than an extreme position, closer in fact to the Nordic countries than to the US, and with a level of mobility that is not obviously lower than that of other major European societies such as France, the former West Germany and Italy.[4] However, the results of these later studies of income mobility, which do not fit well with the favoured narrative, have been simply ignored within British political and policy discourse on social mobility.

What, then, is the situation if we turn to studies of comparative social mobility carried out by sociologists and focused on intergenerational class mobility? The first point to make is that in these studies, at least from the 1970s onwards, the distinction between absolute and relative mobility has always been central.

As regards absolute mobility, a large degree of consensus is apparent on the following lines. Total mobility rates can show some rather wide range of variation, depending primarily on the historical development

---

different – or similar – elasticities for quite different reasons. The Sutton Trust report mainly uses the correlation between father's earnings – or family income – and son's earnings. This is a better measure of relative mobility, although still based on the assumption that the intergenerational relation between incomes or earnings is linear, which is known not always to be the case.

[4] See in particular Björklund and Jäntti (2009: fig. 20.1) and the further discussion in Jäntti and Jenkins (2015). Björklund and Jäntti also work with the intergenerational earnings elasticity – while recognising its limitations – but put confidence intervals around their estimates of it for each country that they cover, and these intervals turn out in many cases to overlap. It should also be noted that in later work Blanden (2013) has taken a far more cautious position on the extent of cross-national variation in income mobility than the Sutton Trust report does; that a recent study treating mobility on the basis of a measure of socioeconomic status, combining income and education, has found that among fourteen modern societies the UK had the fourth lowest correlation between parents' and children's status (Ballarino and Bernardi, 2016: fig. 16.1); and that Jerrim (2017b) has directly questioned the idea of Britain as a low mobility society on the basis of comparative analyses relating men's earnings to the educational level of their fathers.

of countries' class structures. The positions of countries within this range are then likely to change over time as the development of their class structures proceeds. In the middle of the last century, the British total mobility rate would appear to have been around the European average – while perhaps being a little below that of the US – and was mainly kept at this level by the increase in upward mobility during the early stages of the expansion of the managerial and professional salariat (see Figure 2.1). Countries with lower total rates were those with still large agricultural sectors characterised by high immobility, such as Ireland or Poland – and, one could almost certainly add, Spain and Portugal – while other European countries, such as France, Italy or Sweden, had higher rates than Britain, mainly because of the outflow of individuals from rapidly declining agricultural classes. However, by the end of the century some degree of convergence in the shapes of the class structures of western societies was in train, and in turn cross-national variation in absolute mobility was reduced. The British total mobility rate changed rather little but that of other countries tended overall to move closer to it. In sum, sociological research on intergenerational class mobility relating to the twentieth century provides no indication at all of Britain being a distinctively low mobility society so far as absolute rates are concerned.[5]

As regards relative mobility, sociologists differ somewhat over the extent of cross-national variation and over the degree to which, insofar as such variation occurs, it is in some way systematic or reflects only historically formed cultural or institutional features of particular societies. According to the liberal theory of the transition from industrial to postindustrial society, as outlined in Chapter 5, a general tendency should prevail for relative rates of class mobility to become more equal – that is, for social fluidity to increase – as an education-based meritocracy comes into being. And some early studies did indeed claim to show a 'world-wide secular trend' in this direction, so that while countries' levels of relative mobility varied, this variation was systematically related to the progress they had made towards postindustrialism. But these studies have been subject to criticism concerning both the comparability of the data used and the methods of analysis applied, and their findings have not been consistently replicated by subsequent

---

[5] See in particular Erikson and Goldthorpe (1992: chs. 3, 6); Breen and Luijkx (2004a, b).

research. A contrasting view, claiming more empirical support, is one that would place greater emphasis on the similarities that exist in levels and patterns of relative rates among modern societies – that is, in their endogenous mobility regimes – even if with some degree of variation of a nationally specific kind. However, what for our present purposes is of main relevance is that regardless of which of these two positions has been favoured, Britain still emerges from the analyses that have been undertaken *as a rather unexceptional case* – somewhat less fluid than the Nordic social democracies or, while they existed, the communist, or 'state socialist', societies of east-central Europe, but more fluid than a number of other western European societies.[6]

The studies referred to in the foregoing are ones based on data collected in different national surveys carried out from the 1970s through to the 1990s and are now therefore somewhat dated. They are also studies reliant on extensive recoding exercises, which have been necessary to bring the data from the national surveys used so far as possible into comparable form. In order to make some advance in both these respects, we go on to present analyses of comparative mobility that are based on a new dataset that extends into the twenty-first century and that derives from a series of surveys *of cross-national design*, thus providing data that have a high degree of comparability from the start. This dataset is constructed from the first five waves of the European Social Survey (ESS), carried out between 2002 and 2010, which involved face-to-face interviews with individuals in probability samples taken from the adult populations of thirty countries. The samples range in size from 4,740 in Germany down to 891 in Italy. We focus on men and women who were aged 25 to 64 at time of interview. In the case of women, we also limit our analyses here to those who, when interviewed, were working full-time. With women working part-time, selection processes and employment conditions vary cross-nationally to an extent that would make separate analyses necessary.[7]

---

[6] The main study claiming a general movement towards greater social fluidity linked to economic development, and from which the phrase 'world-wide secular trend' is taken, is Ganzeboom, Luijkx and Treiman (1989). For critiques, see Wong (1990), Jones (1992) and Erikson and Goldthorpe (1992: chs. 4, 5). The latter authors develop the idea of nationally specific variation around a common 'core' pattern of social fluidity.

[7] This limitation means that in the case of women we have to omit Italy since the effective sample size becomes too small.

For the purposes of establishing intergenerational class mobility rates, survey respondents' class positions at time of interview are related to the class positions of their parents when respondents were age 14 according to the seven-class version of the European Socio-Economic Classification (ESEC), which is in effect a European version of the British NS-SEC (see Table 1.1).[8] Our dataset is obviously restricted in that it allows us to consider variation in social mobility only across European countries. Nonetheless, this would still appear an adequate context within which to examine further the comparative standing of Britain – or, in the case of the ESS, the UK.[9]

We begin with absolute rates. In Figure 10.1 we show the total mobility rates for men (with 95 per cent confidence intervals) using the seven ESEC classes: that is, the percentage of men found in a different class to that of their parents. What should first of all be noted is *the very limited range of cross-national variation*. In almost all cases, the rates fall between 70 and 80 per cent. Second, as regards the position of the UK, it may be observed, first of all, that the total rate, at approaching 80 per cent, is reassuringly close to that which we showed for Britain in Figure 2.3 on the basis of our data from the cohort studies, and then further that, within the range of variation that exists, this rate puts the UK *among the more mobile European societies*.

In Figure 10.2 we show corresponding total mobility rates for women who are in full-time employment. The rates are in general somewhat higher than for men but almost all still fall within the 70 to 80 per cent range; and while there are some differences in the ordering of the countries, the UK with a rate of close to 80 per cent again ranks high.

So far, then, as total mobility rates are concerned, there is no support at all for the idea that Britain is a low mobility society, although cross-national variation in this regard is in fact quite restricted. As we have emphasised, total rates of class mobility are primarily determined by the shape, and changes in the shape, of the class structure; and what can be taken as underlying the large degree of cross-national similarity in these rates that is apparent in Figures 10.1 and 10.2 is the

---

[8] For full details of ESEC, see Rose and Harrison (2010).
[9] For full details of the dataset, see Bukodi, Paskov and Nolan (2017).

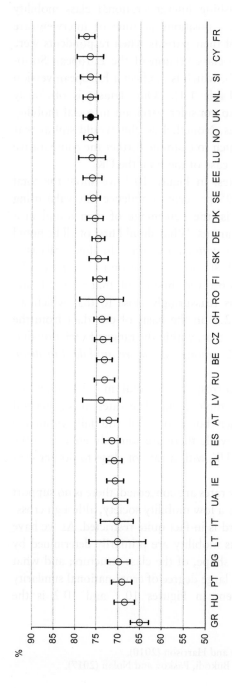

GR: Greece, HU: Hungary, PT: Portugal, BG: Bulgaria, LT: Lithuania, IT: Italy, UA: Ukraine, IE: Ireland, PL: Poland, ES: Spain, AT: Austria, LV: Latvia, RU: Russia, BE: Belgium, CZ: Czech Republic, CH: Switzerland, RO: Romania, FI: Finland, SK: Slovakia, DE: Germany, DK: Denmark, SE: Sweden, EE: Estonia, LU: Luxembourg, NO: Norway, UK: United Kingdom, NL: Netherlands, SI: Slovenia, CY: Cyprus, FR: France

Source: Bukodi, Paskov and Nolan (2017)

Figure 10.1 Total mobility rate (%), with 95% confidence interval, by country, men aged 25–64

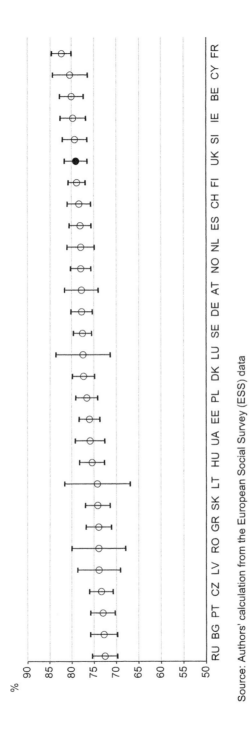

Source: Authors' calculation from the European Social Survey (ESS) data

Figure 10.2 Total mobility rate (%), with 95% confidence interval, by country, women aged 25–64, in full-time employment

continuation through into the twenty-first century of the convergence in the shapes of national class structures that was previously referred to.

It has, however, at the same time to be recognised that this convergence is occurring from sometimes quite different starting points and in different societal contexts; and this is reflected in the fact that, despite the high degree of cross-national similarity in total mobility rates, further analyses, in which we use the hierarchical divisions within ESEC corresponding to those within NS-SEC (see again Table1.1), do reveal greater variation in the relative importance of the upward and downward components of the total rates. Figures 10.3 and 10.4 show for each national case the ratio of the upward to the downward component.

Focusing first on men, it can be seen from Figure 10.3 that the differences in the ratios are quite marked. There are some countries in which the upward component of the total rate is clearly larger than the downward. Most notable in this regard is a geographically contiguous west-central group, comprising Austria, Germany, Switzerland and the Benelux countries, but also included are several southern European countries in our dataset – Cyprus, Portugal and Spain – and Ireland. In all these countries the growth of the managerial and professional salariat would appear to have continued rather strongly over the recent past. In contrast, there are countries in which downward mobility is clearly more common than upward. Included here are countries that were formerly part of the USSR – Estonia, Latvia and Russia itself – together with several other post-communist countries, Bulgaria, the Czech Republic, Hungary and Poland. In these cases, it seems likely that men's mobility chances in particular have been adversely affected by the reduced availability of higher-level positions in declining heavy industries and also by the dismantling of extensive state and party bureaucracies.[10] Finally, there are countries in which the upward and downward components of the total rate are more or less equal. These include the remaining post-communist countries, the Nordic countries,

---

[10] Older respondents to the ESS in post-communist countries will have spent some part of their working lives under communism. But the changes that occurred in these countries during the transition period are known often to have created 'period' as much as 'cohort' effects – i.e. ones bearing more or less equally on individuals of all ages alike. For Russia, where period effects appear to have been particularly strong, see Gerber and Hout (2004).

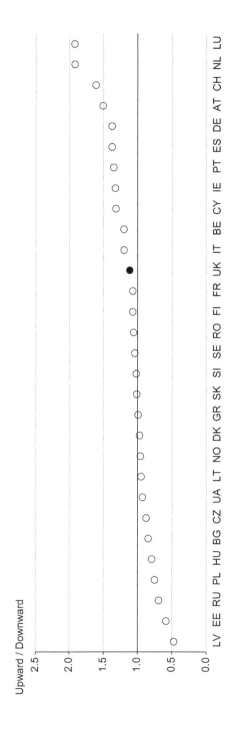

Source: Bukodi, Paskov and Nolan (2017)

Figure 10.3 Ratio of upward mobility to downward mobility by country, men aged 25–64

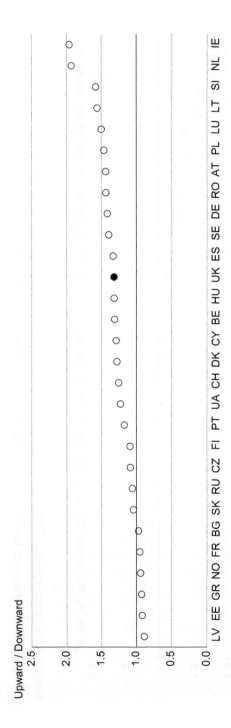

Source: Authors' calculation from the European Social Survey (ESS) data

Figure 10.4 Ratio of upward mobility to downward mobility by country, women aged 25–64, in full-time employment

France, Italy – and the UK. The common factor here would appear to be that the managerial and professional salariat has become more or less stable in size or, at all events, is no longer growing at the same rate as it once did.

Turning to women in full-time employment, in Figure 10.4, we find a generally more favourable situation as regards the balance of upward and downward mobility, which is what might be expected given that these women will tend to be in higher-level employment than those working only part-time. However, while there are no countries in which for women who work full-time downward mobility is clearly a more common experience than upward, there are ones in which the difference is slight. These are mostly post-USSR or other post-communist countries, but Finland and Norway among the Nordic countries are also included and so too is France. The UK appears as one of the countries in which the upward component of the total rate is only moderately higher than the downward.

What emerges from these findings of specific significance for Britain is, we would suggest, the following. If Britain's comparative position is considered together with the trends in upward and downward mobility for men and for women working both full- and part-time that we earlier presented (Figures 2.3 and 2.4) and also with the evidence of the slowing growth of managerial and professional employment after the rapid expansion of the golden age (Figure 2.1), then the distinct possibility arises that Britain could shortly become another country in which individuals' chances of moving down within the class structure are greater than their chances of moving up. We earlier argued that the neglect of this possibility in the political discussion of mobility in Britain can be related to the misplaced concern that has existed over mobility in decline. We may now add that a further factor in its neglect would appear to be the equally misplaced concern over Britain as a low mobility society. So far as cross-national differences exist in total rates of intergenerational class mobility, Britain can in fact be counted as a high mobility society; but it is in the actual, and in the potential future, change in the balance of social ascent and descent that a real mobility problem can be identified.

We now move on to a consideration of relative rates. We follow essentially the same statistical modelling strategy as in Chapter 3. That is, we use the constant association (CA) and uniform difference (UNI-DIFF) models there described, but instead of applying them to class mobility tables for successive birth cohorts in Britain in order to examine change in relative rates over time, we apply them to class mobility tables for the European countries in our dataset in order to examine variation in relative rates across these countries – and to determine the UK's comparative position. Results for men are shown in Figure 10.5 and for women in Figure 10.6.

These figures are to be understood as follows. The average of the UNIDIFF parameters resulting from fitting this model to the mobility tables *of each pair* of countries involved is set at zero, and the individual countries are then ordered in terms of their deviation from this average according to the average of the UNIDIFF parameters from each of the pairwise comparisons in which they were themselves involved. Negative deviations indicate that the odds ratios capturing the association between class origins and destinations in a country's mobility table are uniformly lower than the average – that is, there is greater social fluidity within its class structure – while, conversely, positive deviations indicate that the odds ratios are uniformly higher than the average – that is, there is less social fluidity. It can then be seen from Figures 10.5 and 10.6 that with both men and women in full-time employment, the UK comes close to the high fluidity end of this ordering.

However, what is further indicated, by the country markers being unshaded or shaded, is whether or not *the difference with the UK* is statistically significant so far as the overall level of fluidity is concerned. It turns out that, in the case of men, the UK does not differ in this respect from any of the other fourteen countries that fall below the line of the average, and that, in the case of women, from any of the other fourteen countries that fall below or more or less on this line. In ten of the fourteen comparisons involved for men and in eleven of those for women, the CA model – in this context better understood as the *common* rather than the constant association model – does in fact give an adequate fit to the data, while in the remaining cases this model fits less well but is not improved on by the UNIDIFF model. That is to say, although in these latter cases some differences from the UK exist in the pattern of social fluidity, no systematic difference in the level of fluidity shows up. The point of main importance that emerges is that it is from countries *above* the average line that the UK can be most reliably set apart: that is to say, from countries with class mobility regimes *that entail less fluidity*.

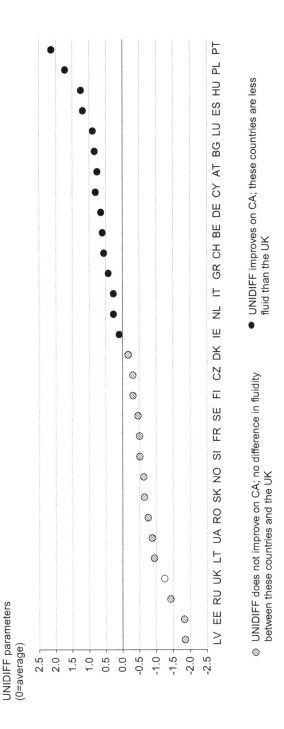

Source: Bukodi, Paskov and Nolan (2017)

Figure 10.5 Country differences in relative rates of social mobility, men aged 25–64

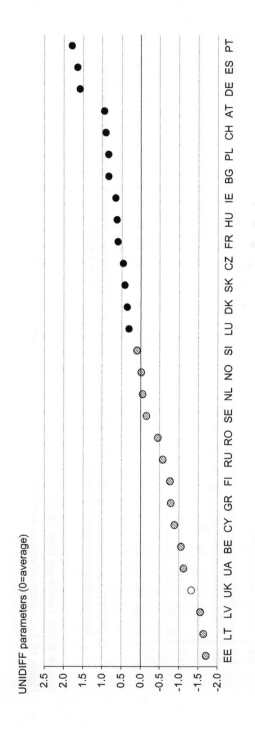

Source: Authors' calculation from the European Social Survey (ESS) data

Figure 10.6 Country differences in relative rates of social mobility, women aged 25–64, in full-time employment

With relative rates of class mobility, just as with absolute rates, there is therefore no evidence whatever of the UK – or, one could safely say, of Britain – being a low mobility society, at all events in a European context. The UK can rather be seen as one of a fairly large number of countries that in fact share largely similar mobility regimes so far as a – comparatively – high level of fluidity is concerned. In the case of men, Figure 10.5 shows that the countries that make up this number fall into three groups: first, the UK plus France and, marginally, Ireland, together with the Nordic countries, forming what might be labelled a west Nordic group; second, those that have emerged from the former USSR; and third, a group comprising several other post-communist countries. The countries with less fluid mobility regimes also fall into three groups: one made up of Austria, Germany, Switzerland and the Benelux countries – that is, the same west-central bloc we earlier identified as having a favourable balance of upward and downward absolute mobility rates – though with the Netherlands now being marginal to the west Nordic group; then one comprising the southern European countries in our dataset, with Italy being possibly marginal to the west Nordic group; and finally one made up of the remaining post-communist countries, Bulgaria, Hungary and Poland. In the case of women, as Figure 10.6 reveals, some differences from this pattern arise, but not for the most part ones of a very substantial kind. And, most relevant for our present concerns, the UK clearly remains in the comparatively high fluidity group.[11]

Given the prevailing insistence in official discourse that Britain is a low mobility society, the results shown in Figures 10.5 and 10.6 may strike some readers as surprising – even implausible. However, in the context of sociological research, past and present, they could not in fact be regarded as at all out of the way. On the one hand, as was previously indicated, in comparative analyses relating to the twentieth century, Britain was not found to have exceptionally unequal relative rates. And, on the other hand, while these earlier analyses did show the Nordic social democracies and also the existing east-central communist

---

[11] For more detailed discussion, see Bukodi and Goldthorpe (2017). A further study of comparative class mobility based on the ESS is Eurofound (2017). This covers a smaller number of countries and, because of a focus on change across (quasi-)cohorts, most analyses are based on a rather crude threefold collapse of ESEC, which makes it difficult to compare the results reported with our own. However, it is again the case that no evidence at all emerges to support the idea of Britain as a society with distinctively low fluidity within its class structure.

societies as having greater fluidity than Britain, more recent research has clearly pointed to the possibility of these differences diminishing. In the Nordic countries it appears that increasing fluidity, rather than being sustained through to the present time, has to be seen as a distinctive feature of certain earlier birth cohorts, so that, through processes of cohort replacement, the level of fluidity has stabilised. And it has been consistently found that in former communist countries economic liberalisation or 'marketisation' and the ending of close state control of the educational system and of its linkages with the labour market, directed towards egalitarian ends, have led to a general decline in social fluidity and, in some cases, of a very sharp kind.[12]

In sum, it is difficult to avoid the conclusion that, rather than the idea of Britain as a low mobility society being derived from any serious examination of the body of relevant research – whether relating to income or to class mobility or to absolute or to relative rates – *it is essentially a political construction*: that is, an idea that it has been found convenient to advance in support of the attempt, made across party political lines, to form a response to increasing inequality of condition in Britain primarily through a policy emphasis on raising levels of mobility.

What, then, are the implications of our findings on comparative mobility in a European context for a better grounded understanding of mobility in Britain?

As regards absolute rates, we can only repeat that what should chiefly command attention in the British case is not the total mobility rate, which, within the limited range of cross-national variation that exists, is quite high, but rather the balance of the upward and downward components of this rate, which is clearly less favourable than in a number of other countries and, on the evidence of trends we have earlier presented, is tending to worsen. This is a matter over which serious political concern would be justified but has, so far, been largely lacking. It is in this connection of some interest to note that in the group of west-central European countries, where upward mobility still predominates over downward, issues of social mobility would appear to have far less political and public prominence than in Britain. This may be due in some part to the fact that in these countries social inequality has

---

[12] On the Nordic countries, see for Sweden, Jonsson (2004) and Breen and Jonsson (2007) and for Finland, Erola (2009); on post-communist countries, see for Russia, Gerber and Hout (2004), for Hungary, Bukodi and Goldthorpe (2010) and for an important comparative analysis, Jackson and Evans (2017).

increased less strongly than in Britain – with therefore politicians feeling less need to focus on mobility. But insofar as mobility arouses less public discussion and anxiety, what may be of main importance is that, despite the comparatively low fluidity that prevails in these countries, the actual experience of mobility among their populations remains similar to that of the British population during the golden age.

As regards relative rates, what would appear to be of main importance is that our findings indicate that rather than European countries varying in their levels of fluidity in some quite continuous way, they tend to fall into a number of groups with more or less distinctive levels. And this in turn suggests that such variation in fluidity might best be understood not by seeking to relate it directly to variation in other macro-social features, such as level of economic development or economic inequality, but rather by considering further the possibility we raised at the end of Chapter 5. That is, that in all societies with a capitalist market economy, a nuclear family system and a liberal democratic polity, some limit exists to the extent to which relative mobility chances can be equalised, primarily on account of the capacity of more advantaged families to use their superior resources, economic but also social and cultural, in order to maintain their children's competitive edge – their greater chances of success in the educational system and in turn in the labour market; and that, as this limit is approached, further attempts to equalise relative chances of class mobility, in having to extend beyond educational policy, will meet with increasing political difficulties.

On this view, certain of the countries in the comparatively high fluidity set that we have identified, that is, the west Nordic group including Britain, could be taken as ones that are coming close to the limit that is suggested, while the post-communist countries in this set are ones *moving away from this limit* as the levels of fluidity they were able to achieve under authoritarian state regulation are now being reduced following their transition to some form of capitalist democracy. At the same time, it can also be recognised that countries may fall some way short of the limit, or recede from it, to differing extents and for quite different reasons.

For example, in such post-communist cases as Bulgaria, Hungary and Poland it would appear that particular features of their transitions have had an especially powerful effect in widening relative mobility chances, thus changing these countries over a period of only a few decades from being probably among those with the highest levels of social fluidity in Europe to being among those with the lowest. However, with the southern European countries included in our analyses, low fluidity has obviously other sources. It would seem likely that in these countries their level of economic development does take on major importance: that is, as regards their still relatively large agricultural sectors, the size of the class of small entrepreneurs within which a marked propensity for immobility, especially for men, is typically found (cf. Chapter 4), and their high educational as well as income inequality. But with the west-central European countries that also show comparatively low fluidity a different situation again has to be recognised. These are economically advanced countries with high standards of living and income inequality that is generally lower than in Britain. In their case it would appear that low fluidity is primarily the result of stratified educational systems coexisting with distinctively strong linkages between their educational systems and labour markets. Or, to revert to the OED triangle, one could say that these countries have lower fluidity than Britain, and likewise France and the Nordic countries, because not only the OE but, perhaps more importantly, *also the ED association* is stronger. There is thus a greater danger of credentialist restrictions on mobility, and education is far more likely to be 'class destiny'.[13]

If such an interpretation of our comparative findings on relative rates of class mobility has any validity, then what follows for Britain is that, as a country coming close to the limit on fluidity that we have proposed, it is one in which attempts to further equalise relative rates – even though, as was shown in Chapter 4, these do remain at the extremes highly unequal – will require political intervention of a kind likely to meet with strong opposition; far stronger than than that raised against present attempts directed primarily at continuing educational expansion and reform. We pursue these issues further in our final concluding chapter.

---

[13] The German case is by far the most studied. For discussion of the 'highly institutionalised' relations prevailing between education, employment and class positions, see Müller and Pollak (2004) and for more detailed analyses, Klein (2011) and Grätz and Pollak (2016). The countries in question may of course benefit in that there are better guarantees of skill in particular occupations: Germany does not suffer from 'cowboy builders'.

Conclusions

In this final chapter we first of all sum up the main findings from the research on which we have reported, and note again where these findings are in contradiction to what is claimed or supposed in current discussion of social mobility in political and policy contexts. We then aim to show how this discussion might in future be conducted on a more secure evidential basis and to bring out some of the implications for policy that would follow.

We list below the leading conclusions that emerge in regard to the substantive issues we have successively taken up in Chapters 2 to 10, basing our analyses throughout primarily on mobility in terms of social class, which, we believe, allows the best estimates to be made of the intergenerational transmission of economic advantage and disadvantage. Relatively minor qualifications that we have previously made to these conclusions are here ignored, but readers are reminded that they do exist.

- Contrary to what has become a widely held view, there has been no decline in absolute intergenerational social mobility in Britain over the recent past, at all events if mobility is treated in terms of class. Men and women born in the 1970s and 1980s are just as likely as those born in the 1940s to be found in different class positions to those of their parents. However, a significant change has occurred in that while earlier, in what has become known as the golden age of mobility, social ascent predominated over social descent, the experience of upward mobility is now becoming less common and that of downward mobility more common. *In this sense*, young people today face less favourable mobility prospects than did their parents or their grandparents. This change is primarily the result of the course of development of the class structure – in particular, of the slowing down of the previous rate of growth of the managerial and professional salariat.

- There has also been no decline in intergenerational class mobility if considered in relative terms or, that is, no decline in social fluidity within the class structure. The relative chances of men and women of different class origins being found in different class destinations have remained remarkably constant over decades. The one exception is a – slight – *increase* in fluidity among women, resulting from some growth in the number of those from more advantaged class origins whose part-time working implies downward intergenerational mobility: that is, women who under existing constraints appear to give priority to family life rather than seeking to exploit their advantages to the full in the context of their own working lives. For the most part, however, what might be called the endogenous mobility regime shows a powerful resistance to change.
- Over-time constancy extends to the pattern as well as the level of relative rates of class mobility. These rates can be shown to be structured by the effects of class hierarchy, class inheritance and status affinity in an essentially unchanging way, and on much the same lines for men and women alike. With short-range mobility transitions inequalities in relative mobility chances are often quite small – 'perfect mobility' is approximated; but with longer-range transitions, as class hierarchy and inheritance effects come increasingly into play, these inequalities widen to a quite extreme extent. Men originating in NS-SEC Class 1 are twenty times more likely to be themselves found in Class 1 rather than in Class 7 than are men originating in Class 7.
- If education is to play the key role in increasing social mobility that is typically assigned to it in political discourse, then certain – often unrecognised – conditions have to be met. The association between individuals' class origins and their educational attainment must weaken, while the association between their educational attainment and their eventual class destinations strengthens, and no offsetting change occurs in the effect of origins on destinations that is *not* mediated via education. However, if education is considered in relative terms, as would appear appropriate insofar as its possible impact on social mobility is concerned, then the associations in question show little change over the historical period that our research covers. It is again the degree of stability of the mobility regime that is notable – despite more or less continuous educational expansion and reform, and often with the express aim of increasing equality of opportunity.

- Even if education is considered in absolute rather than in relative terms – that is, as a consumption rather than an investment good – there is still no evidence of educational inequalities linked to social origins being reduced, at least once social origins are treated in a comprehensive way so as to include parental social status and education as well as parental class. And this finding holds good when early life cognitive ability is also included in the analysis. Considering individuals with similar levels of cognitive ability, those from more advantaged social origins have significantly higher educational attainment than those from less advantaged social origins, and there is little indication of such disparities decreasing over time. Many men and women thus do not realise their full academic potential, and in this way a substantial wastage of talent occurs.

- Analyses of individuals' class histories in relation to their educational attainment show that, as compared with the situation in the first half of the twentieth century, there are now greater numbers of men and women entering higher-level managerial and professional positions directly on completing tertiary education – and remaining in such positions subsequently. But over the more recent past there has been no systematic decrease in the numbers achieving upward mobility during the course of their working lives. The achievement of such worklife mobility is associated with more advantaged social origins and, in some cases, with a relatively high level of cognitive ability, in addition to educational qualifications. When considered *independently of* social origins and cognitive ability, education has not, as seems often believed, increasingly become class destiny. No general and sustained movement towards an education-based meritocracy is apparent.

- The effect of individuals' class origins on their class destinations that is not mediated via education – that is, the so-called direct effect – is yet again a feature of the mobility regime that would appear to have remained constant over time. The direct effect can be shown to be especially marked if social origins are taken to comprise parental status and education as well as class. Both glass ceilings and glass floors are created, and the latter, preventing the downward mobility of individuals of more advantaged origins who have only modest levels of educational attainment, appear if anything the more important. At the same time, though, education pursued over the course of individuals' working lives, if it leads to an improvement in their relative qualifications level, does continue to have an effect on their chances of accessing the salariat and avoiding working-class positions. As regards the mediating factors that underlie the direct effect itself, parental help in the labour market proves to be less important than individual characteristics, such as cognitive ability and internal locus of control – which are themselves associated with social origins – but other factors are also involved including, very possibly, parental wealth.

- Contrary to what has been generally expected, or at least hoped for, lifelong learning – whatever other individual and social benefits it may confer – contributes less to mobility than to immobility in intergenerational perspective. Rather than providing a way in which individuals of less advantaged social origins can compensate for low levels of attainment within mainstream education, it serves as a way in which individuals of more advantaged origins can build on qualifications that they have earlier acquired and, in cases where they have been downwardly mobile at labour market entry, thus improve their chances of counter mobility back to their parents' position. In this connection, further academic qualifications are of far greater value, and especially for men, than are further vocational qualifications.

- Whether class mobility is considered in absolute or relative terms, Britain is not a low mobility society, despite claims to this effect being repeatedly made, notably by the Social Mobility Commission. As regards absolute class mobility, cross-national variation in total rates is not all that wide but, within such variation as exists, the British rate is towards the high end of at least the European range. However, Britain is not among those European countries in which the upward component of the total rate remains clearly greater than the downward, and could be moving towards a situation in which the reverse is the case. As regards relative mobility, Britain again appears at the high end of the European range, being one of group of west Nordic countries whose levels of social fluidity may in fact be approximating a limit for countries with a capitalist market economy, a nuclear family system and a liberal-democratic polity: that is, in the sense that policies aimed at further equalising relative rates will have to be ones going beyond educational expansion and reform and of kind that are likely to be far more strongly contested.

Given these findings, what implications do they carry for a better public understanding of social mobility and for a more securely evidence-based approach to the identification of, and policy responses to, the problems that may be thought to arise? In this regard, we believe it crucial to maintain the distinction we have insisted on throughout between mobility as considered in absolute and in relative terms. Neglect of this distinction is a major source of confusion in much discussion of policy.

So far as absolute mobility is concerned, what most obviously follows from our findings is that it is not the overall level of absolute mobility, or any decline in this level, that constitutes a problem, but rather that rates of upward mobility are falling and rates of downward mobility rising. Where mobility is treated in terms of social class, it is generally found that changes in the level and pattern of absolute rates are overwhelmingly determined by changes in the shape of the class structure, and we have shown that this is indeed the case in Britain today. The end of the golden age of mobility was brought about by a falling off in the rate of growth of the managerial and professional salariat after its rapid expansion over the postwar decades, resulting in a growing number of individuals from advantaged class origins who are at risk of downward mobility. What is therefore implied is that any movement back to the situation of the golden age, when upward mobility predominated over downward, must be dependent upon the further upgrading of the class structure. It is important here to recognise that while achieving a greater equality in relative rates would lead to an increase in total mobility, *it could contribute nothing to the balance between social ascent and descent*. For, as we have emphasised and illustrated in Chapter 3, any such equalisation – any increase in fluidity within the class structure – must raise levels of upward and downward mobility to exactly the same degree.

What policy areas are then of most relevance? Educational policy should not in fact be seen as of primary importance, even if it may have a part to play in supplementing other policies. As we argued in Chapter 2, the supply-side scenario envisaged by Gordon Brown, in which the creation of a highly qualified labour force pulls into Britain a steady stream of 'top end' jobs from around the world, is unlikely to be realised to any significant extent, since Britain, along with other advanced societies, is at an evident disadvantage in the 'global auction' that operates in this regard. Rather, demand for higher-level employment must be essentially created within the national economy; and in this connection it is policy in areas other than education that would appear to have greatest potential – although in current discussion of social mobility this appears to be surprisingly under-appreciated.

This point is perhaps best illustrated in the case of industrial strategy, in which there has of late been a marked revival of interest, as reflected in the publication of government Green and White Papers.[1] A greater role for state intervention is envisaged in influencing not only the *rate* but also the *direction* of economic growth: for example, through measures that seek to improve Britain's poor record in research and development and in technology transfer – moving technological innovation into commercially viable production; that prioritise infrastructural and environmental initiatives; and that make available more 'patient', long-term capital that can enable promising business 'start-ups' to move on to 'scale-ups'. But what is rather remarkable is that in the proliferating discussion of industrial strategy, the implications for social mobility have received very little attention. In her introduction to the White Paper, Theresa May refers to creating 'high quality well-paid jobs right across the country' but makes no explicit linkage to the discussion of social mobility. In the text itself, there is just one reference to mobility. The government, we are told, will 'shortly publish a plan for improving social mobility in England, which will set out how the educational system will expand equality of opportunity': that is, even in the context of industrial strategy it is educational policy that is prioritised in regard to mobility, with the demand side of the matter not being adequately distinguished from the supply side and the confusion between measures relevant to absolute and to relative mobility being all too apparent.[2]

---

[1] HM Government (2017a, b). See also IPPR Commission on Economic Justice (2017) and Heseltine (2017). An academic work that has been of major influence is Mazzucato (2015).

[2] HM Government (2017b: 123). The plan, previously referred to in Chapter 6, n. 16, appeared shortly afterwards with predictable emphases on the importance of school effectiveness and parental behaviour, and with the claim that education would play an 'integral role' in delivering the industrial strategy (Department of Education, 2017: 7). A successful industrial strategy will of course require an appropriately educated and trained labour force; but it would seem desirable, before policy in this regard is developed in any detail, to have some well-considered ideas about how many and what kinds of new jobs are likely to

Policies directed towards the renewal of manufacturing especially, and the more effective exploitation in this regard of the national science and technology base, should in fact be clearly recognised as one major way in which a further upgrading of the class structure could be brought about – not only by increasing the number of higher-level managerial and professional positions but also by offsetting the 'hollowing out' that has resulted from falling numbers of technical and more skilled manual jobs. In turn, and regardless of what might be happening with relative rates, a rise in the upward component of the total mobility rate could be expected to follow – and one that would benefit in particular those localities scarred by deindustrialisation that are regarded as mobility cold spots.[3]

A further policy area of relevance is that of social and of public services more generally. A major driver of the expansion of the managerial and professional salariat that created the golden age of social mobility was the development of the welfare state. And a return to high levels of social investment of this kind does then represent another way in which the upgrading of the class structure could be effected. At the present time much concern is being shown over the possibility of a coming digital and robotics revolution leading to large-scale unemployment or even to 'the end of work'. But this is, in effect, just another expression of the old 'lump of labour' fallacy that within an economy there is always some fixed amount of work to be done. While any period of rapid technological change is likely to be associated with economic and social disruption requiring sustained management, it should be apparent enough, and especially as regards maintaining and advancing the range and quality of services, that substantially greater numbers could be very valuably employed than is presently

---

emerge, and thus to avoid the present situation – which the report did not refer to – in which overqualification and skill shortages appear to coexist. For cogent commentary in this regard, see Peston (2017: 223–4, 230–3).

[3] The Social Mobility Commission has in fact of late taken up this point, even if not giving it any great prominence. It has recommended that 'Central government should put social mobility and place at the heart of the industrial strategy, with a focus on rebalancing economic and work opportunities' and should 'increase the number of high skilled jobs in the regions and particularly in social mobility cold spots, by encouraging and incentivising public sector bodies and private companies to base themselves in those areas' (Social Mobility Commission, 2017a: 9; 2017b: 93).

the case, and often, moreover, at higher levels of employment. For example, in preschool education, childhood and youth services, the health service, the prison service, support for the derelict and homeless, and above all the care of the aged, great individual and societal benefits would follow not only from the expansion of workforces but also from the further upgrading of many personnel to professional standards and status. The crucial issue that arises is, of course, that of how such advances are to be financed: in short, the issue of how gains in productivity and national wealth resulting from technological progress can be directed to this end.

At all events, for present purposes the essential point remains that if current trends of falling upward and rising downward rates of class mobility are to be reversed – or even prevented from becoming more marked – then it is only through the upgrading of the class structure, in one way or another, that this can be achieved. That is to say, within the national economy jobs with employment relations that offer not only relatively high levels of pay but also of income security and stability and career prospects will have to progressively replace jobs in which the employment relations that prevail mean that labour is in effect being reduced to a commodity.

Turning now to relative mobility, it is again the case that the problem that has to be recognised is not that of a decline – not that of an actual decrease of fluidity within the class structure – but rather that of a constancy in relative rates, and one that has persisted over a lengthy period in which attempts have been more or less continuously made to create a greater equality in mobility chances, primarily through educational policies of expansion and reform. What is then implied is that the idea, to which politicians of all parties have resorted, that education can serve as the key means of breaking the link between inequality of condition and inequality of opportunity is seriously flawed. Disparities in the chances of educational success of children from families in more and less advantaged positions persistently show up, even when early life cognitive ability is taken into account, which are in turn reflected in their mobility chances; and in the case of longer-range mobility, such chances diverge to an extent that becomes difficult to reconcile with any conception of equality of opportunity.

The basic failure of politicians in this regard lies, as we have earlier observed, in their inability to grasp, or at all events their unwillingness to accept, that reducing social inequalities in educational attainment as a way of reducing inequalities in mobility chances inescapably involves a zero-sum game. Given the existence of what might be called an objective opportunity structure – in other words, that formed by the class structure as it exists at any one time – any improvement in the relative mobility chances of children of less advantaged class origins can only come about at the expense of a worsening of the chances of children of more advantaged origins. This being so, it is only to be expected that parents with superior resources, economic and also social and cultural, will not remain merely passive in the face of changes in the educational system that appear to threaten their own children's life-chances. They will use their resources as necessary in order to minimise the risks of their children experiencing downwardly mobility. And, as we have suggested, there are good grounds for supposing that the motivation to avoid social descent is yet stronger than that to achieve social ascent. The concern and, for the most part, the capacity of families holding more advantaged class positions to stave off any threat of serious intergenerational downward mobility could in fact be regarded as the key source of the long-term stability that the endogenous mobility regime displays.

What is therefore implied is that if politicians are to pursue any serious commitment to making relative mobility chances more equal, it will be necessary for them to move on from generalities about the importance of raising educational standards and reducing socially linked attainment gaps, on which a broad political consensus exists, and to face issues likely to be of a far more controversial kind.

Thus, even in connection with educational policy, questions arise of how far more advantaged parents' ability to use their superior resources to further their children's educational success should be countered or constrained. For example, apart from raising the quality as well as the quantity of preschool provision for children from disadvantaged backgrounds, should poorer families receive income support specifically for purposes of 'child investments'? Should the ability of well-off parents to employ private tutors for their children be offset by state-funded private tuition as, say, through voucher schemes for children of less well-off parents? Should the various ways in which schools' admissions procedures are exploited by wealthier and better connected and informed parents be made more difficult by introducing selection by lot or by requiring schools to have a balanced intake of pupils in different ability bands? Proposals in all these respects have in fact been put forward by the Sutton Trust and other bodies, but would appear to have received no positive political response.[4] And proposals of a more radical kind – for example, that private schools should lose their charitable status or that, as suggested by Jeremy Corbyn, VAT should be imposed on their fees – have been met with very strongly voiced opposition from Conservative quarters as manifestations of 'class envy' that amount to an illegitimate attempt to undermine parents' rights.[5]

A more fundamental alternative to specific measures of the kind in question can of course also be envisaged, but one that would appear likely to meet with yet wider-ranging sociopolitical dissent. That is, for the perspective on social mobility and social inequality that has so far prevailed in political circles to be directly reversed, so that, rather than increasing mobility, through educational policy, being taken as the preferred solution to the problem of inequality, inequality is recognised as the basic source of the historic ineffectiveness of educational policy in this regard. A general reduction in inequality would then be taken as the prime means of levelling relative mobility chances. Of late, a number of authors have in fact advanced in some detail policy programmes for significantly reducing at least economic inequality, including proposals for more progressive income tax, an inheritance tax, a national pay policy and capital endowments for all at adulthood. But the political viability of such programmes, in the first place in electoral terms, must obviously remain very much in question.[6]

---

[4] See the introductions by Sir Peter Lampl to Kirby (2016), Cullinane et al. (2017), Jerrim (2017a) and Stewart and Waldfogel (2017).

[5] Under New Labour some consideration was given to removing the charitable status of private schools but, instead, a policy was adopted of requiring them to more fully justify this status – with results that do not appear all that impressive. The proposal that VAT should attach to private school fees did in fact receive some unexpected support from Michael Gove – who was then, however, denounced in the right-wing press as a 'class traitor'.

[6] The most important work in this regard is that of Atkinson (2015). But while Atkinson deals very persuasively with objections to his proposals to the effect that they would be detrimental to economic efficiency, that they would be impractical in the face of globalisation, or that within the national economy they could not be afforded, he gives little consideration to whether they could find the political support necessary for their implementation. An interesting sociological commentary is that by Grusky (2017), who suggests that Atkinson's essentially 'technocratic' stance needs complementing by some degree of 'populist' appeal. It is in this connection important to recognise (on the US, see Reeves, 2017) that those benefiting from existing inequalities of both condition and opportunity are

What has, though, at the same time become apparent is that maintaining existing views that would neglect or discount the ways in which inequality of condition impedes equality of opportunity is also facing growing political difficulties. In this regard, developments involving the Social Mobility Commission are of particular note.

Early in 2017 the Commission published an assessment of government policies over the previous twenty years that had been directed towards increasing mobility. The conclusion reached was that the large majority of these had failed to meet their objectives. Of thirty-seven specific policies that were evaluated – most being in the field of education – only seven could be rated as successful. In the discussion of this disappointing record, references were repeatedly made to persisting or widening inequalities – in incomes, in wealth, in housing, in health – that impacted directly on individuals' mobility chances.[7] Then in November 2017 the Commission's annual report appeared and was focused on geographical differences in the prospects of upward mobility for young people of disadvantaged social origins. The report received wide media attention, although largely based on a misunderstanding of what it showed. Contrary to what was generally supposed, the report did not contain any evidence on geographical differences in the social mobility of individuals, whether upward or otherwise. Rather, what were presented were the results of applying to different local authority areas sixteen so-called 'social mobility indicators' – or, more accurately, indicators of *conditions taken to be relevant to the chances of upward mobility*. Some of these indicators related to the educational performance and labour market position of disadvantaged young people – in other words, those eligible for free school meals – but only at an aggregate, area level, while others related directly to such matters as school quality, average wages, prevalence of low wages, home ownership, and the availability of managerial and professional occupations. In other words, local areas were characterised not in terms of the actual mobility of individuals born, or currently

in modern societies no longer a small minority. In Britain even Class 1 now accounts for well over 10 per cent of the electorate and Classes 1 and 2 together for around a third.

[7] Social Mobility Commission (2017a).

living, in them but rather in terms of where they stood on a range of measures of economic and wider social advantage or disadvantage.[8]

It would then be difficult to conclude anything other than that the Commission was becoming increasingly forced to take the position, even if this was nowhere explicitly acknowledged, that rather than mobility being a means of mitigating inequality, inequality had to be seen as fundamentally conditioning mobility. And support for this interpretation is provided by the fact that, shortly after the publication of their report, the members of the Commission collectively resigned. The grounds for this action, as stated by the outgoing chair, Alan Milburn, were that public policy, as thus far conceived and implemented, had failed to improve social mobility, that the present government gave no indication of being ready to take any more serious measures aimed at supporting the 'left-behind communities that had voted for Brexit' or at 'healing social divisions', and that he and his colleagues saw no point in continuing in their efforts 'to push water uphill'.[9]

It would thus appear that at the present time something of an impasse has been reached so far as the social mobility agenda is concerned. While it is becoming increasingly hard in policy circles to ignore the fact that problems of inequality of opportunity cannot be effectively addressed separately from those of inequality of condition, there is no evident political basis for a more integrated approach.

---

[8] Social Mobility Commission (2017b). Acknowledgement that the report does not in fact contain any analyses of geographical variation in social mobility rates, since no databases adequate to the purpose exist, is tucked away in a methodological appendix (Appendix 1). It would have been helpful, and appropriate, if this limitation of the report had been clearly stated at the outset. How well the indices used would correlate with actual mobility is unknown but it may be observed that they do not always correlate very highly with each other.

[9] See *Sunday Times*, 3 December 2017. Given this strong position, it is, however, somewhat strange to find that in their earlier report calling for new thinking on mobility – and despite the chair's recognition that the 'social mobility agenda has tended to be skewed towards children and the educational system' to the neglect of the labour market – the Commission still made recommendations that were heavily concentrated on school effectiveness and parental behaviour on much the same lines as the Department of Education report referred to in note 2 above. The only recommendation directly concerning inequality of condition was that the government should have the 'ambition' to make the UK the country with the lowest level of low pay within the OECD (Social Mobility Commission, 2017a: 5, 9).

One question that arises is then that of whether any way remains through which a viable attempt might be made at reducing inequalities in relative mobility chances: that is, without the emergence of some significantly new political conjuncture. In the light of our research findings, it is possible to suggest one approach that could be pursued and which need not be politically divisive but that would, however, again require a major reorientation of thinking that has for long been largely shared across the political spectrum. What would be entailed would be the following: a move away from an uncritical acceptance of the idea of education as 'the great equaliser' and of an education-based meritocracy as a generally desirable end state; a recognition that, insofar as the association between individuals' social origins and their educational attainment is not weakened, education often serves in effect to *restrict* mobility; and, in turn, a concern to prevent any unnecessary transfer of educational inequalities into inequalities in chances of – upward – mobility in the course of working life.

In Chapter 6 we have shown that there is a wastage of talent in that many individuals of high cognitive ability, but coming disproportionately from disadvantaged social backgrounds, do not fulfil their academic potential at least so far as the attainment of formal qualifications is concerned. The implication of this is that within the labour force there are likely to be some significant number of men and women who are actually capable of undertaking a higher level of work than that in which they are presently engaged. And in Chapter 7 we have further shown that over the postwar years levels of upward mobility achieved in the course of working life have been largely maintained, that educational qualifications are not the only or always the dominant factor in such mobility, and that cognitive ability and perhaps other individual attributes also play a part. We would then see here a positive tendency as regards equality of opportunity that should be sustained and as far as possible strengthened. With many occupations, mainly professional and technical, it is of course the case that certain standards of competency need to be guaranteed a priori, and this is best done by appropriate qualifications being entry requirements. But there are many other occupations, including relatively high-level ones as, say, in management in the services sector and in general administration, where what is of main importance, apart, perhaps, from basic standards of literacy and numeracy, is simply an individual's demonstrated capacity to do well the work that is involved; formal qualifications are of far less relevance in assuring competency, and a demand for them may amount to no more than a credentialist restriction on access.[10]

To return to the point we made at the end of Chapter 7, we would therefore see advantage in at least as strong a concern being shown with employers' internal promotion policies as with their recruitment policies. Employers could be encouraged, or indeed required, to have programmes in place that would help to establish that they are in fact exploiting to the full the human resources that are available in their existing workforces: that is, by providing detailed information on the promotion opportunities open to employees at all levels, ensuring that inappropriate qualifications barriers are not imposed, and, where potentially successful candidates could benefit from it, providing in-house preparatory training. In short, the credentialist 'closure' of positions should be minimised. Any improvement in the chances of upward worklife mobility for able individuals from disadvantaged social origins that followed from such initiatives could well entail worsening chances for less able individuals from more advantaged origins with perhaps higher levels of formal qualification. That is to say, a zero-sum game would, all else being equal, again be in operation. But, as well as this being less apparent than in the case of attempts at increasing equality of mobility chances through educational policy, there would in any event be fewer possibilities for countervailing action.

Finally, though, whatever might be achieved through seeking to remove credentialist barriers, and indeed whatever possibilities for further policy interventions might exist under different political conditions, we would still wish to return to our argument that some limit must exist on the extent to which inequalities in relative mobility chances can be reduced in societies with a capitalist market economy, a nuclear family system and a liberal democratic polity. Within capitalist market economies, wide inequalities in incomes and in economic conditions more generally are inevitably produced – individuals in different class positions live in the different economic worlds that we

---

[10] It could in this connection be thought generally encouraging that according to a recent OECD report the UK, along with Sweden, is distinctive in that variation in years of education, which could be taken as a proxy for qualifications, has no greater impact on differences in earnings than variation in literacy proficiency, whereas in most other countries the impact of the former variation is significantly greater than that of the latter (OECD, 2017: fig. 2.5).

referred to in Chapter 1. Within nuclear families there is a natural tendency for one generation to seek to pass on to the next such economic and wider social advantages as it may have gained – parents want 'to do the best they can' for their children, using whatever resources they have available for the purpose. And within liberal democratic polities any proposed interventions that aim at modifying these essentially inegalitarian processes must, as well as winning political support, electoral and otherwise, be consistent with recognised individual rights. If, then, as we have also argued, Britain is, along with a number of other societies, approaching the limit in question, how further might it be possible to go in equalising relative mobility rates, even supposing policies more radical than those that have been so far pursued?

Through measures of the kind we have previously referred to aimed at restricting the 'commodification of opportunity', within the educational system especially, some check could certainly be placed on the ability of better-off parents simply to buy advantage for their children or at all events this could be made a good deal more expensive; and more general redistributive policies would evidently help to 'level the playing field' so far as the provision of the material conditions conducive to educationally effective parenting is concerned. Insofar as any reduction thus achieved in educational inequalities was reflected in the labour market, some further equalisation of relative mobility chances could then be expected to follow.

However, it has to be recognised that while in these ways the effects of economic inequalities among families might be mitigated, the effects of inequalities in social and cultural and what we have referred to as specifically educational resources need be little changed. And, as is now well established, and as we have at various points illustrated, these latter inequalities are also strongly, and perhaps increasingly strongly, associated with children's attainments in the educational system – and subsequently. Inequalities of the kind in question have then to be recognised as in some large part lying beyond political reach. To take what have become the paradigm cases in this regard, parents who read their children bedtime stories or engage with them in 'supper table debates' give them clear developmental advantages. But to prevent parents from doing these things would be neither feasible nor in any event desirable. The crucial fact that has to be faced is that many activities that could be regarded *as constitutive of family life* serve in themselves to create significant inequalities of opportunity among children from their early years onwards, and in turn play an important part in maintaining intergenerational immobility.[11]

What our argument amounts to is then that, given its established economic, familial and political institutions, *some* degree of inequality in relative mobility chances, and quite possibly at the extremes of a marked degree, has to be accepted as an integral and persisting feature of British society: that is, as following directly from the existence of the institutions in question – which may, of course, on other grounds be valued. As philosophers have had occasion to point out, there is rarely 'lexical ordering' in sociopolitical values or principles; not all of what might be regarded as 'good things' go consistently together.

This being the case, we are led to the conclusion that the primary policy emphasis so far as social mobility is concerned could be most effectively placed on initiatives of the kind earlier discussed that would impact on *absolute* rather than relative rates, and, specifically, through contributing to the upgrading of the class structure. Although industrial strategy and the progressive development of social and public services may well themselves entail political conflict, as regards mobility it is a positive-sum rather than a zero-sum game to which they could be expected to lead: that is, to a situation in which opportunities for upward mobility into more advantaged class positions generally increase, while the risks of downward mobility from such positions decrease – or in other words, to the same situation as prevailed during the golden age. This outcome would not be affected if relative rates remained unchanged, as indeed they did throughout the golden age. And it is in this connection also relevant to note again that what individuals actually *experience* is mobility, or immobility, in the

---

[11] For a sociologically and philosophically informed discussion of the issues that arise, see Brighouse and Swift (2014). The main attraction of preschool programmes for children from disadvantaged backgrounds lies in the possibility of their 'compensating' for their families so far as their educationally relevant development is concerned. There is evidence that such programmes can have some success, and without subsequent 'wash-out' effects, *but only* if they are of an intensive and high-quality kind; or, as Gilbert (2017: 103) has put it, if, as in the US Abecedarian project, they provide 'a substitute family of highly-motivated professional caregivers who work to educate and socialize the children from 7:30 a.m. to 5:15 p.m. five days a week from infancy through age 5'. For a useful review of the present British situation, see Stewart and Waldfogel (2017).

absolute sense, and that while relative rates are important indicators, for social scientists and for policy makers, of the extent to which inequality of opportunity exists in a society, it is unlikely that they greatly impinge on the consciousness of its lay members.

Moreover, if as a result of class structural change a return could be made to a situation in which upward mobility was again more widely experienced than downward, this would in fact provide the most favourable context for further attempts at reducing inequalities in relative rates. Just as policies aimed at income redistribution are more likely to be politically viable when incomes are generally rising, so policies aimed in effect at redistributing mobility chances may meet with less resistance when the general tendency is for people to move up rather than down. In particular, the fear of downward mobility, which, we have argued, chiefly motivates those in more advantaged class positions to oppose or to seek to circumvent egalitarian reforms, may be expected to be less where individual instances of such mobility are only rarely encountered than where, as in Britain today, they are becoming increasingly frequent and thus far more visible.

The preoccupation with educational policy as the primary means of creating more equal mobility chances has, in the light of all the historical evidence, to be seen as misguided. Educational expansion and reform over the last half-century or more *have* widened opportunity in the sense that more individuals of all social origins alike have been able more fully to realise their academic potential. And it is on making further progress in this regard – on reducing the significant wastage of talent that still occurs – that those who work within the educational system should be required, and allowed, to concentrate, rather than having imposed upon them, under an unduly instrumental view of education, the leading role in overcoming problems of inequality of opportunity in a wider sense, the main sources of which lie in fact outside of educational institutions. Efforts can still be made to deal with these problems, as far as is possible, through other forms of policy – ones that will need to be aimed in one way or another at reducing the effects of inequalities of condition. But insofar as social mobility *per se* is to remain a concern – rather than just a convenient topic for political rhetoric – the main focus should be on policies for economic and social development of a purposive kind. That is, for development directed towards the creation of a technologically and

economically more efficient and also more humane form of society that
would lead, through changing demand conditions, to a steadily
increasing number of men and women, of all social origins, being
able to move into class positions in which they could enjoy economic
well-being, security and stability and the prospect of advancement over
the course of their working lives.

References

Abbott, A. and Tsay, A. 2000. 'Sequence Analysis and Optimal Matching Methods in Sociology: Review and Prospect', *Sociological Methods and Research*, 29: 3–33.

Adonis, A. 2012. *Education, Education, Education: Reforming England's Schools*. London: Biteback.

Aisenbrey, S. and Fasang, A. E. 2010. 'New Life for Old Ideas: The "Second Wave" of Sequence Analysis Bringing the "Course" Back into the Life Course', *Sociological Methods and Research*, 38: 420–62.

Aldridge, S. 2001. 'Social Mobility: A Discussion Paper'. Cabinet Office Policy and Evaluation Unit. London: Cabinet Office.

Andrews, J. and Perera, N. 2017. *The Impact of Academies on Educational Outcomes*. London: Education Policy Institute.

Arum, R. and Müller, W. (eds.) 2004. *The Re-emergence of Self-Employment*. Princeton University Press.

Atherton, G. 2017. *The Success Paradox: Why We Need a Holistic Theory of Social Mobility*. Bristol: Policy Press.

Atkinson, A. B. 2015. *Inequality*. Cambridge, Mass.: Harvard University Press.

Atkinson, A. B., Maynard, A. K. and Trinder, C. G. 1983. *Parents and Children: Incomes in Two Generations*. London: Heinemann.

Ballarino, G. and Bernardi, F. 2016. 'The Intergenerational Transmission of Inequality and Education in Fourteen Countries: A Comparison'. In F. Bernardi and G. Ballarino (eds.), *Education, Occupation and Social Origin*. Cheltenham: Edward Elgar.

Banks, J., Smith, Z. and Wakefield, M. 2002. *The Distribution of Financial Wealth in the UK: Evidence from 2000 BHPS Data*. London: Institute for Fiscal Studies.

Bauman, Z. 1982. *Memories of Class: The Pre-History and After-Life of Class*. London: Routledge.

Beck, U. 1992. *Risk Society*. London: Sage.

Belfield, C., Crawford, C., Greaves, E., Gregg, P. and Macmillan, L. 2017. 'Intergenerational Income Persistence within Families'. IFS Working Paper W17/11. London: Institute for Fiscal Studies.

Bell, D. 1972. 'On Meritocracy and Inequality', *The Public Interest*, 29: 29–68.

1973. *The Coming of Post-Industrial Society*. New York: Basic Books.

Bernardi, F. and Ballarino, G. (eds.) 2016. *Education, Occupation and Social Origin*. Cheltenham: Edward Elgar.

Betthäuser, B. and Bourne, M. 2017. 'Understanding the Mobility Chances of Children from Working Class Backgrounds in Britain: How Important are Cognitive Ability and Locus of Control?' University of Oxford, Department of Social Policy and Intervention.

Björklund, A. and Jäntti, M. 2009. 'Intergenerational Income Mobility and the Role of Family Background'. In W. Salverda, B. Nolan and T. M. Smeeding (eds.), *The Oxford Handbook of Economic Inequality*. Oxford University Press.

Blanden, J. 2013. 'Cross-Country Rankings in Intergenerational Mobility: A Comparison of Approaches from Economics and Sociology', *Journal of Economic Surveys*, 27: 38–73.

Blanden, J. and Machin, S. 2007. *Recent Changes in Intergenerational Mobility in Britain*. London: Sutton Trust.

Blanden, J., Gregg, P. and Machin, S. 2005a. 'Educational Inequality and Intergenerational Mobility'. In S. Machin and A. Vignoles (eds.), *What's the Good of Education?* Princeton University Press.

2005b. 'Intergenerational Mobility in Europe and North America'. London: Centre for Economic Performance, LSE and Sutton Trust.

Blanden, J., Gregg, P. and Macmillan, L. 2007. 'Accounting for Intergenerational Income Persistence: Noncognitive Skills, Ability and Education', *Economic Journal*, 117: C43–C60.

Blanden, J., Goodman, A., Gregg, P. and Machin, S. 2004. 'Changes in Intergenerational Mobility in Britain'. In M. Corak (ed.), *Generational Income Mobility in North America and Europe*. Cambridge University Press.

Blanden, J., Buscha, F., Sturgis, P, and Urwin, P, 2012. 'Measuring the Earnings Returns to Lifelong Learning in the UK', *Economics of Education Review*, 31: 501–14.

Boden, R. and Corden, A. 1994. *Measuring Low Incomes: Self-Employment and Family Credit*. London: HMSO.

Boliver, V. and Swift, A. 2011. 'Do Comprehensive Schools Reduce Social Mobility?' *British Journal of Sociology*, 62: 89–110.

Breen, R. 2010. 'Educational Expansion and Social Mobility in the 20th Century', *Social Forces*, 89: 365–88.

Breen, R. and Luijkx, R. 2004a. 'Social Mobility in Europe between 1970 and 2000'. In R. Breen (ed.), *Social Mobility in Europe*. Oxford University Press.

2004b. 'Conclusions'. In R. Breen (ed.), *Social Mobility in Europe*. Oxford University Press.

Breen, R. and Jonsson, J. O. 2007. 'Explaining Change in Social Fluidity: Educational Equalization and Educational Expansion in Twentieth Century Sweden', *American Journal of Sociology*, 112: 1775–810.

Breen, R., Luijkx, R., Müller, W. and Pollak, R. 2009. 'Non-Persistent Inequality in Educational Attainment: Evidence from Eight European Countries', *American Journal of Sociology*, 114: 1475–521.

2010: 'Long-Term Trends in Educational Inequality in Europe: Class Inequalities and Gender Differences', *European Sociological Review*, 26: 31–48.

Brighouse, H. and Swift, A. 2014. *Family Values*. Princeton University Press.

Britton, J. Dearden, L., Shepard, N. and Vignoles, A. 2016. 'How English Domiciled Graduate Earnings Vary with Gender, Institution Attended, Subject and Socioeconomic Background'. IFS Working Paper 16/06. London: Institute for Fiscal Studies.

Brown, P., Lauder, H. and Ashton, D. 2011. *The Global Auction: The Broken Promises of Education, Jobs and Income*. Oxford University Press.

Bukodi, E. 2017. 'Cumulative Inequalities over the Life-Course: Life-Long Learning and Social Mobility in Britain', *Journal of Social Policy*, 46: 367–404.

Bukodi, E. and Goldthorpe, J. H. 2009. 'Class Origins, Education and Occupational Attainment: Cross-Cohort Changes Among Men in Britain'. Centre for Longitudinal Studies, Working Paper 2009/3. London: Institute of Education.

2010. 'Market versus Meritocracy: Hungary as a Critical Case', *European Sociological Review*, 26: 655–74.

2011a. 'Class Origins, Education and Occupational Attainment in Britain: Secular Trends or Cohort-Specific Effects?, *European Societies*, 13: 345–7.

2011b. 'Social Class Returns to Higher Education: Chances of Access to the Professional and Managerial Salariat for Men in Three British Birth Cohorts', *Longitudinal and Life Course Studies*, 2: 185–201.

2016. 'Educational Attainment – Relative or Absolute – as a Mediator of Intergenerational Class Mobility in Britain', *Research in Social Stratification and Mobility*, 43: 5–15.

2017. 'Social Inequality and Social Mobility: Is There an Inverse Relation?' Barnett Papers in Social Research, 17–11. Department of Social Policy and Intervention, University of Oxford.

Bukodi, E., Bourne, M. and Betthäuser, B. 2018. 'Wastage of Talent? Social Origins, Cognitive Ability and Educational Attainment in Britain', *Advances in Life Course Research*, 34: 34–42.

Bukodi, E., Dex, S. and Goldthorpe, J. H. 2011. 'The Conceptualisation and Measurement of Occupational Hierarchies: a Review, a Proposal and Some Illustrative Analyses', *Quality and Quantity*, 45: 623–39.

Bukodi, E., Erikson, R. and Goldthorpe, J. H. 2014. 'The Effects of Social Origins and Cognitive Ability on Educational Attainment: Evidence from Britain and Sweden', *Acta Sociologica*, 57: 293–310.

Bukodi, E., Goldthorpe, J. H. and Kuha, J. 2017. 'The Pattern of Social Fluidity within the British Class Structure', *Journal of the Royal Statistical Society*, series A, 180: 841–62.

Bukodi, E., Paskov, M. and Nolan, B. 2017. 'Intergenerational Class Mobility in Europe: A New Account and an Old Story'. Institute for New Economic Thinking, Working Paper 2017–03. Oxford Martin School.

Bukodi, E., Goldthorpe, J.H., Halpin, B. and Waller, L. 2016, 'Is Education Now Class Destiny? Class Histories Across Three British Birth Cohorts', *European Sociological Review*, 32: 835–49.

Bukodi, E., Goldthorpe, J.H., Joshi, H. and Waller, L. 2017. 'Why have Relative Rates of Class Mobility become More Equal among Women in Britain?' *British Journal of Sociology*, 68: 512–32.

Bukodi, E., Goldthorpe, J. H., Waller, L. and Kuha, J. 2015. 'The Mobility Problem in Britain: New Findings from the Analysis of Birth Cohort Data', *British Journal of Sociology*, 66: 93–117.

Burgess, S. 2014. 'Understanding the Success of London's Schools'. University of Bristol, Centre for Market and Public Organisation.

Burnett, D. 2016. *The Idiot Brain*. London: Norton.

Buscha, F. and Sturgis, P. 2017. 'Declining Social Mobility? Evidence from Five Linked Censuses in England and Wales, 1971–2011', *British Journal of Sociology*, 67: 1–32.

Byford, M., Kuh, D. and Richards, M. 2012: 'Parenting Practices and Intergenerational Association in Cognitive Ability', *International Journal of Epidemiology*, 41: 263–72.

Cabinet Office, 2008. *Getting On, Getting Ahead: Analysing the Trends and Drivers of Social Mobility*. London: Cabinet Office.

Caliendo, M., Cobb-Clark, D. A. and Uhlendorff, A. 2015. 'Locus of Control and Job Search Strategies', *Review of Economics and Statistics*, 97: 88–103.

Carey, N. 2012. *The Epigenetics Revolution*. London: Icon Books.

Causa, O., Dantan, S. and Johansson, A. 2009. 'Intergenerational Social Mobility in European OECD Countries'. OECD Economics Department Working Papers, no. 709. Paris: OECD.

Chan, T-W. 2018. 'Social Mobility and the Well-Being of Individuals', *British Journal of Sociology*, 69: 183–206.

Chan, T.-W. and Goldthorpe, J. H. 2004. 'Is There a Status Order in Contemporary British Society? Evidence from the Occupational Structure of Friendship', *European Sociological Review*, 20: 383–401.

2007. 'Class and Status: the Conceptual Distinction and its Empirical Relevance', *American Sociological Review*, 72: 512–32.

Charles, M. 2011. 'A World of Difference: International Trends in Women's Economic Status', *Annual Review of Sociology*, 37: 355–71.

Chartered Institute of Personnel and Development 2015. *Over-Qualification and Skills Mismatch in the Graduate Labour Market*. London: CIPD.

Collins, R. 1979. *The Credential Society: An Historical Sociology of Education and Stratification*. New York: Academic Press.

Connolly, S. and Gregory, M. 2008. 'Moving Down: Women's Part-Time Work and Occupational Change in Britain', *Economic Journal*, 118: F52–76.

Conservative Party 2008. *Through the Glass Ceiling*. London: Conservative Party.

Cox. D. R., Jackson, M. and Lu, S. 2009. 'On Square Ordinal Contingency Tables: A Comparison of Social Class and Income Mobility for Same Individuals', *Journal of the Royal Statistical Society*, series A, 172: 483–93.

Cullinane, C., Hillary, J., Andrade, J. and McNamara, S. 2017. *Selective Comprehensives 2017: Admissions to High-Attaining Non-Selective Schools for Disadvantaged Pupils*. London: Sutton Trust.

D'Addio, A. C. 2007. *Intergenerational Transmission of Disadvantage: Mobility or Immobility across Generations: A Review of the Evidence for OECD Countries*. Paris: OECD.

Dämmerich, J., Vono de Vilhena, D. and Reichart, E. 2014. 'Participation in Adult Learning in Europe: the Impact of Country-Level and Individual Characteristics'. In H.-P. Blossfeld, E. Kilpi-Jakonen, D. Vono de Vilhena and S. Buchholz (eds.), *Adult Learning in Modern Societies: An International Comparison from a Life-Course Perspective*. Cheltenham: Edward Elgar.

Deary, I. J., Strand, S., Smith, P. and Fernandes, C. 2007. 'Intelligence and Educational Achievement', *Intelligence*, 35: 13–21.

Department of Education 2017. *Unlocking Talent, Fulfilling Potential: A Plan for Improving Social Mobility Through Education*. London: HMSO.

Dex, S, and Bukodi, E. 2012. 'The Effects of Part-Time Work on Women's Occupational Mobility in Britain: Evidence from the 1958 Birth Cohort Study', *National Institute Economic Review*, 222: 820–37.

Dex, S., Ward, K. and Joshi, H. 2008. 'Changes in Women's Occupations and Occupational Mobility over 25 Years'. In J. Scott, S. Dex and

H. Joshi (eds.), *Changes in Women's Employment over 25 Years.* Cheltenham: Edward Elgar.

Elias, P. and McKnight, A. 2003. 'Earnings, Unemployment and the NS-SEC'. In D. Rose and D. Pevalin (eds.), *A Researcher's Guide to the National Statistics Socio-Economic Classification.* London: Sage.

Elliott, J. and Shepherd, P. 2006. 'Cohort Profile: 1970 British Birth Cohort Study (BCS70)', *International Journal of Epidemiology*, 35: 836–43.

Elliott, J., Miles, A., Parsons, S. and Savage, M. 2010. 'The Design and Content of the "Social Participation" Study'. Centre for Longitudinal Studies, Working Paper 2010/3. Institute of Education, University of London.

Erikson, R. 2016. 'Intergenerational Associations of Stratification Dimensions – Do they Change and, if so, in Concert?' European Consortium for Sociological Research, annual conference, Oxford.

Erikson, R. and Goldthorpe, J. H. 1992. *The Constant Flux: A Study of Class Mobility in Industrial Societies.* Oxford: Clarendon Press.

2010. 'Has Social Mobility in Britain Decreased? Reconciling Divergent Findings on Income and Class Mobility', *British Journal of Sociology*, 61: 211–30.

Erikson, R., Goldthorpe, J. H. and Hällsten, M. 2012. 'No Way Back Up from Ratcheting Down: A Critique of the "Micro-Class" Approach to the Analysis of Social Mobility', *Acta Sociologica*, 55: 211–29.

Ermisch, J. and Francesconi, M. 2004. 'Intergenerational Mobility in Britain: New Evidence from the British Household Panel Study'. In M. Corak (ed.), *Generational Income Mobility in North America and Europe.* Cambridge University Press.

Erola, J. 2009. 'Social Mobility and Education of Finnish Cohorts Born 1936–75: Succeeding while Failing in Equality of Opportunity', *Acta Sociologica*, 52: 307–27.

Eurofound 2017. *Social Mobility in the EU.* Luxembourg: Publications Office of the European Union.

Flynn, J. R. 1987. 'Massive IQ Gains in 14 Nations: What IQ Tests Really Measure', *Psychological Bulletin*, 101: 171–91.

Francis, B. and Hutchings, M. 2013. *Parent Power? Using Money and Information to Boost Children's Chances of Educational Success.* London: Sutton Trust.

Friedman, S. 2014. 'The Price of the Ticket: Rethinking the Experience of Social Mobility', *Sociology*, 48: 352–68.

2015. 'Habitus Clivé and the Emotional Imprint of Social Mobility', *Sociological Review*, 64: 129–47.

Friedman, S., Laurison, D. and Macmillan, L. 2017. 'Social Mobility in Contemporary Britain: New Insights from the Labour Force Survey'. London: Social Mobility Commission.

Galindo-Rueda, F. and Vignoles, A. 2005. 'The Declining Relative Import-ance of Ability in Predicting Educational Attainment', *Journal of Human Resources*, 40: 335–53.

Gallie, D. 2000. 'The Labour Force'. In A. H. Halsey (ed.), *Twentieth-Century British Social Trends*. London: Macmillan.

Gallie, D., White, M., Cheng.Y and Tomlinson, M. 1998. *Restructuring the Employment Relationship*. Oxford University Press.

Ganzeboon, H.G. B., Luijkx, R. and Treiman, D. J. 1989. 'Intergenerational Class Mobility in Comparative Perspective', *Research in Social Stratifi-cation and Mobility*, 8: 3–84.

Gerber, T. P, and Hout, M. 2004. 'Tightening Up: Declining Class Mobility during Russia's Market Transition', *American Sociological Review*, 69: 677–703.

Giddens, A. 1994. *Beyond Left and Right*. Cambridge: Polity Press.

Gilbert, N. 2017. *Never Enough: Capitalism and the Progressive Spirit*. Oxford University Press.

Gigerenzer, G. 2008. *Rationality for Mortals*. Oxford University Press.

Girod, R. 1971. *Mobilité sociale*. Geneva: Droz.

Glass, D. V. (ed.) 1954. *Social Mobility in Britain*. London: Routledge.

Gloster, R., Buzzeo, J., Marvell, R., Tassinari, A., Williams, J., Williams, M., Swift, S. and Newton, B. 2015. 'The Contribution of Further Education and Skills to Social Mobility'. Department of Business, Innovation and Skills, Research Paper, 254.

Goldstein, H. and Woodhouse, G. 2000. 'School Effectiveness Research and Educational Policy', *Oxford Review of Education*, 26: 353–63.

Goldthorpe, J. H. 1980/1987, 2nd edn. *Social Mobility and Class Structure in Modern Britain*. Oxford: Clarendon Press.

  1982. 'On the Service Class, its Formation and Future'. In A. Giddens and G. Mackenzie (eds.), *Social Class and the Division of Labour*. Cam-bridge University Press.

  2005. 'Progress in Sociology: the Case of Social Mobility Research'. In S. Svallfors (ed.), *Analyzing Inequality*. Stanford University Press.

  2007. *On Sociology*, 2 vols. Stanford University Press.

  2013. 'Understanding – and Misunderstanding – Social Mobility in Britain: the Entry of the Economists, the Confusion of Politicians and the Limits of Educational Policy', *Journal of Social Policy*, 42: 431–50.

  2014. 'The Role of Education in Intergenerational Social Mobility: Prob-lems from Empirical Research in Sociology and some Theoretical Pointers from Economics', *Rationality and Society*, 26: 265–89.

  2016. 'Social Class Mobility in Modern Britain: Changing Structure, Constant Process', *Journal of the British Academy*, 4: 89–111.

Goldthorpe J. H. and Mills, C. 2004. 'Trends in Intergenerational Class Mobility in Britain in the Late Twentieth Century'. In R. Breen (ed.), *Social Mobility in Europe*. Oxford University Press.

Goldthorpe, J. H. and McKnight, A. 2006. 'The Economic Basis of Social Class'. In S. L. Morgan, D. B. Grusky and G. S. Fields (eds.), *Mobility and Inequality*. Stanford University Press.

Goldthorpe, J. H. and Jackson, M. 2007. 'Intergenerational Class Mobility in Contemporary Britain: Political Concerns and Empirical Findings', *British Journal of Sociology*, 58: 525–46.

2008. 'Education-based Meritocracy: The Barriers to its Realisation'. In A. Lareau and D. Conley (eds.), *Social Class: How does it Work*. New York: Russell Sage Foundation.

Goldthorpe, J. H. and Mills, C. 2008. 'Trends in Intergenerational Class Mobility in Modern Britain: Evidence from National Surveys, 1972–2005', *National Institute Economic Review*, 205: 83–100.

Goos, M. and Manning, A. 2007. 'Lousy and Lovely Jobs: The Rising Polarization of Work in Britain', *Review of Economics and Statistics*, 89: 118–33.

Grätz, M. and Pollak, R. 2016. 'Legacies of the Past: Social Origin, Educational Attainment and Labour-Market Outcomes in Germany'. In F. Bernardi and G. Ballarino (eds.), *Education, Occupation and Social Origin*. Cheltenham: Edward Elgar.

Gray, J. L. and Moshinsky, P. 1935. 'Ability and Opportunity in English Education', *Sociological Review*, 27: 113–62.

Green, F. and Zhu, Y. 2010. 'Overqualification, Job Dissatisfaction, and Increasing Dispersion in the Returns to Graduate Education', *Oxford Economic Papers*, 52: 740–63.

Grusky, D. B. 2017. 'Reducing Inequality in a Populist World', *Revue Française de Sociologie*, 58: 199–205.

Gugushvili, A., Bukodi, E. and Goldthorpe, J. H. 2017. 'The Direct Effect of Social Origins on Social Mobility Chances: "Glass Floors" and "Glass Ceilings" in Britain', *European Sociological Review*, 33: 305–16.

Gutierrez, O. M., Micklewright, J. and Vignoles, A. 2014. 'Social Mobility and the Importance of Networks: Evidence for Britain'. IZA Discussion Paper 8380. Bonn: Institute for the Study of Labour.

Hakim, C. 2000. *Work-Lifestyle Choices in the 21st Century: Preference Theory*. Oxford University Press.

2004. 'Lifestyle Preferences versus Patriarchal Values: Causal and Non-Causal Attitudes'. In J. Zollinger Giele and E. Holst (eds.), *Changing Life Patterns in Western Industrial Societies*. London: Elsevier.

Halpin, B. 2014. 'Three Narratives of Sequence Analysis'. In P. Blanchard, F Bühlmann and J.-A. Gauthier (eds.), *Advances in Sequence Analysis: Theory, Methods, Applications*. Berlin: Springer.

Halsey, A. H. 1977. 'Towards Meritocracy? The Case of Britain'. In J. Karabel and A. H. Halsey (eds.), *Power and Ideology in Education*. Oxford University Press.

HM Government 2009a. *New Opportunities: Fair Chances for the Future*. London: HM Government.

  2009b. *Unleashing Aspirations: The Final Report of the Panel on Fair Access to the Professions*. London: Cabinet Office.

  2011. *Opening Doors, Breaking Barriers: A Strategy for Social Mobility*. London: Cabinet Office.

  2012. *Opening Doors, Breaking Barriers: A Strategy for Social Mobility: Update on Progress since April 2011*. London: Cabinet Office.

  2017a. *Building our Industrial Strategy*. Green Paper. London: HM Government.

  2017b. *Industrial Strategy: Building a Britain Fit for the Future*. White Paper. London: HM Government.

Heckman, J. J. and Mosso, S. 2014. 'The Economics of Human Development and Social Mobility', *Annual Review of Economics*, 6: 689–733.

Herrnstein, R. J. and Murray, C. 1994. *The Bell Curve*. New York: Free Press.

Heseltine, M. 2017. *Industrial Strategy: A Response to the Government's Green Paper*. London: self-published.

Hirsch, F. 1977. *Social Limits to Growth*. London: Routledge & Kegan Paul.

Hobbs, G. and Vignoles, A. 2010. 'Is Children's Free School Meals Eligibility a Good Proxy for Family Income? *British Educational Research Journal*, 36: 673–90.

Holford, A. 2017. 'Access to and Returns from Unpaid Graduate Internships'. University of Essex, Institute for Economic and Social Research.

Hout, M. and Di Prete, T. A. 2006. 'RC28's Contribution to Knowledge: an Assessment and an Agenda for the Future', *Research in Social Stratification and Mobility*, 24: 1–20.

Ioannides, Y. M. and Loury, L. D. 2004. 'Job Information Networks. Neighborhood Effects and Inequality', *Journal of Economic Literature*, 42: 1056–93.

IPPR Commission on Economic Justice 2017. *Industrial Strategy: Steering Structural Change in the UK Economy*. London: Institute for Public Policy Research.

Ishida, H. Müller, W. and Ridge, J. M. 1995. 'Class Origin, Class Destination, and Education: A Cross-National Study of Industrial Nations', *American Journal of Sociology*, 101: 145–93.

Jablonka, E. and Lamb, M. 2013. *Evolution in Four Dimensions*. Cambridge, Mass.: MIT Press.

Jackson, M. and Evans, G. 2017. 'Rebuilding Walls: Market Transition and Social Mobility in the Post-Socialist Societies of Europe', *Sociological Science*, 4: 54–79.

Jackson, M., Goldthorpe, J. H. and Mills, C. 2005. 'Education, Employers and Class Mobility', *Research in Social Stratification and Mobility*, 23: 3–34.

Jackson, M., Erikson, R., Goldthorpe, J. H. and Yaish, M. 2007. 'Primary and Secondary Effects in Class Differentials in Educational Attainment: The Transition to A-Level Courses in England and Wales', *Acta Sociologica*, 50: 211–29.

Jäntti, M. and Jenkins, S. P. 2015. 'Income Mobility'. In A. B. Atkinson and F. Bourgignon (eds.), *Handbook of Income Distribution*, vol. II, Amsterdam: Elsevier.

Jenkins, A., Vignoles, A., Wolf, A. and Galindo-Rueda, F. 2003. 'The Determinants and Labour Market Effects of Lifelong Learning', *Applied Economics*, 35: 1711–21.

Jerrim, J. 2017a. *Extra Time: Private Tuition and Out-of-School Study, New International Evidence*. London: Sutton Trust.

   2017b. 'The Link between Family Background and Later Lifetime Income: How does the UK Compare with Other Countries?', *Fiscal Studies*, 38: 49–79.

Jerrim, J., Choi, A. and Simancas, R. 2016. 'Two-Sample, Two-Stage Least Squares (TSTSLS) Estimates of Earnings Mobility: How Consistent are They?', *Survey Research Methods*, 10: 85–102.

Jones, F. L. 1992. 'Common Social Fluidity: A Comment on some Recent Criticisms', *European Sociological Review*, 8: 233–7.

Jonsson, J. O. 2004. 'Equality at a Halt? Social Mobility in Sweden, 1976–1999'. In R. Breen (ed.), *Social Mobility in Europe*. Oxford University Press.

Jonsson, J. O. and Mills, C. 1993. 'Social Class and Educational Attainment in Historical Perspective', *British Journal of Sociology*, 44: 213–47, 403–28.

Jonsson, J. O., Mills, C. and Müller, W. 1996. 'A Half-Century of Increasing Educational Openness? Social Class, Gender and Educational Attainment in Sweden, Germany and Britain'. In R. Erikson and J. O. Jonsson (eds.), *Can Education be Equalized? The Swedish Case in Comparative Perspective*. Boulder, Col.: Westview Press.

Jonsson, J. O., Grusky, D. B., Pollak, R. and Brinton, M. C. 2009. 'Micro-class Mobility: Social Reproduction in Four Countries', *American Journal of Sociology*, 114: 977–1036.

Kangas, O. and Rostgaard, T. 2007. 'Preferences or Institutions? Work-Life Family Opportunities in Seven European Countries', *Journal of European Social Policy*, 17: 240–56.

Kahneman, D. 2011. *Thinking Fast and Slow*. London: Allen Lane.

Kirby, P. 2016. *Shadow Schooling: Private Tuition and Social Mobility in the UK*. London: Sutton Trust.

Klein, M. 2011. 'Trends in the Association between Educational Attainment and Class Destinations in West Germany', *Research in Social Stratification and Mobility*, 29: 427–44.

Kounali, D., Robinson, T., Goldstein, H. and Lauder, H. 2008. 'The Probity of Free School Meals as a Proxy Measure for Disadvantage'. University of Bristol, Centre for Multilevel Modelling Research.

Kuha, J. 2013. 'A Note on the Imputation of Missing Data'. University of Oxford, Department of Social Policy and Intervention.

Lareau, A. 2003. *Unequal Childhoods*. Berkeley: University of California Press.

Laurison, D. and Friedman, S. 2016. 'The Class Pay Gap in Higher Professional and Managerial Occupations', *American Sociological Review*, 81: 668–95.

Leitch, S. 2006. *Prosperity for All in the Global Economy – World Class Skills*. Norwich: HMSO.

Li, Y. and Devine, F. 2011. 'Is Social Mobility Really Declining?', *Sociological Research Online*, 16(3): 4.

Li, Y. and Heath, A. F. 2016. 'Class Matters: A Study of Minority and Majority Social Mobility in Britain', *American Journal of Sociology*, 122: 162–200.

Liberal Democrats 2009. *Report from the Independent Commission on Social Mobility*. London: Liberal Democrats.

Loury, L. D. 2006. 'Some Contacts are More Equal than Others', *Journal of Labor Economics*, 24: 299–318.

Lucchini, M. and Schizzerotto, A. 2010. 'Unemployment Risks in Four European Countries'. In D. Rose and E. Harrison (eds.), *Social Class in Europe: An Introduction to the European Socio-Economic Classification*. London: Routledge.

Macmillan, L., Tyler, C. and Vignoles, A. 2015. 'Who Gets the Top Jobs? The Role of Family Background and Networks in Recent Graduates' Access to High Status Professions', *Journal of Social Policy*, 44: 487–515.

McGee, A. 2015. 'How the Perception of Control Influences Unemployed Job Search', *Industrial and Labor Relations Review*, 68: 184–211.

McGovern, P., Hill, S., Mills, C. and White, M. 2007. *Market, Class and Employment*. Oxford University Press.

McKnight, A. 2015. *Downward Mobility: Opportunity Hoarding and the Glass Floor*. London: Social Mobility and Child Poverty Commission.

McRae, S. 2003. 'Constraints and Choices in Mothers' Employment Careers: A Consideration of Hakim's Preference Theory', *British Journal of Sociology*, 54: 317–38.

Marks, G. N. 2014. *Education, Social Background and Cognitive Ability: The Decline of the Social*. London: Routledge.

Mazzucato, M, 2015. *The Entrepreneurial State*. New York: Public Affairs.

Milanovic, B. 2016. *Global Inequality*. Cambridge, Mass.: Harvard University Press.

Millerson, G. 1964. *The Qualifying Associations*. London: Routledge & Kegan Paul.

Mills, C. 2015. 'The Great British Class Survey: *Requiescat in Pace*', *Sociological Review*, 63: 393–9.

Mills, C. and Payne, C. 1989. 'Service Class Entry in Worklife Perspective'. ESRC Social Change and Economic Life Initiative, Working Paper 10.

Ministry of Education 1959. *15 to 18*. London: HMSO.

Müller, W. and Pollak, R. 2004. 'Social Mobility in West Germany: The Long Arm of History Discovered?' In R. Breen (ed.), *Social Mobility in Europe*. Oxford University Press.

Nathan, G. 1999. *A Review of Sample Attrition and Representativeness in Three Cohort Studies*. Methodological Series 13. London: Governmental Statistical Service.

Nicoletti, C. and Ermisch, J. 2007. 'Intergenerational Earnings Mobility: Changes across Cohorts in Britain', *B.E. Journal of Economic Analysis and Policy*, 7: 1–36.

ONS 2005. *The National Statistics Socio-Economic Classification: User Manual*. London: Palgrave Macmillan.

2010. *Trends in All-Cause Mortality by NS-SEC for English Regions and Wales, 2001–03 and 2008–10*. London: ONS.

OECD 2010. 'A Family Affair: Intergenerational Social Mobility across OECD Countries'. In *Economic Policy Reform: Going for Growth*. Paris: OECD.

2017, *Educational Opportunity for All: Overcoming Inequality Throughout the Life Course*. Paris: OECD.

Osborne Groves, M. 2005. 'Personality and the Transmission of Economic Status'. In S. Bowles, H. Gintis and M. Osborne Groves (eds.), *Unequal Chances*. Princeton University Press.

Paterson, L. and Ianelli, C. 2007. 'Patterns of Absolute and Relative Social Mobility: A Comparative Study of England, Wales and Scotland', *Sociological Research Online*, 12(6): 15.

Payne, G. 2017. *The New Social Mobility: How the Politicians Got it Wrong*. Bristol: Policy Press.

Pearson, H. 2016. *The Life Project*. London: Penguin.

Peston, R. 2017. *WTF*. London: Hodder & Stoughton.

Pfeffer, F. T. and Hällsten, M. 2012. 'Mobility Regimes and Parental Wealth: The United States, Germany and Sweden in Comparative Perspective'. University of Michigan, Population Studies Center.

Phelps Brown, H. 1977. *The Inequality of Pay*. Oxford University Press.

Picketty, T. 2015. *Capital in the Twenty-First Century*. Cambridge, Mass.: Harvard University Press.

Power, C. and Elliott, J. 2006. 'Cohort Profile: 1958 British Birth Cohort (National Child Development Study)', *International Journal of Epidemiology*, 35: 34–41.

Raffe, D. 1979, 'The "Alternative Route" Reconsidered: Part-time Further Education and Social Mobility in England and Wales', *Sociology*, 13: 47–73.

Reeves, A., Friedman, S., Rahal, C. and Flemmen, M. 2017. 'The Decline and Persistence of the Old Boy: Private Schools and Elite Recruitment 1897 to 2016', *American Sociological Review*, 82: 1139–66.

Reeves, R. V. 2017. *Dream Hoarders*. Washington DC.: Brookings Institution.

Reeves, R. V. and Howard, K. 2013. *The Glass Floor: Education, Downward Mobility and Opportunity Hoarding*. Washington DC: Brookings Institution.

Richards, L., Garratt, E. and Heath, A. F. 2016. *The Childhood Origins of Social Mobility: Socio-Economic Inequalities and Changing Opportunities*. London: Social Mobility Commission.

Rose, D. and Pevalin, D. (eds.) 2003. *A Researcher's Guide to the National Statistics Socio-Economic Classification*. London: Sage.

Rose, D, and Harrison, E. 2010. *Social Class in Europe*. London: Routledge.

Rose, D., Pevalin, D. and O'Reilly, K. 2005. *The National Statistics Socio-Economic Classification: Origins, Development and Use*. London: Office of National Statistics and Palgrave Macmillan.

Routh, G. 1981. *Occupation and Pay in Great Britain*. Cambridge University Press.

1987. *Occupations of the People of Great Britain*. London: Macmillan.

Saunders, P. 1996. *Unequal but Fair: A Study of Class Barriers in Britain*. London: Institute of Economic Affairs.

2010. *Social Mobility Myths*. London: Civitas.

Savage, M. 2015. 'Introduction to Elites: From the Problematic of the Proletariat to a Class Analysis of "Wealth Elites"', *Sociological Review*, 63: 323–39.

Scase, R. and Goffee, R. 1980. *The Real World of the Small Business Owner*. London: Croom Helm.

Shaw, B., Baars, S. and Menzies, L. 2017. *Low Income Pupils' Progress at Secondary School*. London: Social Mobility Commission.

Schoon, I. 2010. 'Childhood Cognitive Ability and Adult Academic Achievement: Evidence from Three British Cohorts', *Longitudinal and Life-Course Studies*, 1: 241–58.

Sellström, E. and Bremberg, S. 2006. 'Is There a "School Effect" on Pupil Outcomes? A Review of Multilevel Studies', *Journal of Epidemiology and Community Health*, 60: 149–55.

Social Mobility and Child Poverty Commission 2013. *State of the Nation 2013*. London: HMSO.

2014. *Elitist Britain?* London: HMSO.

2015. *State of the Nation 2015*. London: HMSO.

Social Mobility Commission 2016. *State of the Nation 2016*. London: HMSO.

2017a. *Time for Change: An Assessment of Government Policies on Social Mobility 1997–2017*. London: HMSO.

2017b. *State of the Nation 2017*. London: HMSO.

Sorokin, P. A. 1927. *Social Mobility*. New York: Harper.

1959. *Social and Cultural Mobility*. Glencoe, Ill.: Free Press.

Stewart, K. and Waldfogel, J. 2017. *Closing Gaps Early*. London: Sutton Trust.

Sturgis, P. and Buscha, F. 2015. 'Increasing Inter-Generational Social Mobility: Is Educational Expansion the Answer? *British Journal of Sociology*, 66: 512–33.

Sullivan, A., Parsons, S., Green, F., Wiggins, R. D. and Ploubidis, G. 2017. 'The Path from Social Origins to Top Jobs: Social Reproduction via Education', *British Journal of Sociology*, doi: 10.1111/1468-4446.12314

Swift, A. 2004. 'Would Perfect Mobility be Perfect?', *European Sociological Review*, 20: 1–11.

Tilly, C. 1998. *Durable Inequality*. Berkeley: University of California Press.

Torche, F. 2015. 'Analyses of Intergenerational Mobility: An Interdisciplinary Review', *Annals of the American Academy of Political and Social Science*, 657: 37–62.

Tuckett, A. and Field, J. 2016. *Factors and Motivations Affecting Attitudes Towards and Propensity to Learn Through the Life Course*. London: Government Office for Science.

Vandecasteele, L. 2016. 'Social Origin, Education and Socio-Economic Inequalities: Trends in the United Kingdom'. In F. Bernardi and G. Ballarino (eds.), *Education, Occupation and Social Origin*. Cheltenham: Edward Elgar.

Wadsworth, M., Kuh, D., Richards, M. and Hardy, R. 2006. 'Cohort Profile: the 1946 National Birth Cohort (MRC National Survey of Health and Development)', *International Journal of Epidemiology*, 35: 49–54.

White, C., Glickman, M., Johnson, B. and Corbin, T. 2007. 'Social Inequalities in Adult Male Mortality by the National Statistics Socio-Economic Classification, England and Wales, 2001–03', *Health Statistics Quarterly*, winter: 6–23.

White, M. 1991. *Against Unemployment*. London: Policy Studies Institute.

Williams, M. 2013. 'Occupations and British Wage Inequality, 1970s–2000s', *European Sociological Review*, 29: 841–57.

2017a. 'Occupational Stratification in Contemporary Britain: Occupational Class and the Wage Structure in the Wake of the Great Recession'. *Sociology*, 51: 1299–317.

2017b. 'An Old Model of Social Class? Job Characteristics and the NS-SEC Schema', *Work, Employment and Society*, 31: 153–65.

Williams, M. and Koumenta, M. 2016. 'Occupational Class, Flexible Working, and the Emergence of Zero-Hours Contracts: Occupational Differentiation in Employment Contracts Redux'. University of Surrey Business School.

Winship, S. 2017. 'Economic Mobility: A State-of-the-Art Primer'. Washington, DC: Archbridge Institute.

Wolf, A. 2002. *Does Education Matter? Myths about Education and Economic Growth*. London: Penguin.

Wolf, A., Jenkins, A. and Vignoles, A. 2006. 'Certifying the Workforce: Economic Imperative or Failed Social Policy?' *Journal of Education Policy*, 21: 535–65.

Wong, R. S.-K. 1990. 'Understanding Cross-National Variation in Occupational Mobility', *American Sociological Review*, 55: 560–73.

Young, M. 1958. *The Rise of the Meritocracy*. Harmondsworth: Penguin.

Index